THE JOURNAL OF A SOUTHERN PASTOR

THE JOURNAL OF A

Southern Pastor

J. B. GREMILLION

FIDES PUBLISHERS ASSOCIATION

CHICAGO, ILLINOIS

922

The Library of Congress Card Catalog Number: 56-11630

Nihil Obstat: Albert L. Schlitzer,
C.S.C., S.T.D.
Imprimatur: ✠ Leo A. Pursley, D.D.,
Apostolic Administrator of
the Diocese of
Fort Wayne, Indiana

© Copyright, 1957, Fides Publishers Association, Chicago, Illinois

 55

Manufactured by American Book–Stratford Press, Inc., New York, N. Y.

CONTENTS

v

ACKNOWLEDGMENTS

The author wishes to acknowledge the following periodicals, in which sections of his book have previously appeared and from whose editors he has received permission to reprint: *America, The Commonweal, Social Order, The Interracial Review, Community,* and the *Bulletin* of the National Catholic Educational Association.

PREFACE

By John LaFarge, S.J.

These are the experiences of a working parish priest, a man intensely convinced of the layman's function in the Church. They demonstrate, blow by blow, a broad concept of that function: the layman seen in relation to the total mission of the Church in the contemporary world, and a very definite idea as to how the layman can find ways to fulfill that mission.

This intimate story of the goings-on in St. Joseph's Parish, jotted down helter-skelter, over a relatively short space of time, calls for some hurrah for the pastor, as well as for the unusual body of men and women who are cooperating with him. The parish is suburban, and about fifty percent of its members are college graduates. The scene is the new South, bustling Shreveport, where pleasant, leisurely ways of a Louisiana past are being rapidly pushed aside in the explosions of industrial and commercial development. The days are past when front-porch talk could agreeably substitute for front-line action. Some of these Catholic souls who work with their spiritual leader are a minority within a minority. Catho-

1

lics of whatever description, however, are legitimately
called upon to take their own constructive part in the
problems of the entire community: to make their own
spiritually motivated contribution to its needs.

The more skeptical will ask: why go to so much
trouble? Why this detailed plan of adult education which
Father Gremillion and his brother priests are elaborat-
ing? Why lay such emphasis on the true notion of man,
or Christian humanism; on the natural law and the concept of Christian democracy and the problems of the social order; on the relation of Church and State, on tor-
menting questions which are not contained in our pocket
catechisms and about which there is some argument, even
among the faithful? Would not the spiritually starving
masses be more helped by a few basic truths clearly
formulated, dramatically declared; why so much discussion?

The answer is simple. The great basic truths do need
to be enunciated, and repeated without intermission.
But the Church's full mission to the contemporary world,
the world right here in the United States, cannot be fulfilled by simple, dramatic appeals of word or example
alone. The ancient, normal path to the knowledge of the
truth—under the grace of God—is the hard discipline of
study, reason and deliberation. Such study and deliberation are most urgently needed precisely at the spot where
the Catholic—the member of Christ's Mystical Body, the
bearer, as it were, of the personality of the Church in his
own humble person—meets the world day by day; in the
trade or profession, in the home and neighborhood life:
that is to say, in existence. Lectures can aid, and text-
books can guide, but it is only through discussion, conference, planned meetings of minds that conclusions on

such problems become truly *one's own,* and are seen in their real dimensions. These, after all, are the dimensions of the charity of Christ.

As for the how of such self-formation, the Shreveport story describes a method and an institution. Father Gremillion's method is a schedule of adult education, somewhat breathtaking in its variety, and rather heavily schematized. The institution is his Collegium, a solemn enough title, but adopted, I imagine, with the intention of showing that the participants mean business. Furthermore, his Operation Shreveport is reassuringly free of a yearning to be unique. It is carried out in the great line of modern apostleship throughout the Christian world, and with the Catholic Committee of the South, and, locally, with the gracious cooperation of his own Bishop and fellow clergy of the Alexandria diocese. The varied and truly Christlike pastorate that the author has set for himself is based upon a profound philosophy of the parish itself: in the author's own words "a family of families in Christ," that gathers as the people of God each Sunday in order to worship God not just as private individuals, but "as a community of God's children, publicly professing our thanks and praise, our weakness and love." Every parish priest is intimately conscious of the complex of infinite details, the hidden grandeur of this little world of souls, striving, falling and rising on their way to Heaven. But he can never quite convey the idea to those who have not had the same experience.

"When you encounter human persons," said the late apostle of lay action, Emmanuel Mounier, "you encounter suffering." The bitterest sufferings are not always those of the more conventional type, but are rather the inner trials created by scarifying violations of justice, charity and human dignity. The experience of such "encounters" forms also the story of this Deep South parish. It has still a long road to travel before such unwelcome contradictions cease to trouble its progress. But, said the same Emmanuel Mounier, "God invents with us." What counts in the long run is not the cleverness of our own schemes, but the sincerity, humility and perseverence of our effort. Let us hope that the adventure of one parish will encourage countless other such "families of God" to strike out bravely on their way.

New York
August 15, 1956

PROLOGUE

Two years ago M. Jacques Maritain told me I should keep a journal. He surprised me pleasantly. He could not have devised a greater compliment. Seated in the living room of his home on Linden Lane hard by the Princeton campus I resolved to follow the great thinker's counsel. If he who had written so much, so well, and with such depth and scope encouraged me to write, then write I would.

Actually M. Maritain confirmed and re-activated resolutions which had been firmly resolved several times past. Urgings to start journals and to jot down thoughts and scribble comments on the passing scene have harassed me like the symptoms of a chronic ailment. But my resolves have been hot and cold, barometric ups and downs, malarial alternating currents of chill and fever and chill again. Is the urge to write a malignancy, or a pregnancy portending a fruitful and blessed event? If a pregnancy then this volume might well be the crowning miscarriage after years of false inceptions and abortive gestations. One never realizes how much fortitude it takes to write a book, or how little fortitude one possesses until he starts and stops a dozen times. From the file

5

cabinet womb of foetal creations: correspondence, programs, bulletins, newsletters, speeches, articles and sermons, jottings, comments and marginal notes, first chapters of books and first acts of plays stillborn—from this
miscellany of matter and spirit I beget this journal of a
Southern pastor, induced by M. Maritain's midwifery.

Many undertake journals without foreseeing publication. So they contend. They just felt the impulse, a matter of self-expression, of wanting to speak out—like the
mocking bird warbling at midnight when countryside
ears are pillowed in sleep.

The setting down of thoughts on paper necessitates the
clarification of that vague dimly-seen hazy world we call
the conscious. And that is good. To form a sentence a
man must form an idea. And begetting an idea is good in
itself regardless of the idea's content. This mirrors the
eternal generative act by which God the Father begets
and enunciates the LOGOS, the Idea Who is His Son. To
His image and likeness we are made. So we too beget and
enunciate ideas—small snivelling ideas, inane silly ideas,
tentative ideas and once in a while great and enduring
ideas. Such is man's nature, a derelict of Adam's Eden
days.

So a man can write a journal without writing for an
audience just as God begets the Divine Word for endless
ages without concern for an audience in the timelessness
before creation. Then by creation God begets His Own
audience. We creatures exist to applaud God, encore
after encore. "Clap your hands, all ye nations!"

The Trinity needs no audience and no applause; still
our God-given purpose is to behold and applaud the
Trinity. Here lies the master paradox of human existence. Church and parish, pastor and people exist pri-

marily for this self-same purpose: to behold, to acclaim and to love the triune God, in Himself and mirrored in His creatures. The parish is the basic working unit within the Church toward the fulfillment of this exalted purpose. I write as pastor of such a parish striving to fulfill a purpose so exalted.

I stress the striving rather than the fulfilling. I tell about failure and hate and sin, as well as I tell about glory and godliness, because I write about human beings, my parishioners, my friends and myself. We do not go toward God in an antiseptic atmosphere, and we do not proceed alone. We uncover God through and with and in our brother creatures. God speaks to us with the tongues of angels and through the mouth of miry mud; He reveals Himself through man and matter, to whom both we are all relatives by blood. We work out our salvation by weekday wear as well as by Sunday rest; by pounding a typewriter and pounding pavement, as well as pounding our breast with *mea culpas*. Christ worked our salvation during the thirty years of His carpenterhood at Nazareth as well as during the three hours of His victimhood at Golgotha. The parish exists to wash all creation with His Blood. Another tension arises: Whereas the Church (Who is Christ) is not of the world, the Church is very much *in* the world. The Church is hierarchy AND PEOPLE. The Church through the laity must incarnate Christ into society, in the life and work of men; family, economy, body politic and the rest.

How does the parish fulfill this role within the Church? Can pastor and people impact the downtown world? Or is this beyond our scope, the role of other organs of the Mystical Body? Abbe Michonneau and Canon Cardijn debate these questions. The social encyclicals, Cardinal Suhard and others clarify the issues by degree.

Another dilemma. Semantics enter in. How can we have a *Catholic parish?* a universal parochialism? a world embracing narrowness? We must see the parish as the cell of the much greater Body. Else the cell dies, or worse yet blocks the flow of life and grows to canker. The parish must not be parochial but Catholic, KATHOLIKE, universal.

Further queries fill a pastor's journal: the role of the laity, the forming and activating of lay leaders, a life-giving liturgy, ministering to the whole people whether Catholic or not, strengthening the family under the barrage of materialism and keep-up-with-the-Joneses-itis, envisioning the whole world from a parish of the provinces. No region of our nation is more provincial and self-conscious than the South. The current integration of the Negro has exacerbated that apartness. These observations take cognizance of this as it does of other social realities.

This journal is not a unified study of parish sociology. It is very personal, introspective, volatile. I am unlike God in the timelessness before He created His audience world: I crave an audience. Hence this is not a diary destined for the eyes of God and mine alone. No dark and devious secrets, no heart-rending drama of a soul's climactic struggle, but a simple sharing as in conversation with my people, sharing thought and feeling about God and man as together we proceed toward the dark door of death. I am priest of Christ with the flock confided to his care to teach and to guide, to love and to sanctify, to try and fail and try again. And the flock provides means for the shepherd to work out his own salvation. Christ gives all the commission of helping all to know and love and serve Him: this we call the communion of saints. We push and pull each other along the road to paradise. The parish is the communion of saints in seminal microcosm.

St. Joseph's parish is located in the residential suburbs of a city numbering some 160,000 people, a city typically southern in racial and religious complexion. Some 33% of the population is Negro; some 7% Catholic. Our suburban area is predominantly white. The Negroes are segregated in thirteen city ghettos, only one of which borders our parish. Our local economy is based on petroleum and natural gas, cotton, cattle and lumber. In its atmosphere and outlook Shreveport is more Texas than Old South. Much of the population is Texas-born; we bask in the reflected splendor of that incandescent blowtorch a mere eighteen miles to the West. Our main thoroughfare is, of course, Texas Street.

More than ninety percent of our parishioners own their homes. More accurately they are paying installments each month and will own them in fifteen to twenty years. Payments also come due monthly on auto, furniture, church building fund, TV and hospital bills. Add the doctors to the creditors, especially the obstetricians and pediatricians because most couples were married since the war and children parade the aisles at every Mass in para-liturgical procession. Homes are in the twelve to twenty thousand dollar bracket. Men occupy managerial and professional positions as doctors, lawyers, engineers and geologists, corporation officers and department heads, educators, bankers, contractors, brokers, realtors, sales managers and regional name-brand representatives. Their incomes range from five to ten thousand dollars a year. Most of it they pre-spend on installment plan. Debt is normality.

Half of the parents have college backgrounds, of whom only about 15% have attended Catholic colleges. And a very important feature: about 50% are mixed marriages, mixed that is in the religion of the spouses; one being Catholic, the other not. On the whole ours is a religion-minded community; certainly 90% profess membership in some church.

In short the five hundred fifty formally Catholic families of St. Joseph's reside in *suburbia Americana,* the new sociological darling, the current object of affectionate attention from swarms of statisticians and research analysts. Shopping centers and community clubs and double car ports abound. Gadgets galore protrude from wall and ceiling of the newer homes; to maintain the electric dishwasher, dryer, percolator, laundry and other handy machines requires more than a handyman's native skill. It's a bluff world of baby-sitting and mower-borrowing, but extremely complex in its interdepend-encies. How many persons serve me each time I draw a glass of water from the kitchen tap, how many humans bring my poached egg from the cackling hen. That's why we enter a new era: man's relation to man assumes greater import than man's relation to things. And again: the whole wide world would remake itself to the image and likeness of *suburbia Americana,* deny the temptation though some might.

Seven years ago my bishop sent me here to establish our parish. This is not a parish biography. It is too sketchy, incomplete. In fact much attention falls upon extra-parochial interests, a major concern being the impact of Christ in the Church upon the community and the world, with especial concern for the role of the parish and the laity.

We who are the Church continue Christ in time and space. The perceptive student of history pierces beyond the surface debris of mere war and dynasty to discern close interrelation between the dominant ideas and the human events of a given period, between the ideals and values derived by society's thinkers from their concept of truth and the cultural temper to which these ideas and ideals give birth. The study of history is primarily the study of the incarnation of ideas, the idea becoming the flesh of the social body. The *Alter Christus,* priest of the Logos, might summarize his mission with this Ciceronian phrase: *Verbum incarnadum est.* The Word must be made incarnate. The layman partakes of the same mission. He must incarnate Christ in his workaday world. Priest and laity *together* form the Church and redeem every chink and clod of God's genesis.

Ideas take on flesh, become incarnate in the managerial, political, family and work life of my parishioners; in the Monday morning real life situations of the operating room, editorial staff, court chamber, bargaining table, directors' conference, labor halls, country club barbecues and legislative floors. By their agency the idea becomes the act, economic theory the contract, social concept the custom, political ideal the statute.

Church and parish have primary jurisdiction and control over the gifts of Redemption, Sacraments and Sacrifice. But that Church which continues the God-Man must needs show concern over the gifts of Creation as well, soil and seeds, ore, rain and sea and sun, created by God for every man. Concern, but not control: that is the formula. And in this temporal order, it gives rise to vibrant tensions. Christ redeems man through His Church and redeems His material creation through man: economic, political, family man; learning, teaching, aesthetic man; striving, working, sweating man; suffering, worshiping, penitent man. The layman's role is manifold. At the parish and community level we have barely begun to perceive his breadth, depth and dimension. These jottings offer no definitive survey. Quite the opposite these are inklings and surface glimmers.

A penultimate point. "Two years ago M. Jacques Maritain told me I should keep a journal," opens this prologue. Be duly warned that I admit the temptation to inveterate name-dropping. The name-dropper exalts himself upon the shoulders of the great and near-great. He peppers his conversation with direct quotes from renowned personalities. Name-dropping tempts most of us and many succumb. The first lieutenant exudes: "As the general observed to me yesterday. . . ." The third assistant pastor confides: "Between us here's what the cardinal really intends. . . . " The fourth clerk to the second undersecretary of the Department of Agriculture reveals: "The President's personal farm program envisions. . . . " Mrs. Klymer breathes over her tea: "At the Les Madames reception Mrs. Gabfiest agreed with me. . . . " And the bench warmer: "I signalled the quarterback to kick. . . . " It was fourth down and twelve yards to go; Mrs. Klymer protested the smog; the President's revelation came via TV; the cardinal's intentions by pastoral letter; and the general addressed his division on July Fourth. To the uninitiated name-dropping conjures visions of a tête-à-tête among the powers behind the thrones. Be thou initiated! I too am tempted to name-dropping or its reasonable facsimile.

When I mention Bishops Wright and Sheen, Christopher Dawson and Arnold Toynbee, M. Maritain, Father LaFarge or Monsignor Ligutti the connection might be tenuous indeed. Perhaps I have merely read their books and seen them in the hazy distance of a lecture stage. Perhaps again we have talked by the hour or for days on end. Perhaps the context will clarify the true relationship and perhaps befog it. Regardless I register now an indebtedness to these and many others who have stimulated and inspired me through their words and work. Among these I must single out my own Bishop Greco, my priest friends and the parish flock the Bishop has committed to my charge: to teach, to rule and to sanctify. They have taught me much by their life and love and sacrifice.

Lastly, this is not a final book. Rather the opposite, it is tentative, probing, provisional. It does not answer questions, it raises them. It does not offer solutions but states problems. It reflects the growing maturity of the Church and people of America, just past awkward adolescence and inquiring now into our adult being with a Socratic "know thyself." It reflects too the self-consciousness of the "post-Christian West," realizing now that our science has made of this world a neighborhood, a physical unity in woeful need of the one Truth and Love of Son and Spirit Who Alone can make of the whole human family Community-in-Christ.

The awakening has begun.

❖

AWAKE, SLEEPER!

Ephesians 5:14.

One evening when St. Paul was preaching in Troas "a young man named Eutychus, who was sitting at the window, was overcome with drowsiness and . . . he went fast asleep and fell down from the third story to the ground and was picked up dead." That Paul then raised him to life brings no surprise. But how astonishing that the man fell asleep at all. If Paul's preaching was as thunderous as his letters how could any one cat nap? More logically the man's defenestration would result from the Apostle's tornadic vehemence blowing the hearer out of the window. But Luke who was present states he fell asleep, and Luke the physician ought to know.

Paul must have felt humbled at losing even one of his listeners. Falling asleep was bad enough, but to point up the boredom by so dramatic an exit as falling three stories dead to the ground smells of sabotage.

15

Already in apostolic times the paralysis of sleep crept into the Church. Through the centuries sleep has benumbed this member of Our Lord's Mystical Body, then another. Like the ebb and flow of the ocean tide, history records the deterioration and reform of the Church's organs; now this, now that; now here, now there. By 1900 this drug-like paralysis reached a peak. Only a slightest fraction of the Whole Body showed some sign of life; the great bulk of the Body—the laity—barely ever budged.

It lay inert, showing little inner-activity, adhering to Our Lord's Body as though a mere extraneous accretion, rather than a vital participant in the Whole. The great accomplishment of the Popes Pius has been the awakening of the laity to a first glimmer of their Christ-being, to a dawning consciousness of who the laity are.

The awakening has begun. But it is still early in the morning, very early indeed. The whole organism, clergy and laity, is still stiffly drowsy from the long hibernation. The fullness of conscious aliveness must still reach the extremities of Our Lord's Body.

1. Winter Weekend

ANOTHER Knights of Columbus weekend for leaders underway. Sorry to leave midway but Saturday confessions begin in a couple of hours; I had to get back home to the parish. Everything at Lafayette's in good hands. They don't need me whole time. Many others can take over. Jaubert and Reggie (K of C leaders), Fathers DeBlanc and Sigur (Newman Chaplains) with their THINK group nucleus have all it takes and more. Then the Fathers Bordelon join them tomorrow.

We're getting somewhere; last night convinced me. Sixty men spending Friday through Sunday knocking heads and rubbing minds together. After this blockbuster they will never be the same. "What Christ expects of the practical Catholic" will take on new dimensions of breadth and depth. That narrow "no meat on Friday, Easter duties, Mass on Sunday" concept of the practicing Catholic must open wide to embrace the whole Christ who lives in every man of every nation, race and time. We must throw off the bonds of selfish individualism which mummy-wraps the Mystical Body and paralyzes our people into concentrating only on *my* soul and *my* salvation, *my* Christ and *my* Communion. This weekend is a retreat—a retreat from the silence of never asking questions about Negro Samaritans and Zacheus usury, a retreat out of the shell of self into the society of the whole Christ, the universal Church KATHOLIKE.

About a year ago we began these seminar workshops. I remember their genesis. We had gathered at the Newman Center of Louisiana State University in Baton Rouge—five or six K. of C. state officers, diocesan chaplains and our host Monsignor Tracy, state chaplain. At this day-long meeting to formulate the year's program we laid groundwork for closed weekend retreats by a thousand men, for four giant Christ the King rallies, for nocturnal adoration in parish churches on First Friday eves, for religion contests and similar good works. A program to arouse pride among the fifteen thousand men composing "the strong right arm of the Church" in Louisiana.

But through that day of self-congratulation and wistful hope a sting of the conscience buffeted us. The month previous the Kefauver Committee on crime had come to New Orleans and scapelled out nauseous corruption. TV, radio, headline spewed it forth. The stench exposed from our own state's social body wrinkled nostril and forehead. All agreed that this collapse of public morals rendered the work of the Knights doubly necessary. Sighs of misgiving abounded in the upper room of the Newman Center. "We're just not effective enough. We have a good program, but . . . well, we're not reaching the areas of life where Christ is most needed." And from which He is most habitually exiled.

While the year's plan for retreats and rallies, corporate Communions and contests took shape in the course of the day, organizational self-appraisal dominated. An impromptu examination of group conscience resulted: Emphasis has been properly placed on personal sanctity. The man who knows his Faith and frequents the Sacraments, who lives a good family life and "gives a good example," who stands up for the Church and shushs snide snaps at the pastor—this Knight is the good Catholic, the prototypal practical Catholic. All to the good, but now all obviously insufficient. Bringing God into the private life of the person is *sine qua non,* but some short circuit has obstructed the expected overflow of godliness into the public life of society. Private morality is insulated from public morality. Pious exercises and vigils infuse body and soul of retreatants and nocturnal adorers with abounding grace and goodness but somehow the body and soul of society languish moribund as ever. The American bishops call this communal malady secularism in their 1947 statement.

Such were the misgivings voiced that day a year ago in Baton Rouge as the Knights re-examined their crowded and worthy program. The modern Knight is dubbed and sent forth "to do good." In the colossal complexity of today's world he fights a lonely battle, a defensive rearguard skirmish. The fight to avoid positive evil plus the temptation of succumbing to the miasma of neutrality toward God overshadows hope of permeating the environment with Christ's truth, justice and love. Individual good example "shines forth to illumine the darkness and the darkness does not comprehend it." Holding one's own becomes the sufficing victory, with emphasis on "one's own."

So these men came to realize that by and large the really critical problems of our day remain untouched by the state's only organization of Catholic laymen. The fifteen thousand soldiers of Christ who are in the best position to bring Him into the marketplace have no program for training, no marshalling ground, no concerted plan of attack. They exert precious little group impact upon the most pressing social issues of our changing South: racial discrimination and segregation, civil rights, labor-management teamwork, share-cropping, migrant workers, the fading family farm, dislocations arising from heightened industrialization, "the welfare state," education without God, corrupt politics, and the influence of other social realties upon the family—like housing, living family wage, public welfare, high health costs, recreation, social security. In fact we drew the sad conclusion that many men are infected with anti-Christian attitudes especially in the gnarled problems of racial tension, labor relations and the plantation system. How many Knights really grasp what those social encyclicals are all about? that socio-economics must be subject to the moral law of Christ's justice and love?

At this point State Deputy Charles Jaubert, lawyer by profession and one of those Catholic college graduates who has not "failed," voiced the need for a school, center or similar means by which adults could grow to a deeper understanding of the Church's social doctrine. The three day institutes were then conceived of which the current Lafayette weekend is the fourth.

About sixty persons are participating; a selected cross section of businessman, Chamber of Commerce executive and union organizer, public school teacher, college dean and housewife, priest and sister, lawyer and doctor, contractor, mayor and mechanic. By tomorrow night they will know each other by name and feel a surprising solidarity; rubbing minds together in argument and wee-hour bull sessions, tasting the unity of the one Truth;

community Mass and meals will see to that. The solidarity however must not induce soporific security. The weekend will shake their complacency, shock the *status quo*. Our blockbuster handle fits the experience: exploding rock-ribbed conservatisms, clearing out blind alleys and dead ends, unveiling fresh horizons, casting fire upon the earth. The seminar-panels seek no final nor flitting solutions. We want to light up the sky with that vision in lack of which the people perish. We want the men to glimpse even hazily of Our Lord's blueprint for His City of the God-Man. In upbuilding His City we work out our salvation; in perfecting God's raw creation we perfect ourselves to the image and likeness of our Creator God. That's what the blueprint reveals to him who will decipher it. The weekend would but awaken the sleeper and ignite the torch to fuse Christian meaning into the stress and strain of our workaday world.

The three day experience avoids handing out ready-made plans, seeking rather to goad the participant into decision and action flowing from their own *esse Christianum* (their inner Christ-being) in the unforeseen contingencies and challenges of their personal vocation and group status. The institute provides an initial glimpse of the whole Christ (who is the Church) living on in time and space through and in us, priest and people, living in the world He came to save. The whole Christ is longer and deeper and wider than the world itself; our arms and minds and wills must extend to embrace Him. That's why we jam-pack so much material into the block-buster weekend. Subjects march on each other's heels in close order drill. A sampling from the mimeographed program:

A glance at the day's news.

Is Christ interested in social issues?

The "practical Catholic" and the problems of society.

The return of our exiled Christ: restoring to Him His creation.

Today's approach inadequate?

The scope of parish and organizations: Holy Name, Confraternity of Christian Doctrine, CYO, Councils of Catholic Men and Women, Knights of Columbus, St. Vincent de Paul and others.

The Mystical Body at work.

One total Apostolate: clergy and laity together.

Night prayers in common and compline.

I led the panel on these subjects last evening. Over a score joined in the melee. The Christianity of the many bears no relevancy to the events of the day. Sunday religion remains on the pantry shelf, canned and vacuum-packed to prevent contamination by weekday woe and weal. Vital bonds between Christ and His people must be forged.

Today after morning prayers and the Holy Sacrifice, a homily, Communion and breakfast, last evening's theme was developed further:

Society and the nature of man.

The institutions composing society: family, economy, body politic, education, others.

The Church's apostolate through institutions: Pius XI.

Why we must have lay apostles.

Particular competence and role of the layman.

Baptism and Confirmation: Sacraments of Apostolicity.

The layman receives his "orders" through the sacraments.

And his commission via the living magistry of Pope and Bishops.

After two hours hammering at this armory of the spirit we turn to the field of battle, spending Saturday and Sunday probing society's institutions, sector by sector. The first brush is in the realm of intellect and idea, the struggle for the minds of men:

The purpose and status of formal education in our civilization.
The Catholic school system.
   Raison d'etre, vocations, lay teachers, secular institutes.
The tax-supported system: its philosophy.
   Bringing God into the public school.
The Catholic college; has the graduate failed parish and Church?
Secular universities and the Newman foundation.
How make Newman centers more effective? The Oxford plan.

Then we take on the economy, a couple of hours surveying that great sweaty arena of human endeavor by which the raw creation of soil and sun, water and ore, sea and seed become warm milk for baby's bottle, Johnny's shoes and bike, ball and book, wall and roof to make the house that Mom and Dad might make a home.

Why did God create natural resources?
Why do men work? Personal and social purposes.
How can an economy provide a living-family-saving wage?
Organization: of capital and labor to become the team.
A voice and a vote; political and economic democracy.
Rural Louisiana; decentralized industrialization.
Ideal of the family farm; urban living.
Factory farm successor to the plantation.
Sugar workers and migrant laborers.
The National Catholic Rural Life Conference.
A F L co-op–union among truck and fruit farmers.

Each of these areas could engage the group for many hours, but we shake loose from each in quick succession. This get-together cannot provide definitive answers. All we can hope for is a dawning realization that Our Lord is as interested in work and home and family wage as we are, that His rule of right and wrong must pacify the economic jungle of unconditional *laissez-faire,* and that all Leos, Piuses and labor priests are inadequate unless Joe Smith does his part in keeping with his talents great or small, through his organization, factory or farm. It takes a dialectical crowbar to pry loose the group and move along. Then the next subject really grips them because it cuts across the entire society and digs roots deep in history and human emotion:

> The principles for restoring race relations in Christ:
>> One God and Father: one human family.
>> One Savior and Church: one Mystical Body of Christ.
>> One nation and community.
> Segregation and discrimination must go:
>> Conveyances and public places.
>> Employment opportunity and wage; F. E. P. C.
>> Education: "Equal but separate?"
>> Housing, zoning ordinances.
>> Social equality and friendship.
>> Interracial marriage.
>> The ultimate aim: total integration.

This explosive issue usually convulses the weekend more than every other. Louisiana Catholicism exposes now its most gnawing weakness. Are we also guilty of racism? Inheriting from our grandfathers an economy and sociology based on slavery and the dominance of one race over another, what have we done to redress the wrong? How remove this occlusion in the flow of Christ's

Blood that He may cleanse and nourish His Whole Body?
The arm of God is long and strong, the Love of Christ
can melt the hardest hearts. We can become true brothers
some way, some day. But will the Lord suffer our pride
in patience much longer—or the Negro?

The body politic next occupies our reeling participants:

Government and the nature of man.
The welfare state and principle of subsidiarity.
Duties of Christians as citizens: public morals, spoils.
Relation of Church and State.
Our interdependence as one world.
Population vs. resources; immigration.
United Nations; F A O, W H O, Point IV.
The world apostolate; the missions, role of the laity.
    Special position of Louisiana toward Latin America.
    Latin college students in our state.

And following this look at the human family over all
horizons the weekend concludes its dizzy pace with con-
siderations on the Christian family apostolate, liturgy in
the home, dating and courtship, Cana and marriage preparation. In the closing hours of Sunday afternoon each
strives to perceive how he can convey home something of
the spark and flame which enveloped him these three
days. Can he form a group in parish or town, along bayou
bank or country lane? Will he pursue the vision he has
beheld? Will he witness to Christ? Will he act alone and
with others? For this he is sent forth with the Benediction
of our Eucharistic King—as we are all sent in the diversity
of our ministries by Him and His Vicar, by our shepherd-
successors of Peter and James and John.

These are my thoughts back home on Saturday night.

Confessions are over now; tomorrow Paul's epistle on charity, THE epistle of Paul. Reading over these scribbles I wonder that we would presume so much. Why not stick to the tried and true like altar society, benefits and Holy Name breakfasts, building fund drives and sick calls? All good and fine. But enough? Do we ever do enough? Can we presume not to presume to do more for Christ, to widen His embrace? Our good Ordinaries approve our effort; by word and letter Archbishop Rummel, Bishops Jeanmard and Greco commend the Knights for these leader-formation weekends.

And who would be a priest at all without presumption? How I presumed the strength and grace of Christ when I said in the confessional a few moments ago: "I absolve you from your sins in the Name of the Father and of the Son and of the Holy Spirit. Amen."

Bob Baker just stepped in for extra survey cards. Two of his block captains ran short. Guess there are more families in that new subdivision than we at first figured. Two o'clock. The captains started their Sunday house to house calls an hour ago. Should finish at three. Of course, they'll hit a few snags.

"Receive them as my emissaries and representatives," I told the people this morning. " 'As the Father has sent me, I also send you,' says Christ to the priest. As Christ has sent me, I also send these men to you, our parishioners. He who receives them receives me." Rebuffs will be few if any at all. The people mean well. They want to be led to Christ despite the flesh and the devil and all his pomps.

Driving Denny Morris over to the bank a half hour back to deposit the collection (biggest in history!) we

saw a couple of the men making their rounds, bruising
their knuckles not for the sake of Fuller Brushes or auto
insurance but for Christ.

St. Paul's classic on charity for the Epistle today. In-
triguing how words lose their power, how they peter out!
They grow old and tired and empty. Charity is a wornout word. To the mind's eye it conjures visions of charity
balls and benefits, "Buddy, can ya spare a dime?", a
Christmas basket duly motioned and seconded and
carried and minuted and reported back to committee by
the women's auxiliary.

Charity flamed for St. Paul. Charity burned and pushed
and pulled, scouring the heart clean of trivial trash and
sundry little hates. Charity bound the fragments of the
universe and held them one. Charity tied God to Man in
Christ, and fused all men in Him. Charity left mother
and father, and home and hearth—tramped deserts and
suffered shipwreck, a night and a day in the salty sea, and
thrice bore forty lashes less one. For Paul charity flamed
and consumed the innards of man. Now charity writes a
dollar check (deductible) for the Red Cross and pins a
blood red cross on the coat lapel. But charity spears no
heart and spurs no man to move. Barnacled with the
incrustation of a century's half-hearted humanitarianism
(a heavy word!) charity wallows a derelict in the slimy
slough of enlightened self-interest. Supposing Christ had
pleaded enlightened self-interest in the Garden of Gethsemane. To Paul charity means the life of man because
it means man's life-giving love. A love embracing all with
the all-embracing Heart of Christ. He would not use
this wornout word to pour himself out to us today.

This I explained to the people this morning in the

pulpit. But what word, what sign of sound would Paul
pen in his Epistles to the Americans? Love is the closest,
I guess. But even there what poverty of expression.
L-O-V-E. A beautiful word. A beautiful sound. Visions
of young love and mother love and Divine Love and sex
love and puppy love. That's the rub; it means too many
things. What an impasse for the human mind striving to
conceive and to communicate its innermost realities.

I recall Father William Russell's gentlemanly disgust
with the Trinity College coed who couldn't grasp the
concept of loving God "because you can't put your arms
around Him." God as a triple-threat Clark Gable—a new
kind of blasphemy. But there it is: the roar of the Holy
Spirit enflaming feeble fishermen and assorted bodily
squeezes, squishing lips and such, all going by the same
sign of sound—LOVE.

We call God the Unutterable, the Ineffable. So much
is unutterable for man because we are so limited by matter, time and space; so woefully walled in. Three dimensions not being prison enough, Einstein adds a fourth.
And what little spirit we do have cannot breathe where
it will without an unwieldy scaffolding of shaky adjectives
to carry the thought home. What confusion of identity;
love: young, mother, divine, sex and puppy!

Monday morning appraisal of yesterday's Confraternity
of Christian Doctrine survey. About 90% of our families
were contacted and cards in the rectory by 8:30 P.M. The
cards tell many a sad story. Divorces. Children unbaptized. Tepidity toward Christ. Fallen-aways by the
dozen. Somehow though I don't feel discouraged. I knew
it all along in general, if not by name and phone number. Besides these people don't really hate God; they're

not malicious. They don't know God well enough to hate Him. He loves them all, and some day they might awaken and love Him back.

Wedding rehearsal at St. John's last evening. Took over an hour, what with five brides and groomsmen, and two very vocal mothers-in-law-to-be. All the flowers and candles and solos and tedious "to-do" can gnaw the nerves, but after all it's the greatest event since the youngsters were born. Why shouldn't they frame the setting with gorgeous gilt? Non-essential to the Sacrament, true. But why not use silk and satins and sobbing sopranoes to underline the import of the two become one in Christ.

Now I must get a hair cut, over to St. Ann's for the sisters' confessions, to the VA hospital to smile with Bob Kavanaugh drying up with Hodgkins disease, then to St. John's to witness John and Betty giving themselves to each other " . . . for better or for worse until death do us part." Brave words, in Him Who strengthens them and me.

2. First Week of Lent

THEY TALK of facing reality. "Face the facts. Call a spade a spade. You've got to be a realist."

Mother Church is the realist, especially on Ash Wednesday. No namby-pamby pussyfooting with her. She covers over no grimy clay with morticians' grassy green. She loves her children so she wants them to know the truth. She says it with ashes, black and bold and straight to the point: "Remember, man, that thou art dust, and to dust thou shalt return."

From his courtroom bench the judge sentences the criminal to twenty years and a day, to life imprisonment, to hang by the neck until dead. On Ash Wednesday I pass sentence on all my parish flock. The Communion Table, the place of the morning's Agapé, becomes the bar of divine justice. "The wages of sin is death." The sadness of it all, that we should all be doomed to die. The faces turn up to me bravely, bravely facing the sentence of death. All I condemn to die because we all share the same humanity.

I pass from mother to child, from grandfather to son and babe in arms, from youth to lovely maiden. On each forehead I trace a cross of ashy dust, a father sentencing

his children to die, engraving the TAU mark on head
and heart: "Remember, John and Jane, that thou art
dust . . . " Dust?—these cherubic cheeks? this open maiden
loveliness? this cutely pugged nose? this carefully dis-
hevelled hair? Ashes?—this manly skull firm beneath my
thumb? this fertile brain, source of engineering marvels? these pulsing temples, founts of fortune-seeking
drive and managerial skill? Slime?—these pools of infant
innocence holding back the tears? Why should a baby
ever die?

How can a father sentence his sons and daughters to
death, to waste again into the dust from whence they
came?

Great is the God Who compounded such beauty from
dust, and compounded such dust from nothingness.

Annie Gibson in to line up details for the visit of
Betty Schneider, national director of Friendship House.
Circle 5 has courageously transferred their meeting here
for Betty's talk Monday evening, despite fear that some
might renege. And the men's group takes responsibility
for hosting.

Many poor people in trouble today, adultery and
drinking and birth control and even a little hate. They
talk and talk and beg for an easy way out, but there is
none. I show them the crucifix and we talk about yesterday's ashes. They leave unburdened a bit, stumbling on
as though Simon of Cyrene had just happened along.

Allen Lanier called up last night. In town on business.
Utilizing his Annapolis training, he has engineered a
novel type of barge float for oil derricks in the coastal

tidelands. Succeeded in selling Oceanic Oil Co. on the idea. A two million dollar initial investment. Again, how one must think big. Why not such largeness of concept in our plans with Christ? Is He less willing to listen than the district manager of Oceanic Oil Co.?

Allen wanted to report on the success on the Lafayette weekend. Race relations and family life panels especially good. He admitted being somewhat dazzled by the size of the job ahead. He's exactly the type of leader we must develop. The man who has the guts to proposition Oceanic Oil Co. to the tune of two million dollars has the makings of the leader who dares to restore all things in Christ, including the oil industry. We plan dinner together when he returns in a couple of weeks.

Bill and Mary Jackson just in from Lafayette phone in expressing their pleasure with the weekend, too. Much give and take. It seems that I confused the racial issue Friday evening at the opening session by saying thoughtlessly (and foolishly) that I had had three white and three Negro couples to the rectory for dinner together, "just to show it can be done." But Bill cleared up the motives and smoothed objections in my absence. Wonder what Mrs. Adrianeaux will do about the interracial CCD meeting at her home, especially knowing Bishop Jeanmard's wishes? Judge Dalfume helped greatly with the announcement that two Negroes had just served on the grand jury of Acadia Parish.

Emile Reggie has been in town most of the week lining up details for the K. of C. State Convention in May. Sessions with him Wednesday A.M. here in the rectory, Wednesday evening with convention committee downtown and last evening at local council meeting. Jim Farley unable to speak. Discuss Martin Durkin and Henry Ford.

Yesterday noon we got together eight men from the two THINK groups for lunch with Emile at the Chef to honor our State Deputy and re-hash the state of the world. Good to get the gang together. Much "stuff" discussed. Race issue dominates. Slim to speak at Southern University in Baton Rouge Monday; some AFL connection because Lige Williams, State Labor Federation president, is on it. Red explains Betty Schneider's appearance on Monday evening to tell about Friendship House. Leonard comments on the L. S. U. stadium vs. library controversy—"the animal vs. the spiritual of man." He is mailing out fifty copies of the *Shreveport Times* editorial to acquaintances over the state thumping for the university library over the stadium.

We hurriedly analyze the whole "stuff" movement, especially the weekends. Excellent reports on the Lafayette affair just past. End up with Red and Leonard responsible for promoting an all day confab here in Shreveport —start with Community Mass, meals together, twenty-five chosen and briefed men digging into some three or so specific fields, e. g., race, economy and family—with lay apostolate dynamics interwoven and dominating. Have three or four from Natchitoches, Alexandria and Monroe present, and send three or four men thither later for similar Sundays in each place. This to serve as pilot model for sessions all over Louisiana, by and large in county seats—Opelousas, Abbeville, Thibodaux, Lake Charles. The day long session idea is promoted by Emile and Charlie Jaubert because the weekends do not reach the natural leader of mediocre dedication; at first he will not leave home for an entire weekend. Further, those in attendance at Baton Rouge, New Orleans and Lafayette weekends in past five months are mostly local, and too much coming and going to work up intensity and *esprit de corps* as generated originally at Alexandria a year ago. Same time and talent could put on ten or twelve Sunday punches in the coming year reaching two to three hundred community leaders covering the whole state: leaders in business, labor, politics, education, professions, etc. Then occasional weekend for selected elite from each section to stimulate their growth and develop higher echelon state and region wide leadership.

Re Betty Schneider: Father Louis recounts Washington Friendship House experiences. We broach Shreveport possibility—near Booker T. Washington High School. LaFarge's *No Postponement* just read by one of gang: "Don't agree with all of it. But someone must go ahead of us to pull us along, and we must push ahead to pull rank and file laggards along. We're making progress but have such a long way to go." Negro employment by corporations as accountants and geologists and office managers held back by "social equality" issue. Only outlet for college grad in South is teaching, and very recently a few lawyers and doctors. Only total integration can remedy this customed-in-concrete discrimination by our local corporations. Otherwise the Negro will remain the janitor and window washer.

How we cover the waterfront of God and man in an hour and a half—half-baked assuredly. But a little warmth from the heart of Christ feels comforting in the cold, cold world in which these men buy and sell and legislate and insure and whose fragments they bind together with the baling wire of Paul's charity.

Monsignor Ligutti scribbles a note from La Paz, Bolivia. He cannot do the article for AMERICA on the Manizales Latin American Congress on Rural Life Problems. Never in one place long enough. He's written to Father Hartnett suggesting I ghost it for him from Ligutti's mimeographed Andean Notes, or that Father Bill Gibbons or Fred McGuire be approached. Monsignor waxes enthusiastic: "Saw Grail girls in Puno [where is that? They're accompanying Bishop Lane of Maryknoll.] Really, Father Joe, this has been a great experience [and he's had 'em]. They felt this A.M. for Lima. As I stop here and there I can see the results: Unbelievable! Thank God for all. Got here this noon. Will cover Bolivia in one week. Then to Argentina, Chile, Paraguay, Brazil. Keep me in your prayers."

Compare him with whom but Paul whose range was limited by the pillars of Hercules. Paul didn't aim beyond Spain. But Luigi Gino Ligutti, he embraces the whole two and a half billioned world in his embrace of Christian love because he like Paul loves all that he knows, and LGL has the advantage of 20th century geography. Who will be his Luke?

CCD men here this Saturday afternoon to work out details for tomorrow's initial lectures launching our adult education experiment. In the survey last Sunday eighty-three signed up for the Church History course by Father Scherer and a hundred eighty enrolled in my *Reason Why* series. Many of these are probables and "we hope's." Attendance by such a great number is out of the question. Two hundred would be grand. The men line up the chairs and welcomers and book salesgirls. Mary's Workers will serve the coffee.

Dr. Bozek pleads that I stress the "What science tells us about God" theme due to the expected presence of several doctors, geologists and others whose positivistic training has encased their minds with scientistic bias. Their intellects are prisoners of sense data. To them the five senses become ultimates instead of avenues to supraphysical truth. All reality must be laboratory tested. They still want to precipitate Omnipotence to a filterable residue; Eternity must be sychronized with a stopwatch; Immensity measured with a slide rule; the Light of Total Truth spectroscoped into bright hands of blue and yellow and red; Absolute Intellect scrutinized under the microscope and the pungency of Divine Wit litmus-tested for acidity; the centrifugal Good of the All-embracing Will atomized in a whirling cyclotron. Sense becomes an end instead of a means. They reduce the whole of reality to direct sense experience. Why? By what reasoning? From which premises? Sense data now and forever world without end. Amen. That's the great "taken for granted" base of surface sand on which wobbles the impressive sky scraping super structure of scientism. And for all their methodic scholarship and admirable painstaking observation these gifted searchers cannot see those feet of clay.

If only these dedicated scholars would delve beneath the surface into the metaphysical. What a great intellectual synthesis could then come forth from the chrysalis of the senses. How sad if all our great scientific achievement becomes a terminus tomb instead of a maturing stage in the metamorphosis of man. Only Christ can call

Lazarus forth from this tempting tomb, and loose the precious silken shroud of sensate science which cocoons him.

Two hundred fifty-seven jammed the two lectures last night. Really, the drive which impelled them to come is their inner yearning for God, the Truth, Whole and Entire. Some only curious? But what is curiosity but a conscious emptiness seeking to be filled. The curious are basically humble folk, aware of their own deficiency. Their intellects need truth like famished bellies need bread. Truth is the meat of life. Some placate this yearning prodigal son-wise with swine husks, the fibrous shuckings of Ultimate Reality. God made us all with an appetite insatiable save by the taste of His Own Divinity. Insofar as each creature participates with Him and in Him and through Him and by Him in the experience of existing, that being possesses something of the divine and possesses in consequence by its own participated truth the power to please the yearning intellect. But with a passing pleasure only because the human intellect yearns for the Infinite. So knowledge of creatures never satisfies totally; it whets the appetite and leads man on to God. In *Genesis* Moses recounts that God the Creator saw the earth and the moon, the trees and herbs, the birds and whales and four-footed animals each according to their kind—all these He saw and saw that they were good. Creatures for the first time were perceived as true and good. And aptly this first perception of the truth and goodness of every creature came from their Creator, the Source of their truth and goodness because He is the Source of their being.

We have in our parish about a dozen geologists, a comparable number of engineers and doctors and lawyers. At least 40% of the men hold college degrees. To a man they have struggled in private and in public in the arena of "science vs. religion." Some have lost their faith completely, embracing sceptical positivism. Some have resorted to a Cartesian evasion; they are Christians on Sunday and "scientific" during the week. Most of them just muddle through, never clarifying the mud in their minds; for these all light is twilight. Others—a few others —have found the truth of both science and religion without conflict, but rather arm-in-arm perfecting man's grasp of God as the Alpha and Omega of the whole and glorified by His Creation blueprinted by science.

The truth enjoyed by these last gains currency today at the very top of the intellectual spring. But cultural lag dams and slows the flow of truth. From Millikan and Hubble to high-school physics and Sunday magazine supplement the lag measures about twenty-five years. When my parishioners and I attended Louisiana State a mere twenty years ago, chemistry and zoology and social science were still incensed as demi-gods by the high priests of materialism.

Today amoral scientism is arraigned in the court of the ideas of the world. Science comes now to be recognized as a mere creature once worshiped as divine. A sacred cow, the current best-seller irreverently heckles. Science is not master of its own fate, how then can it direct the rest of the world? Science is but an instrument, a morally neutral instrument capable of good or evil. The society of men must then utilize this instrument, dominate and harness it, not be harnessed by it. Man is master over science; sense constrained science is not equal to man. To wed such science for better or for worse is not only a marriage beneath man's dignity; it is emotionally unsatisfying, logically repugnant and ontologically impossible of consummation.

The doctors and geologists and chain store managers present last night to hear "What science tells us about God" begin to understand all this as they seek the ultimates—the Where from? the How? and the Where to? of life. Even LIFE magazine (to some, more influential than the Bible) searches their souls:

> "It is the apparent loneliness and singularity of our planet in a hostile universe that evoke the deeper questions: How was the earth created? When did it come into being? What is its fate? The concept of a random universe, existing without origin or destiny, is meaningless to the human animal who lives in a dimension of time. Man has always postulated a Creation, and *Genesis* speaks with universal accents in its mighty opening phrases: 'In the beginning God created the heaven and the earth. And the earth was without form, and void; and darkness was upon the face of the deep. . . .' In its assault on these uttermost questions modern cosmogony impinges on the ancient realm of religion. The striking fact is that today their stories seem increasingly to converge. And every mystery that science resolves points to a larger mystery beyond itself." (LIFE, Dec. 8, 1952.)

And the quasi-pantheistic postulate of the eternity of energy fizzles as the cyclotron tells its tale and the two hundred inch telescope sounds the depth of space. At some point in the past it all began—electrons began spinning, atoms began splitting, galaxies began exploding, solar systems began to be—at some point IN TIME.

> "It was not until the discovery of radioactivity around 1900 that the age of the earth could be fixed with approx-

imate precision. For the radioactive elements, such as uranium, thorium and radium, decay at fixed rates that are independent of heat, pressure or any external influence. Each loses in a given period a certain proportion of atoms which then undergo a long series of transformations at a fixed, known rhythm, ending up eventually as atoms of lead. One gram of uranium, for example, yields $1/7,600,000,000$th of a gram of lead per year. So it is possible to weigh the amount of uranium in any bit of radioactive rock against its residue of lead and thus calculate how long ago the deposit was formed.

"Careful analyses of radioactive rocks in all parts of the world have failed to disclose any older than two and a half billion years—these are in South Africa—thus pointing to the conclusion that the earth's crust solidified about three billion years ago. Other approaches to the problem—calculations of the ratio of salt in the ocean to the amount of salts annually conveyed by rivers to the sea, as well as recent studies of stellar combustion and galactic movements—all indicate a beginning, a creation fixed in time. The date always falls within certain crude limits, never less than two billion years, never more than four or five. And so the earth did not exist always. Yet it is older far than man from his brief temporal perspective ever surmised till now." (LIFE, Dec. 8, 1952.)

THE UNIVERSE AND DR. EINSTEIN recently published by William Sloan and written by Lincoln Bennett summarizes the demise of the philosophic concept of eternal physical energy (and eternal matter, because physical energy and matter are essentially identical):

"If the universe is running down and nature's processes are proceeding in just one direction, the inescapable inference is that everything has a beginning: Somehow and some time the cosmic processes were started, the stellar fires ignited, and the whole vast pageant of *the universe brought into being.*

"Most of the clues, moreover, that have been discovered at the inner and outer frontiers of scientific cognition suggest a *definite time of creation.*

"The unvarying rate at which uranium expends its nuclear energies and the absence of any natural process leading to its formation indicate that all the uranium on earth *must have come into existence at one specific time.* . . .

"So all the evidence that points to the ultimate annihilation of the universe points just as definitely to its inception fixed in time." (*The Universe and Dr. Einstein,* by Lincoln Bennett; William Sloan, Publisher.)

Why my concern with meteors and Messier 84 and mesons? What's that got to do with the Eucharist and adultery and Christ crucified? Plenty, almost everything. We now see energy and matter as identical, matter being frozen or congealed energy. Atheistic materialism is grounded on the premise of eternal physical energy.

We are engaged today primarily in a combat of ideas. Ideology is no idle word. It means the study of the seed-idea. Christ is first of all an IDEA, THE Idea. "The Word (LOGOS in Greek, VERBUM in Latin, also IDEA in English) was made Flesh and dwelt amongst us." Christ is the eternal IDEA generated eternally by the eternal Intellect of the Father. By becoming Flesh He joins the eternal Spirit to temporal physical energy (and/or matter). By postulating the eternity of physical energy scientism endows energy with God-like attributes. If energy (and/or matter) is eternal it too can say, "I am Who am." It becomes *a se;* it can explain itself. It is accountable to no one. The Flesh can then ignore the Word! Matter flaunts the Spirit, and since the material is so obvious to man's five senses, matter soon becomes dominant, the master and source of spiritual manifestations. Matter, energy, FORCE become the absolute.

The seed-idea of atheistic materialism is the eternity and primacy of physical energy. The seed-idea of Christianity is Eternal Spirit creating, upholding and rendering intelligible temporal exhaustible energy. Through Christ God is in the world, dwelling in the world, loving the world, but is not of the world. Never forget "God so loved the world that He gave His only begotten Son." By no means is Christianity otherworldly in an absolute sense. "He (Christ) was in the world and the world was made through Him." (John I, 10.) The Spirit through Christ has primacy in the world of matter as well as in the world of spirit.

The ideology of Communism grounds itself on the postulate of bourgeois scientism that the world of matter exercises primacy, the so-called spiritual manifestations of thought and human creativeness being merely manifestations of the material matrix. Now that true science destroys the myth of eternal energy and the motherhood of matter, atheistic materialism will starve to death.

The few have gone the whole way along the Red road charted by scientism. The many do not pursue their premises to the logical catastrophic end. Some lingering nostalgia of Christian humanism diluted into humanitarianism holds them from the precipice of pessimism.

Most Christians are to some degree influenced by the sacralization of science. Religion becomes a formality, divorced from "the facts of real life." Part of the man says, "I believe in God the Father Almighty," part of the time. Another part of the same man says, "Hmmm . . . ," tongue in cheek.

I want my people to know God totally and without reserve. For this we were born and for this we came into the world. The wondering, wonderful and wonderfilled curiosity of men of science patiently piercing ever deeper into the inner and outer frontiers of matter tell us evermore about God and His creatures. The decisive truth that energy and matter are not eternal is one of the greatest advances in the battle of ideas since the preliminary bouts of the sixteenth century. The revolt of creature science against the Creator God has netted the calamitous ruins of all war—shattered minds and wills and shattered spirit, hate fragmentizing family and community, nation and world held together only by the inflexible cement of force.

How good to shout from the housetops: "Force is not all, energy is not eternal—only One can say, 'I am Who am!' Him alone we kneel down and adore!"

After ninety minutes of this we broke up for evening coffee and talk. Their minds are alive and curious, thank God. Bishop Greco and Monsignor Vandegaer came in about 9:30 P.M. from Confirmation. The Bishop chatted with the people in his fatherly manner.

Then he, Monsignor and I rehashed the whole business till after eleven. The Bishop sees and applauds our purpose and approach. We had quite a time discussing why a hypothetical 400-inch telescope might never glimpse a glowing galaxy moving away from us at the speed of 187,000 miles per second because it would emit its light at only 186,000 miles per second. But can anything travel faster than the speed of light? Any material thing, that is?

3. Race

THE INTERRACIAL MEETING in the cafeteria tonight to hear Betty Schneider on Friendship House has brought criticism from parishioners and others. Nothing serious but just enough to perk my ears and give me a temptation to anger to overcome. After the 9:00 A.M. Mass yesterday the four men were chatting on the front walk loudly enough to catch my ear. I sauntered up:

"You're pushing this nigger business too far, Father. It's all right to give the nigger better wages and more schooling, but this business of social equality, no sir! You're from the South, too, aren't you? You know we've gotta keep segregation and we're GONNA keep segregation."

"Yes, I'm from the South, south Louisiana on top of it. Born and reared on a cotton and cane farm down there. My dad had Negro share-croppers—maybe that's what opened my eyes. My grandad fought in the Confederate Army. I remember when my grandmother's personal slave servant died. Yes, I'm from the South and I've a lot to make up for."

"Well, Father, what are you aiming at? Why did you invite those colored folks for a meeting here? Are you trying to break down the wall of segregation?"

44

"Sure, I'm trying to destroy segregation."

"You don't mean you're for social equality, too!"

"Sure, I am. I frequently have Negro friends in for dinner at the Rectory."

"What! We didn't know that. Teddy Roosevelt got me mad when he had Booker T. Washington for lunch. But I then found out that he was just having a sandwich at his desk and Booker T. walked in so he just offered him a sandwich. That wasn't as bad as it sounded."

"Well, now let's get this straight once and for all. That's not the way it happened with me. I have invited Negroes over several times. We sat down at the dinner table and ate and talked. They're my friends. Some of the people I most admire in the whole city. This is my home. I can invite whom I wish to visit me. I can choose whom I will, black, brown or yellow as my friends. If you don't want them at your home that's your choice. But don't try to tell me whom I can ask to my dinner table."

"Well, I'll be . . .! What'll the neighbors think? You're looking for trouble. There'll be riots and bloodshed. That's what fanaticism will do. And the niggers don't want to mix. Why the other Sunday one of the ushers tried to make a black man get out of the last pew and move up front. And he didn't want to cause any fuss; he was satisfied just where he belonged in the back pew."

"We're having a meeting tomorrow night—Negroes and whites together to hear about the work of a wonderful band of thorough-going Christians. If you wish to come, you're welcome; if you don't want to come, then just don't come. And about segregation in church, several years ago I instructed the ushers to seat Negroes anywhere in Church and preferably NOT in the back pews. There are thirty pews in Church, if a Negro is in pew number ten and you don't want to sit there you have twenty-nine other pews to choose from."

So the music goes round and round. Only four actual complaints to my face thus far. More underneath; I hear rumblings. Even the usual talk of burning crosses but I know that's just talk. We must understand the irrational in man. Only radical Christianity can root out this irrational element. Christ is such a radical by suburban American standards. But the great thing about Christ is that into the gaping wounds caused by the rooting-up He pours the soothing ointment of His love. Do I?

So much has happened in these whirlwind two days.

Betty Schneider entranced her seventy-five listeners Monday evening. About twenty Negroes came, mostly from Father Tony Walsh's parish. Like the whites they varied happily in age: high-school youth, young and middle-aged couples. Betty shoots straight from the shoulder, backs down to no one (not even on FEPC). She affects no bombast and seeks no martyr's crown. Nobody feels sorry for her or her cause. Rather one knows that she has the key to happiness in her sense of mission: losing her life she has found life and found it more abundantly. She's more to be envied than pitied: that was the audience reaction over the coffee and chatter which followed the question period.

A buffet at the Gibson's preceded the meeting. Father Gaudin, pastor of St. John's, added much by his presence and sensible words. Mr. Lorraine came out with his story about the usher in heaven demanding non-segregated seating, and he invited all in the hall to "close your eyes and see if you can tell the difference."

Tuesday morning we go through Booker T. Washington High. Mr. Brown spent an hour and a half showing us around. Betty compares the plant to only one other—white or Negro: Father Flanagan's Boys Town. At noon her bus leaves for Memphis without her. By now she's definitely interested in Shreveport.

Unable to reach Bishop Greco by phone (he's somewhere in the missions), we drive into Alexandria at 8:00 P. M. hoping to see him. By now Eric, Annie and I know a lot about Friendship House. The Bishop walks in a bit after nine. Within an hour he has invited Friendship House into the diocese and appointed me chaplain. Betty's flabbergasted.

By the time we leave at 10:30 P. M. a tentative plan shapes up: two staff workers, preferably one a southerner, to come into Shreveport about October; a beginning budget of $300.00 monthly; limited and short-term financial help from the Bishop; FH on its own thereafter with assistance of friends near and far; careful choice of storefront site and living quarters; volunteers and program flexible to needs. Betty understands this first venture South might require adaptation. And we understand that she must propose all this to eleven other members of FH's national council. But anyway we are far beyond the hoping stage! I had hoped all this would happen in ten years at best.

Wednesday noon some ten men discuss the whole business from scratch with Betty. Fathers Gaudin and Bryant present from St. John's. Not only approval but enthusiasm. One question: Should staffers live in Negro homes at beginning? Should we risk the possibility of legal action invoking the state law against the races occupying the same residence unless the Negro be a servant? Betty is very loathe to relinquish this basic Friendship House prin-

ciple of sharing the very life and condition of the Negro.
The lawyers among us perforce uphold the "law and
order" principle (admitting all the while the ordinance
to be against natural law) "to avoid the greater evil" of
possible violence and stonings, verbal abuse, etc. Father
Bryant insists these fears are unfounded, that the staff
should rent rooms with Negro families and ride out the
consequences. We shall see.

The interracial just seems to dominate this week.

After *au revoirs* to Miss Schneider yesterday afternoon
I went to a Council of Social Agencies meeting. President
Wesley Etheridge with an ill-concealed look of great
expectations asks me to meet with him and three Negro
leaders at the high school at 7:00 P. M. First we have a
briefing over dinner with Milam Brownson and Luke
Buchanan.

Our city Negro house-to-house survey revealed that of
11,002 colored dwellings in Shreveport some 7,000 are
substandard, only confirming factually the impression
anyone would get from the most casual ride through the
slums. We have emphasized housing as second only to
education in the priority of Negro problems. Now that
education rapidly improves, housing becomes definitely
number one.

Among the myriad factors restraining progress here
Milam Brownson and Nelson Dalson, who certainly know
the field, place first: lack of financing: insurance and mort-
gage companies not interested because servicing loans of
$5,000.00 costs as much as $10,000.00 loans, and many
other reasons including prejudice, i.e. pre-judging Negro's
ability and determination to make monthly payments;
and secondly, the relative high cost of "treating raw land,"

providing streets, sewerage, drainage and utilities is almost as expensive for a $5,000.00 home as it is for a $15,000.00 residence, especially if the lots are about the same size.

Consequently, no financiers offer their money on long terms for low cost housing. They have other safer markets for their funds. This leaves the field open to the occasional plunger seeking a killing at extreme rates of interest and with only eight to ten years to pay out. And this leaves the slum-dwellers in the slums. They have no place to move to.

Through some concatenation of circumstance, the Drydock Savings Bank of New York wants to invest one million dollars in 200 Negro homes priced at $5,000. And looking over the nation they are investigating Shreveport because our survey provides the information they seek, and principally because of the history of the Negro-white cooperation during the past three years. The two hundred homes on an excellent forty-acre site would require a down payment of $400.00 including title costs, and monthly payments of $37.50 for 20 years. Four rooms plus bath, 672 square feet; slab floor, cement block walls; streets curbed and paved; all utilities piped in; lot 42 by 120 feet; FHA approved; and the monthly payment includes all taxes and rent, as well as paving and sewerage fees.

We ask Dr. B. N. Morrow, President of the Negro Chamber of Commerce, Lister Reed, head of the Carver YMCA, and Aldo Simmons, principal of the high school, to serve on an advisory committee as spokesmen for the Negro community. Would they like these homes? the location? Can they afford them? What part can Negro realtors and builders play in the project? And so forth and so on into the night.

The Drydock Savings Bank is making an experiment in a new and difficult field. They are not after a killing; 4½% interest is all they want; they'll barely break even. If successful many other lending institutions will follow their lead as a social responsibility. If this fails other pioneers will be retarded for several years. Local conditions of interracial harmony hold the key of make or break. That's why one of the bank vice-presidents is in town from New York this week to case the community himself.

Wes Etheridge and I share all this with the three Negro leaders in preparation for a more decisive meeting Sunday afternoon. So far so good.

The National Conference of Christians and Jews held their annual brotherhood luncheon at noon. Judge Moynihan of Detroit spoke with better effect than usual. For the first time in four years I did not speak to any groups during brotherhood week. I wonder at the necessity or benefit of standing up once a year and reminding people that we shouldn't hate each other. There's a hollow sound about the whole deal. And then how in the world can we sincerely plead brotherhood in view of race segregation and all its works. Besides I'm tired of so many public appearances. I'm talked out. Think I'll take a sabbatical from luncheon clubs. They can be so superficial. Sing a song and slap a back; we do no wrong, and that's a fact! We kick up a fuss; so rah, rah for us! Still they fill a need, a yearning of some kind. Is the need artificial, the yearning manufactured? What a mess we humans be?

Dr. Martin Louverture celebrates the second anniversary of his arrival in Shreveport. Some ten of his friends gathered in his office at two this afternoon (Sunday) for a glass of champagne and an hour of good talk.

Dr. Morrow impresses me more and more. His grandfather was a slave; owned by others as a piece of property. His father was a sharecropper; owned little or nothing; uneducated. Now here's Dr. Morrow, an M.D.; financially affluent, leader of his people, respected as well by our white community. What white man can point to a like record! None had to climb out from such depths of economic and social suppression. I am proud to call men like him my friends. They prove the improvability of the Negro as a people; they substantiate our hope for the future.

Mr. Wright, principal of Midway High, attracts my attention, sensible and soft-spoken. Had heard him emcee several affairs like the scout banquet earlier this month, but this presents our first opportunity to converse.

Again, what can the Negro college graduate do in Shreveport besides teach? Educators already exceed the number of openings. Of the thousands of positions offered college men by Gulf Refining, Texas Eastern, Libbey-Owens Glass, United Gas and their fellow corporations, practically none are open to Negro graduates. Whites and Negroes don't know each other well enough to attempt the close association of office work as accountants or teaming up on geological or engineering problems. That's why fair employment practices are so closely related to total acceptance. True social justice hinges on social equality. There's no half-way. Total integration is the sole answer. Very few interracial marriages need result and what if they do! Human acceptance is the basic problem.

Most of my parishioners never conversed with an educated Negro. They only know the Negro as a janitor or

cook or hoe-hand. Many of them lovable characters, yes.
But a people numbering millions can't remain "characters"; they want to be just plain people, fellow beings
in the human family. That's why cultured Negroes have
such a role to play and why we must provide opportunities for white leaders to meet colored leaders as equals.

We discussed, too, the necessity for colored leaders to
give of themselves to their race. Too often the more gifted
among them regard their people as fair game with a merci-
lessness imitative of the most tough-hided whites. Those
endowed by God with greater intelligence, personality
and drive, and particularly those who have the great advantage of a higher education must see their duty before
Christ to utilize these gifts not solely for the aggrandize-
ment of themselves and their families but for all of their
brothers. They must grasp "noblesse oblige." Good to hear
that at a recent get-together this group discussed: "What
has the Negro done for the Negro?"

To Martin's home for dinner and music and more talk
with friends, most of whom are on the faculty of Texas
Southern University, Houston.

At five back to Washington High for joint meeting of
the Survey Steering Committee and FHA men on the
million dollar housing project of the Drydock Savings
Bank. For three hours we explore all the angles. A joint
letter to the bank is being drafted when I must leave for
our lecture course.

By actual count 190 attended the second installment of
"What Science tells us about God," and 54 heard Father
Scherer's history lecture covering the second century of
Christianity.

Among the bull sessions that continued till ten thirty

or eleven was one with Raymond Wilson and Leonard Warren on the source of human rights. True to his Harvard Law School training Raymond admits no relationship whatever between God and human rights: We have rights just so long as the courts so interpret the constitution, and to the extent that the interpretation of the courts is acceptable to a majority of the people. There is no such thing as natural law by which man derives ineradicable rights from his very being as created by God. The Constitution preamble's "that all men are endowed by their Creator with certain inalienable rights," represents a passing phase in the minds of doctrinaires one hundred eighty years ago which certainly does not apply today. Totalitarianism is right if a majority of the people want it. By education we must guide them elsewhere, but there are no absolute moral principles rooted in human nature by God. The temporal and the eternal, the natural and the supernatural, matter and spirit, the city of man and the city of God are irreconcilable, in no way penetrating each other, absolutely repugnant; the one does not depend upon or derive from the other in any manner, shape or form.

Leonard and I are both breathless to have these basics of positivistic secularism so baldly embraced not by some long-haired Ivy League theorist but by a practicing lawyer in Shreveport, Louisiana. Raymond wants to talk more. And we, also, certainly want to and will. A really good THINK session in the offing.

4. The Church in Spring

To MARYHILL YESTERDAY for our first Monday of the month day of recollection and diocesan clergy conference.

Cardinal Stritch will be the guest of honor at the Centennial celebration of the founding of the Diocese on May 20th and 21st. In the centennial committee we iron out details for two hours.

Fathers Marvin, Roland and I obtain permission from the Bishop to make the Catholic Committee of the South convention in Richmond, April 21-24, and to continue on a ten day *dulce et utile* trek through Washington, New York, Grailville, Chicago and Des Moines. Bishop Greco plans to make the convention himself. He is especially pleased to learn that laymen of the diocese are also on the program. We discuss lay leadership training with him.

To Marksville in the evening. Bert Thomas accepts definitely a place on the program. Long distance to Tom Layne routs him out of bed and he, too, gives the greenlight. Whether their wives will accompany them is questionable, what with five babies between them. It takes heroism for the married to dive into the active apostolate. They're so badly needed that we'll just have to have more heroism.

In Mansura we pull out the road maps and plan the trip, straining chevy's theoretical abilities to the utmost. Take the train overnight back to Shreveport in time for the 8:15 children's Mass.

Mother Angelique, Provincial of the Sisters of Divine Providence, in from San Antonio for visitation. These mother superiors are great women. What a load to carry! Some eight hundred sisters in seventy schools and hospitals and mission centers. All growing by leaps and bounds but the number of vocations does not increase. Maybe the new juniorate will help.

We will not get a fourth Sister here in September. Employing a third lay teacher means a ratio of three and three. More and more our Catholic school system must depend upon lay teachers. The change is not an unmitigated evil. Laymen have their contribution to make *if* they are trained and have a *sense of mission*.

Lord, we beseech you, hear us. Pastors of huge schools who "wouldn't have a layman" on their forty Sister faculties should reconsider their attitude. Certainly these good priests have an apostolic interest in the spread of God's Kingdom outside their own circumscribed bailiwick. If they would release a fourth of their sisters and substitute lay teachers we could open many more schools, especially in our no-priest-southland. I will be happy to know that we can preserve in our school a half and half ratio of sisters and lay teachers.

The big news of Mother's visit: after a century and more the Sisters' habits will be changed. They don the new outfits for a fashion show. Simpler, less encumbered. No more pressure on the ears; the heavy starched crown is gone; now they can hear. The blinders are cut back;

now they can see. Ah! the *magnum mysterium* of the changelessness of Sisters' habits. Does God's immutability reflect more strongly in His whole creation? They become something more than sacramentals which are after all channels of grace only *ex opere operantis*. In some way or other clothes must play an abiding role in women's lives. If you can't change the styles every spring and fall, then make the change every thousand years. The changelessness then becomes more appealing than the seasonal change. After all Sisters are consecrated to God, with solemn vows of poverty, chastity and obedience, but they are still women.

When Pope Pius XII is canonized the second nocturn of the breviary lessons shall state in stentorian Latin that while history testifies to his victory over Fascism and how he conquered Stalin's Reds without a single armored division, his singular accomplishment was "mutationem modernam monialium vestimentorum veterum suaviter et fortiter, sine sanguine et sine matrum superiorum singulo decapitatione, effici . . . to have effected the change of Sisters' vesture by firm and persuasive means, without the shedding of blood and without the decapitation of a single mother superior." Breviary in English by then?

THE SILVER CHALICE review by Father Denny Curren drew a hundred seventy-five last evening. Father Denny held them for better than an hour mixing his best chuckles with worthwhile historical notes of the early Church and well received moralizing. He's down to 269 pounds now. He gave me the perfect jibe for my introductory remarks with: "Sure, Joe, and I used to hit 325; I no longer have to go to the tractor company to weigh!"

Amazing how the people go for these book reviews.

More symptoms of intellectual and spiritual hunger, I guess. Must have them more often.

Bob Kavanaugh died this morning at the Veteran's Hospital. Hodgkin's disease had dried his manly thirty-three year old body to a shriveled skeleton. His mother wisely permitted an autopsy because "it might help some other mother's son."

We live in the valley of death. Just finishing architecture at Miami University when stricken a year ago, Bob loved to build strong and straight like his own marble-muscled body. Now it returns to mother earth. He was ready for the summons. Had friends read to him Thomas Merton aloud to the very end. And Christ came.

How senseless all life would be did we not know Christ. How awful it must be not to know Him. Life without God sketches no pattern, makes no sense. The fool makes no sense from minute to minute; the God-less make no sense from life to life.

First Friday means all-day adoration of Our Lord in honor of His Sacred Heart.

Enthroning the Eucharistic Christ in the monstrance and singing praises to His Loving Heart is a solid and satisfying devotion. Then we follow Benediction with the Stations of the Cross, following Christ from pillar to post. That's solid and satisfying, too.

De gustibus non est disputandum. And undoubtedly tastes vary in the devotional life of the many. So Mother Church countenances all manner of religious expressiveness. There are many ways of saying, "I love You." Now and then I become concerned with the emphasis placed by some propagandists on the superficial paraphernalia

of certain devotions. This past week such a propagandist
hawked his wares here in Shreveport. He is a brother on
national tour "selling" a good thing: devotion to Our Lady
of Fatima. But what an atmosphere he builds up with
handbills, tree bark, Lucia's Communion veil, patches of
Francisco's pants, photos of "the well where the angel
appeared" and other assorted museum pieces. Add the
breathless pace of his apocalyptic voice and his stage presentation of religion degenerates to the stratum of a patent
medicine hawker. As a couple of parishioners put it, "It
smelled of witchcraft."

Naturally he stressed Holy Communion on the first
five Saturdays. But to judge by his emphasis the Body of
Our Lord is not the important Thing. THE point is
FIRST and FIVE and SATURDAY.

The avidity of people for Necedah and Konnersreuth
worries me. Even Herod wanted to see Christ work wonders. Cardinal Ottavianni, Assessor of the Holy Office, has
reason to be concerned. We pastors have not given his
warnings sufficient prominence in view of this current
fever for the marvelous. This fever is rather easy to explain. The world's in a mess. The world's torn asunder
by hate. Only love can cure this hate. But love is so demanding, so much more difficult than gallivanting around
to gawk at visions.

Confraternity of Christian Doctrine Executive Board
met this afternoon, some eighteen men and women.

The adult education movement takes on shape and
heftiness. We'll aim at two six weeks courses each year,
one term in the spring and one in the fall, on Sunday
evenings 7:30 through 9:00 P.M., followed by the coffee
hour with its invaluable bull sessions. We work up a two

year program of studies, with at least three of the terms covering history: Term I—the Apostles through Charlemagne (33 to 850 A. D.); Term II—post Charlemagne to the treaty of Augsburg ending the religious wars (850 to 1648); Term III—through today. Suggested other courses besides my current *THE REASON WHY* (fundamental apologetics) are the Life of Christ, Marriage and Family, the Liturgy, the Social Doctrine of the Church, the Sacraments, Fundamentals of Moral Theology and many more. No lack of material. And unless I am badly misjudging there is no lack of sincere interest. With our full-hearted concern for our school system for children we have woefully neglected our adults.

The CCD Board favors sponsoring monthly forums open to all during the slack period between the more formal six-week courses. Wagner heads a committee to work these up with panels on the Church and: Point Four, Labor Unions, Race Relations, Spain, the U. N., Dr. Conant, Merton and the like, together with book reviews and a look-see at current events through the lens of eternity. By questionnaire these men will solicit suggestions from those now attending the CCD courses.

We will build this into something worthwhile. How our people need the stimulation of truth. How little we give them in a twelve minute sermon.

Today we celebrate the Fourth Anniversary of St. Joseph's Parish.

Four years ago we offered together for the first time the Sacrifice of the Mass as a family of families. Everybody felt ill at ease that first Sunday in the Broadmoor Theatre. The inclined floor, the dim lights, the lack of windows and kneelers, the folding altar for thirteen months were bad enough. To top it all as we made our sanctimonious entry the marquee and sign boards proclaimed the week-end attraction like Bette Davis in THE GREAT SINNER, and Bobby Breen in STAIRWAY TO HEAVEN, CHICKEN EVERY SUNDAY, and BRINGING UP FATHER.

In THE SUNDAY SOWING, our weekly bulletin, making its debut the Second Sunday of Lent, 1949, we said:

"Christ in the Neighborhood—
> And Jesus came near and touched them, and said to them, 'Arise and do not be afraid.' (From today's Gospel.)

"Some 1900 years ago God felt that he was too far away from His children on earth. Seated on His Throne in Heaven the physical obstacle of distance as well as the psychological barrier of fear separated the Father from His sons and daughters. God didn't like this situation, so He did a very simple yet aweingly dramatic thing. He came down here on the planet Earth to live with us for a while.

"He wanted to be close to us, and wanted us to be close to Him. So He gave us a chance to see really what He was like, a chance to talk with Him and walk with Him. As Christ, the God-man, He rubbed shoulders with His children, that knowing Him better we might love Him more dearly, and loving Him we might serve Him more loyally.

"Through the powers He entrusted to His Apostles and their successors, Christ continues His divinely human companionship. In the Holy Eucharist He reaches into every nook and cranny of the world.

"And today He comes to Broadmoor. . . .

"HOMELESS—We have no ornate House in which to welcome Christ. We have as yet no well-appointed Temple in which to offer Him hospitality. However, don't fret too much; He isn't tempermental. Christ has occupied temporary quarters before. Remember, there was only a stable on the first night He arrived.

"And He knows that we'll build Him a fine Home just as soon as possible, especially since Joseph the Carpenter is so personally interested and Mother Mary won't be standing idly by." (end quote from our parish bulletin Vol. I, No. 1.)

Who shall say what a parish is? Who shall discourse on its nature? Who shall proclaim its glory?

A parish is a holy thing, a holy place where God meets man and man meets God. It is Moses on Mount Sinai, the shepherds and magi in Bethlehem, the marriage feast of Cana, the Sea of Galilee with its stormy boat rides and crowded shores; it is the Garden of Gethsemane and the crowning with thorns, the Cross on Golgotha and "Alleluia, He is risen!," the flames of Pentecost and Paul in the Athenian forum—all woven into one strand and reaching through the arches of the years and the minutes of space to March 8, 1953 and unto the consummation of the world.

God love our people and all who dwell here and do not know Him, and one another.

Several letters this morning:

Father Maurice Shean will meet with us next week in Simmesport to work on the Richmond Convention and Catholic Committee of the South policy meet for August. This opens up great possibilities and responsibilities. Dr. George Mitchell of Southern Regional Council, Atlanta, to meet with the men at Marksville Monday evening.

Emile Reggie, Charlie Jaubert, Father Oswald Sigur et al will gather at Father Marvin's to plan further K. of C. social action leadership training next Friday.

Jeanne Plante writes from Grailville about Sallie Collett's article for the *Sunday Visitor*, and Sallie writes about her future in the apostolate.

Betty Schneider: "I'm still reeling at the turn of events in Shreveport. Everybody is quite excited about it all and I have already gotten letters out to the various staffs so that we can come to some decision in the month as to how we will proceed in Shreveport. As I told you, I'm somewhat sure that we'll go ahead on it. However, I don't make those kind of decisions myself.

"Meeting you all . . . dispels a lot of false ideas I had about Southerners."

I note well that she does not say "*whether* we will proceed in Shreveport," but "*how* we will proceed. . . ." Christ, You must really want this Friendship House here. If not You had better start permitting the expected obstacles to pop up mighty soon and stop nipping them in the bud.

Tomorrow's my birthday. Thirty-four. The children surprise me with a Missa Cantata a day early and "Happy Birthday to you!" in assembly. They are a lovely, loving bunch.

Vladimir Polivka recounted his experiences with the Reds in Prague, Czechoslovakia, to the Mother and Dad's Club this evening. He has real ability and charm. Was on verge of doctorate in law at Charles University. Now in undergraduate scholarship at Centenary.

He escaped in 1948, during the February coup. Was in

Stuttgart about same time I was inspecting DP camps for NCWC with Monsignors Ligutti, Mulroy, Loftus, Fathers Kelly and Scheidler. Revives the nightmare memories of the hunger and cold and misery and despair of those millions.

And as a further refresher on global human misery Monsignor Swanstrom of NCWC Relief Services mails in the two thousand paged "Hearings before the President's Commission on Immigration and Naturalization." Twenty hundred eighty-nine pages saying God made the world and all its space and natural resources for all the human family. So many Catholics meet this terrific problem by making novenas and nothing more. To beg God to perform miracles to do our work as citizens of the world is the refuge of laziness and the subterfuge of callousness if not outright hate. Christ did not abrogate but confirmed by His Own Life the commandment: "By the sweat of thy brow . . . ," and added ". . . and thy neighbor as thyself."

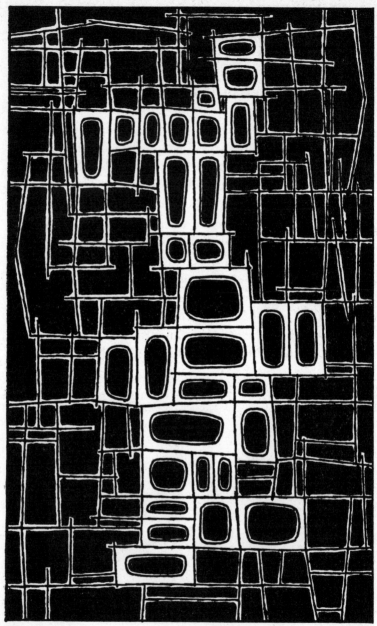

"You and you and you and I are One and We."

❖

GREAT IS MY
CONFIDENCE IN YOU

2 Corinthians 7: 4

We have had a lot of polio in Shreveport during the past five years. Now the Salk vaccine has marvelously reduced the dread scourge. Before immunization took control we saw in sadness quite a number of victims, some our own children. The peak crisis of fever and pain filled with fear of death lasts only a few days. Now the onslaught subsides; little Johnny will live. But the heart-rending struggle to overcome paralysis begins, the struggle to revivify nerves, to trigger dead reflexes, to rebuild wasted muscles, to coordinate the whole body. Massage, tedious exercise, racklike stretching, near scalding heat treatments continue by the hour and by the day, by the month and through the year.

And what has happened to Johnny's spirit? Does he

still hope to walk again? Yesterday he wiggled his toes, in two weeks doctor says he might turn his ankle sidewise, in a couple of months maybe bend the knee. Then braces will be fitted. How long before he will confidently arise and walk!—Run? Ask not the question.

For some time yet the Church will ask of the till recently paralyzed laity, "What can you do? What weight can you bear?" To the extent we feel the sense of life-with-the-Whole, to the extent we feel wanted and trusted, to the degree we have trial and error exercise, to that degree we have confidence in our own powers. We live in a day of great expectations because the members now hear (and begin to understand) the Head saying: "You and you and you and I are One and We."

1. Lay Leaders

PREPARING THE TALK for the Catholic Committee of the South convention in Richmond coming this month has forced me to reflect on our experiments of the past two years. What have we learned about lay leader formation which might interest the clergy of Virginia and the South. My THINK group notes, week-end programs and correspondence files bulge with tentative indications.

In September 1951 AMERICA ran an article on "the failure of the Catholic college graduate," particularly how he falls short of his promised contribution to parish life. I wrote a four page commentary to Father Bob Hartnett; since then the editor of AMERICA and I have exchanged a score of letters debating the problem. Our Catholic school system is THE strength and signal mark of the Church in the U. S.; our achievement and hope for the future should be gaugeable by the participation of our finished product, the college graduate, in Catholic life. If he has "failed" we have here a serious indictment of the whole apostolate of the Church.

Archbishop Lucey of San Antonio, episcopal chairman of the lay organizations of N. C. W. C., worries about the state of affairs. Some two years ago he and Father Phil

Kenney of N. C. W. C.'s Washington headquarters got some forty priests together in New Orleans to chew on this question for a couple of days. Archbishop Rummel and other ordinaries of the province partook in the give and take. Father Kenney assigned me to analyze the status of men's organizations in the province of New Orleans.

The conclusions of two years ago still hold today: The scope of Holy Name, St. Vincent de Paul, C. C. D., K. of C. and D. C. C. M. activity is much restricted. The critical problems daily headlined are barely touched by group awareness or action, nor by the individual Catholic conscience. In their programming our organizations seem quite insulated from "outside" realities like industry-labor tensions, race relations, plantation tenancy and migrant workers, educational and governmental philosophy, the institutional and political impact upon the family by housing, hospitalization, welfare aid, etc. And the Archbishop of San Antonio inserted world affairs into my litany of omissions.

Our most talented men do not give their time and thought to our Church organizations. The men who have succeeded in business and the professions, farm and labor circles, those who have a voice in "higher politics," community affairs, service and civic clubs, educational and other top policy-making roles tend to remain *Sunday* Catholics only. These social institutions form the very fabric of our society; these are the precise areas of life from which Christ is exiled. Could these born leaders as militant Christians re-orient their institutions toward a Christian society?

Some opined that we priests might fear an intelligent, militant laity, that we feel much more at home with the pious old reliables who will never counter our opinions and to whom explanations are unnecessary because "Father's the boss." Too, we might place an exaggerated value on obvious piety and a heavy penalty on intelligence and depth in choosing leaders. Or for that matter, do we make any attempt whatsoever at selecting and forming lay leaders. Does the city politician demand more innate leadership ability of the ward boss, the army of the commissioned officer, than we demand of our co-workers? Or do we want only yes men? And we have a penchant for the mass approach; we count effectiveness by numbers.

The bill of fare offered by our parish and organizational life tastes insipid to the average college man, hopelessly flat and out of touch with boiling reality for the exceptional gifted person. Much becomes puerile, an insult to his dignity and capabilities. Quoting now from my letter to Father Hartnett: "The college grad finds no attraction in organizing benefits and bingos; 'youth work' in the form of athletics and talent nights and teen-town parties, even catechizing appeal to a very limited number. Snobbish? Yes, and he should be. His call lies elsewhere. Using the college man for this type of parish activity is comparable to using the atom bomb on an infantry platoon. He is so badly needed elsewhere.

"The college graduate must bring Christ into the marketplace, into his profession and business circles, into the institution of which he forms a part, into his civic and political community. He must by his daily influence compound cures for the ills of the social body. He is a trained man in his particular field; he owes Christian leadership to that organ or tissue of the social body of which he is a member.

"To my mind this vocation has precedence over the

demands of the parish proper. Social problems press upon him: racial tensions, management-labor relations, business ethics, political corruption, migrant labor, foreign policy, the philosophies underlying education and law and government, etc. For decades our Holy Fathers have been clamoring for us to realize these facts of life.

"What parish attempts to train and commission the college graduate for work in these areas which compose his daily life? What lay organization embraces these social problems in the scope of its activities? Happily some Catholic colleges of late by dint of a crusading professor here and there conceive of themselves as centers for inspiring this type of leadership rather than for imparting mere technical and academic training in moral surroundings. But once the raw graduate arrives in the parish what vehicle, what channel, what *modus procedendi* does he find by which he might affect the *institutions,* the organs of the social structure in sustained corporate ensemble with his fellow members of the Mystical Body? None. What frustration! What waste!

"Most pastors think in terms only of the spiritual motivation and reform of *individual persons.* They do not understand the institutional pattern of society and the necessity of reforming these institutions. They have only the vaguest concept of what Pius XI means when he says: 'The public institutions of themselves, of peoples, moreover, ought to make all human society conform to the needs of the common good; that is, to the norm of social justice." (Quadragesimo Anno, On the Reconstruction of the Social Order, parag. 110.)

"College graduates compose these institutions (economics, finance, government, education, law, etc.) as well as the parish. In many ways the institution needs his leadership more than the parish does. The Church should provide him with positive concrete means of participation in group thought, group planning and group action for exercising this leadership as well as the spiritual drive of supernatural grace. 'Receive the Sacraments and give a good example' is woefully inadequate in this age.

"We are led to a problem which is much more basic.

"In the juridic structure of the Church the parish is considered to be the fundamental unit. Service to the parish becomes the norm by which an action or person is judged, in this instance the college man. The parish is a geographic entity; mere accident of residence determines its composition. But does function, loyalty and 'belongingness'? Here is a carry-over from the single plane horizontal structure of an agricultural and small town society.

"To my mind this single plane horizontal concept of the Church's structure needs re-examination and radical adjustment to parallel the present day complexities of society's vertical institutions. The lawyer residing in my parish really lives *qua* lawyer downtown. His lawyer-life is his office and books and bar association and the courts and his fellow attorneys. Even in recreation it is likely that he golfs with lawyers and goes to football games with lawyers and has lawyers out to his home for barbecued chicken. The geologist who is his next door neighbor he barely knows. He is more likely to make his acquaintance at a Chamber of Commerce or Rotary Club or business meeting downtown than across the side hedge at home. This is applicable to all the trades, crafts and professions.

"The social problems of our day criss-cross parish boundaries. The accident of parish geography cannot cope with the substance of social and economic reality.

The parish is not a self-contained sociological unit. We must create a juridic entity fitted to the needs and functions of the Church in this day and age. The parish can best serve itself and its people by cooperating in the creation of some type of moral person greater than itself, which is now striving to be born.

"In our efforts here we have come face to face with this basic question. When we try to reduce the Church to its fundamental elements we think of the parish—church and school. The parish *is* not meeting our needs. CAN it do so?—I leave open to discussion, but personally I think not."

In keeping with the theory outlined in this epistle to Father Bob Hartnett our nuclear groups have not in fact been confined to parish boundaries. Fathers DeBlanc and Sigur in Lafayette conceived that group on a community basis; so did Monsignor Vander Putten with the Fathers Bordelon viewing rather the whole Avoyelles county as a sociological unit. Using this Avoyelles group for case history these ten men were selected from four different Church parishes. These rural leaders reside in small towns and villages twenty miles along the Bayou des Glaises highway.

Every two weeks they got together for sessions lasting three and four hours: two doctors, the president of a bank, a lawyer, U. S. department of agriculture official, a feed manufacturer and planter, a lumber dealer and two merchants and farmers. Their ages range from thirty to forty-five. What induced ten very busy men, fathers of growing families, community leaders upon whom everyone calls, to give further hours and intelligent attention to causes which added nothing to their bank accounts and self-aggrandizement? A leader finds the joy of fulfillment in striving for an idea and ideal greater than self.

Men of this caliber develop greater sensitivity to the ills of our social body. Possessed of greater intelligence they perceive and reflect upon the structure of society, its stresses and strains. Ordinary social and business interchange creates an atmosphere which stifles serious conversation. Or the snatches here and there never get far along the way towards a whole view of life. It takes hours to chew over the tangled knot of race relations, right-to-work bills and the welfare state. Starting from the surface of their everyday lives, from the Monday morning need of answering: "What determines a fair wage? Should I okay this loan? At what rate of interest? Should I resort to surgery? The school board threatens the Negro school principal with suspension, say he's too uppity, should I intervene? Another family farm up for sale, should I offer a loan or buy it up myself? What is the moral, as distinct from the strictly legal, merit of this damage suit?"—from the need of solving these day to day dilemmas, these men must establish deep convictions of social justice and love. Mere transient opinions no longer satisfy. They seek roots, the roots of rights and duties, good and evil, roots which sink deep into the nature of man and society. And these roots lead deeper and deeper into "Who is man? Where did I come from? Why am I here? God—Who is God? Why did He make the world? its natural resources? How came I into this stewardship? What!—the Negro *my* brother? How seriously did Christ mean '. . . and thy neighbor as thyself'?"

See. Judge. Act. Specialized Catholic action has reemphasized the applicability of Christian prudence in restoring Christ to the workaday world. The group of eight or ten observes more angles, draws from wider experience; consciences examine each other, Christ's Truth and Love scrutinizes "but everybody does it," a communal *confiteor* often results. The men share each other's light and find strength in the group will, solidifying into group conviction. We seek no immediate action, no startling project. From the inner transformation over the weeks and months action does come forth. Perhaps in the court chamber a Negro mother is called "Mrs." for the first time in the startled judge's memory—the lone act of an individual. Or perhaps group action results; the Knights of Columbus undertake a state-wide program to form social consciences; petitions appear before legislative committees; the way is smoothed for Negroes to enter a college.

The men meet every two weeks, three or four hours at a stretch. We erect no mold nor scaffolding of preconceived blueprint. We must preserve the flexibility and spontaneity characterizing a movement, not crystallize into another brittle bundle of by-laws, dues and motions duly seconded and filed away. "The Spirit breathes where It will," and how and when It will. Why shouldn't a priest devote ten or twelve hours a month to the development of lay leaders? If each year I can help five men grow toward true stature, that to me is time well spent. Christ did not spend all His time on the crowded shores of Lake Genesareth. After a spate of talk and fishing He called Simon Peter, James and John up toward the mountains. In time that nuclear group grew into the Twelve. And Christ is patient, remarkably patient; the work of the Twelve continues today.

A seminary faculty of eight or ten priests devote their full time to training a dozen to fifteen ordinands each year. We priests of the parishes can certainly dedicate some fraction of our week to the intensive formation of a few top leaders to participate in the apostolate of the Twelve, in keeping with the diversity of needs and organs and functions experienced by Christ in His Mystical Body.

2. Christ-in-Community

JULY DRAWS TO A CLOSE. In a couple of weeks we, the Fathers Bordelon and I, head for the Catholic Committee of the South policy meeting at Belmont Abbey. Then we spend the following week giving lectures at Grailville.

The C. C. S. Belmont gathering of thirty and more to mull over the South and see our region as a whole—as God sees it—that week with Fathers Maurice Shean and John Thomas, with fine laymen like Morton Elder and Paul Williams and George Mitchell promises well. And the week at Grailville promises much also; every association with these intense young women of depth and world vision helps me to understand a wee bit better what Christ is all about, 33 and 1953 A.D., next year and next century.

But as the summer breezes by I doubt if any experience will equal the spiritual conferences of the past two Sundays. Sixty odd showed up each evening: parish and community leaders, participants of the various groups, officers of the K. of C. and other organizations; knowledgeable, talented, generous persons almost to a man, many of them husbands and wives who really want to put on

Christ and have Him grow inside both themselves, that they may more truly become conjoined in Him.

Preparing such conferences forces me to dig deeper myself. Then we dig together:

These are conferences on the spiritual life. We all have a spiritual life to some measure, meaning our contact with Christ, the degree to which we know and love Him. Often we prattle away from catechism memory that we exist to know God, love and serve Him, to be happy on earth and in heaven. These phrases flow out without meaning too much. To the extent these words mean something we have life in and of and through the Spirit.

Now and again we must needs withdraw from the pressing demands of business and home, forsake the relaxing small talk of living room and coffee table in order to penetrate more deeply into this more abundant life Christ died to give us. Happily these two evenings husband and wife find unity in seeking Christ together; here seated side by side you ponder the same Truth, thrill to the same Love, follow the same Way, move to the same Life. Too seldom can couples make retreats together. No bond is more precious than a shared-inner-vision, the compenetration of two selves become one in the ictus of a spiritual insight. To be fused into one by the flame of God's love—that's the great grace of the married state.

These conferences differ from our many other Sunday evening gatherings for lectures and forums. The history course and *THE REASON WHY* series stressed the apologetic vein, proving the authenticity of the Gospels, the historicity of Justin Martyr and Ignatius of Antioch, demonstrating the existence of God, reconciling seeming conflicts between science and the supernatural—defending Christ before Pilate, Seneca and Caiphas, Newton,

Darwin and Huxley. Tonight we drop all debate. We set out to prove nothing. We merely open the portal of the soul that Christ can come in.

We must not dwell constantly on proof and demonstration. The continual demand for proof stifles love; stifling love stifles life. We must reach the point with Christ where proof is no longer necessary. Compare your own love for each other: for husband and wife to demand continually: "Well, prove that you love me!" is to kill love. This keeps us on edge. That's the vice of jealousy and mistrust. Because by love we give ourselves to each other; once and for all I'm yours and you're mine. The essence of marriage lies in this giving of one another, the two becoming one—forever.

Now it is much the same with Christ, to demand proof of love stifles love. We smother our spiritual life by constantly challenging Christ's good intentions, by repeatedly asking, "Why did You do this?" and "Why didn't You do it my way?" and "Now prove this to me!" Certainly we act reasonably in examining our Faith, in making more profound our grasp of history and theology, the great truths of Christ and His Church. But truth must lead us further along; truth must lead to love. So the mental gymnastics of piling up quotes from Conway's *Question Box* provides no ultimate; it merely offers means to an end. Too often we bog down in the miasma of means; we never pass from the Alpha to the Omega.

Our spiritual life is our courtship with Christ. Imagine a courtship crammed with nothing but question marks and suspicion. So we start out from the bedrock soaring upwards. We are creatures, children of God, brothers and sisters of Christ, heirs of heaven. From these rooted foundation truths we climb toward Our Lord. We embrace Christ: "I'm Yours and You're mine, and that's that. Let's go on from here."

Individualism has permeated our civilization, even penetrating our spiritual life. Individualism greatly impedes spiritual growth. The ultimate human perversion is to become so wrapped up in the shell of self as to be incapable of loving or of being loved. That's hell: unloving and unlovable. T. S. Eliot explains this in "The Cocktail Party." Each man nourishes within his being a writhing worm of unconditioned self, coiling, uncoiling. We echo and re-echo Adam's yearning to be *too much like God,* to be self-subsistent, sufficient to ourselves. This leads us to despise and deny our state of being, our condition of existence, our creaturehood. The misery gnawing we feel down inside is the ego gnawing on self. We shut ourselves off from Him Who Alone can feed us. We want to be self-contained, independent of every other being, but we find our cupboard bare.

In response to "Who am I?"—and we all ask the question more often than we know—John Smith, 430 Patton Avenue, Shreveport, Louisiana, U. S. A., planet earth, that's a juvenile answer. The shattering truth is that I'm a creature, *ens ab alio,* suspended, hanging in being, dependent for existence second by second upon Him Who truly *IS*, Him who is *ENS A SE,* Being of and by and through Itself.

We will never find happiness—because we will never find love—unless we grasp and accept the truth of our creature-ness, the truth of our no-thing-hood: that the being we possess as our own is a mere radiation, a wavering beam of being shadowed with motes, a ripple of is-ness impaled for the moment onto the screen of time and space. God is the ALL. And we participate ever so slightly in His All-ness.

A further humiliation to our pretensions is that God chooses to give us being and sustain us in life through the agency of our fellow creatures. We rebel against our dependency on God; we rail the more against our dependency upon these beings so close to nothing as we ourselves are. We must gulp down fowl's eggs and the flesh of swine, drink water and breathe air. For the life of the mind and spirit we must depend on the lowly senses, light and sound waves; dead molecule butting against dead molecule brings words to our ears. Alas, even the Word of God reaches us via creature molecules set in motion by the fleshy vocal chords of Moses and Isaiah, Peter, James and John, Pius Twelfth, Bishops Sheen and Greco, and via light waves bouncing from their written thoughts and flickering TV image.

Grace, Christ's light and strength and love, through the sacraments travels along fickle conductors, creature things of passing sight and sound, before losing its impact in the leaden shield of self. There, too often but to wane and fade away, corroded by the acid self that embitters my taste of the misery-me I try to feed upon, insulated from creature and Creator.

God communicates Himself through our fellow creatures. Francis of Assisi saw every creature as a messenger from God. The sun and sea, cricket and donkey each told him something about their common heavenly Father; they spoke of God's power and love and majesty and closeness. Francis loved God in and by and through all he saw and heard. We, on the other hand, regard creatures as sources of *our* power and glory, as objects to be possessed unconditionally, as means of dominating other human beings. We covet. And in coveting we can find no peace. Instead of recognizing our own creaturehood, our own dependent state in which we are fed existence through the stream of fellow creatures flowing from the Godhead, we would reverse the flow of the stream and dominate all creatures so that they then depend on us. Pursuing this course to its ultimate we would manipulate nature in all its manifestations; controlling force and energy in all its variety, do we not then control God from Whom this force and energy purports to flow? Thus we surpass ourselves, we are no longer creatures, no longer dependent. Man is *the master*. We no longer need God. Man controls nature through science. Air and soil and sea are man's to manipulate. Divine Providence is no more. Nietzsche chants the dirge of the death of God. God the Creator does not avenge Himself directly as in Old Testament days. In time the creature turns upon man, upon the would-be god. Our own scientific achievement threatens to pollute the air, shatter the earth and boil the sea. The invisible electron which man has diverted from its appointed course threatens us with cosmic suicide.

Is this God's way of quelling our insurrection? Has God fitted out His creation with a built-in governor so that when one portion of creation asserts to itself quasidivine attributes another creature rises up to smite the rebel down? Like Michael smote Lucifer and evicted Adam. Ah, the tale of human progress: from the Fall to the fall-out.

Be that as it may the spiritual life we develop depends in great measure upon our relation with creatures through which God channels to us existence at all its levels. Soil and manure become the spaghetti and meat-balls which continue our vegetative life of cellular growth. Light rays and sound waves stimulate our ani-mal-shared senses of sight and hearing. These sense stimuli supply the raw data from which the intellect ab-stracts universal ideas. These universals frame targets for the free will, and show us God. And even the life of grace, that supernatural gift by which we participate in the life and love of Christ Himself, that grace comes to us via creature channels: the bread and oil, words and water of the Sacraments and Sacrifice.

And the crucial point—all these life-giving creatures flow from God to us through the ministry of our fellow men. Parents, truckers, farmers, teachers, priests and neighbors bring us God's gift of *is-ness*. The individual does not and cannot stand alone. We are interdependent. We are made for community. We become ourselves most truly when we share ourselves with one another, when we freely fulfill our role of bearing God's quota of being in all its variety to our brother humans, each in keeping with his vocation, talent and station.

Too long has the search for self-identity been walled off within the limited orbit of the individual self. The parish must thaw out the streams of life iced up by indi-vidualism. That's what we mean when we say the parish must generate community, must dig out channels for the flow of the deep waters promised by Christ at Jacob's well. Supernatural goods adhere and engraft themselves on the natural; so the flow of the spirit, of truth and grace, of the more abundant life co-exists to some degree with the current of human living. That is why the parish cannot ignore man's natural needs—the need for human compassion, the need to share joy and sadness, laughter and tears, the need for solidarity, for friendship, for community. That's why an individualist Christianity is a bastard Christianity; warped, perverted.

"I can stand on my own two feet. I am captain of my fate and master of my soul." These are lies. We have other captains and other masters because we have a Father and many brothers. Christ never said, "Go it alone. Carry your own burden. Look out for number one." Just the opposite. He constantly insists that we find strength and realization in one another. "By this will all men know that you are my disciples if you have love for one another. Give *us* this day *our* daily bread; forgive *us our* trespasses—." How could we have forgotten? How could the Sacrament of Communion become Food for *my* soul only, the Sacrifice of Golgotha on the parish altar a mere background for *my* private silent petitions, for *my* health and *my* job and *my* family? How came it about that the Church, the Universal Church, the world and time embracing Mystical Body of Christ has narrowed to *my* road to *my* heaven?

Individualism has shattered our parish life. Each of us seeks to save his own soul, and this usually from a most selfish motive of escaping hell and scraping by over the threshold into purgatory. Love of God has little enough to do with it. We share no unity of prayer and worship, no sense of a shared secret, of a common inner life. The skeleton of surviving oneness is organizational, administrative, spasmodic; based on physical rather than spiritual reality: we just happen to live near this church *building*. The Mass in this *building* is usually short. This *building* in which I attend Mass is air-conditioned. And if any *esprit de corps* appears it tends toward the gladhanding, back-slapping variety imitative of a luncheon club. Now there's nothing wrong with greeting one another, but this should manifest a perduring concern and devotion; Christ-in-you must know and love and greet Christ-in-me. Then our parish begets Christ-in-community.

Our parish must become a community of truth, joined by our deeply held convictions, by our sense of sharing a precious secret. Our parish must become a community of love, admiring each others gifts, rejoicing in our God given talents, Christ-in-me loving Christ-in-you. And from this love must come forth a community of service, bearing one another's burdens, washing our brother's feet, caring for our neighbor's children, helping in the little incidents of every day and the great emergencies of every life—help with the cup of cold water, the bandaid, the pint of blood from the parish bank, the loan from the credit union. Our parish must become a community of worship; we must pray together and for each other, we the One Body kneeling, confessing, adoring the One Spirit.

When we become conscious of this community of life then we become Christ-in-community.

3. The Apostolate to Institutions

THERE DOES exist a South—a South, U. S. A., that is.

This one region of our nation has a type of existence unique to itself, a style of living, an atmosphere and a history which set it off from the rest of the nation. Much of our national development cannot be understood except in terms of this region's relation with the whole—Jefferson's relation with Hamilton and the Adamses, cotton and New England tariffs, raw-boned Old Hickory and the "effete city slickers," slave holders and the abolitionists, Calhoun and Webster and, of course, the fratricidal War between the States. Tussles have cropped up between other provincial entities: mid-West farmers and Eastern railroad barons, Texas ranchers and New York bankers, public land and water vs. private fences and mines and company-owned utilities, between isolationist mid-America and interventionist Atlantic (and now Pacific) sea-boarders. But all these inter-regional tensions fade and pass away compared to the enduring dialectic between North and South.

Because the South does exist, the Catholic Committee of the South exists. A living organism adapts itself to some degree to the environment within which it lives, or

changes the environment. So with the Church, Christ's
Living Body.

The C. C. S. functions by and large in those south-
eastern states which formed the Confederacy. Anchor
your geometric compass at Louisville, protrude the outer
leg six hundred miles to the east, and swing down
through the Carolinas, north Florida, the Gulf South, to
a southwesterly reach near Dallas, Texas: that arc de-
limits the American South, some dozen states of thirty
million people, of whom some one and a half million are
Catholic.

That at most five percent of the region's people are
members of the Church, as compared to four times that
density in other parts of the nation, immediately points
out a southern particularity to which the Church in the
South faces up with its Extension-built missions and
trailer chapels and street preaching. But to muddy up
this demographic sketch half of the South's Catholics reside in one enclave of one state, Louisiana. Some three-
quarter million Catholics live within a hundred or so
miles of New Orleans. This concentration reduces the
Church's representation to some three percent in the
region's remaining half million square miles, the proportion falling to half of one percent in some states like
the Carolinas which boast fewer Catholics than pre-Red
China.

But statistics, figures and number scrabble will never
describe the South. Emotional charges and cultural un-
dertones and livid history flesh out this demographic
skeleton, and make of the region a heaving, pulsating
personality. Cornpone and sowbelly, spirituals and jazz,
cotton and tobacco, textiles and lumber, progress and
reaction, statesmanship and demagoguery, Moses and

Darwin, sharecropping and labor unions, plantation landlordism and hill country yeomanry—all contribute to the temperamental tantrum and stoic nobility of the South.

In 1939 southern bishops, clergy and laity attended a meeting called by the Social Action Department of N. C. W. C. at Cleveland, Ohio. There the idea of C. C. S. was conceived. President Roosevelt had recently described the South as the nation's economic problem number one. The Social Action Department is charged with bettering racial and labor-management relations. The South had its pressing problems in these fields. There, too, the Church's educational system was weakest and its life among the prolific rural families almost nil. Under the sponsorship of southern bishops the Catholic Committee of the South came into being in Atlanta in 1940 dedicated to the difficult task of interpreting and applying Christian principles to the institutions of southern society. In the thirteen years since, Archbishop Rummel has given the C. C. S. the support of his moral authority and vast prestige as metropolitan of the area. Priests like Father Vincent O'Connell, S.M., of New Orleans' Major Seminary, lay leaders like Paul Williams of Richmond and Morton Elder of Birmingham, have kept the vigorous infant alive and kicking. And many have kicked back, trying to crush what is to them an *enfant terrible*.

Two weeks ago some thirty of us spent five days at Belmont Abbey in the Piedmont area of North Carolina. The C. C. S. called together a number of friends to talk things over. In the hospitable *ora et labora* atmosphere of the Benedictine monastery we asked ourselves where have we come from and where are we going. Bishop

John J. Russell of Charleston, presided as episcopal moderator; Father Lou Flaherty of Richmond and Father Maurice Shean, Oratorian Superior from Rock Hill, S. C., organized and ram-rodded the policy meet. Top men pitched in; like Dr. George Mitchell, Director of the Southern Regional Council, Atlanta; Father John Thomas, the Jesuit family sociologist of the Institute of Social Order; Martin Work of the National Council of Catholic Men, Washington.

If ever a few dared to undertake much among the many, the C. C. S. qualifies among those few. The Committee offers a prime example of the apostolate to social institutions, the apostolate for which Pius XI pleaded, a bearing of Christ not merely to individual souls but to the organs of the social body which compose human life: the family, economy, education, body politic and that complex web of customs and mores which become the ethos of a people. The C. C. S. is not properly an action group. It has no canonical status or jurisdictional authority within the Church. Its adherents are volunteers. Like much of the South itself it represents a state of mind, a social view, a direction of the will—fathered by the social encyclicals and striving to impregnate the popes' eternal truths into the temporal realities which are the South.

I cannot measure the impact of the Catholic Committee of the South upon our secular institutions like the press and other mass media, our university and public school system, our new born unions and awakening management. Public statements and small groups C. C. S.-inspired have voiced Christian ideals in the segregation issue when few others dared risk this John the Baptist role. Because of this the New Orleans Commission on Human Rights lives in constant peril of a John the Baptist fate. However difficult to evaluate its effectiveness upon the general public and our non-Catholic neighbors the C. C. S. has borne witness to Christ—and some fraction of the darkness grasps His Presence.

C. C. S. effectiveness within the Church herself stands out more clearly. These effects might be handily termed the three "c's"; communication, consciousness and conscience.

First, because of C. C. S. the Church in the South has been in *communication*. To a degree much greater than would have otherwise resulted clergy and lay leaders forge a chain of hands stretching from Richmond to Raleigh and Gastonia county, through Savannah, Atlanta, Birmingham and Mobile, via Biloxi to New Orleans, Lafayette and Arkansas. Despite our geographic spread we are in touch with the larger Body. And happily in recent years Archbishop O'Boyle of Washington and Bishop Molloy of Covington have extended our sense of oneness northward to the Mason-Dixon line.

Second, this regional oneness has begotten regional *consciousness*, an awareness of and for the Church striving here: not a perverted provinciality, but a sense of solidarity, of caring about the Church as a Whole, for building up the Body of Christ under the surroundings particular to the South. In April we gathered in convention at Richmond. Laymen and priests from our three Louisiana dioceses spent three days with clergy and laity from the missionary, sparsely Catholic Bible-belt. We talked and prayed, argued, ate, laughed and worried together. The five or six student leaders representing the Newman Center of Southwestern Louisiana Institute now orientate their thinking and apostolic zeal toward helping the Glenmary and the other missionaries in the foothills of the Smokies. We all now more clearly see that Catholic Louisiana must set an example of inter-racial justice and charity which can set the compass for the whole South. Father Smith roaming the four counties of Allegheny hills forming his forty family parish feels less alone as he peruses the monthly newsletter C. C. S. circulates to continue this south-wide community sense. We each have someone else to mention occasionally in the memento for the living.

And then the C. C. S. does much to form the *conscience* of the southern Church. The conscience makes practical judgments of right and wrong. Are we not at times creatures of our environment rather than its creators? Do we not at times sway with the wind? The C. C. S. strengthens our corporate conscience and often has been its voice. And, too, the Committee has balanced the South's individualism with the integral truth of the sociality of man; a social justice and social charity can be conceived and brought forth only by a *social* conscience, seeing mankind in all his manifold inter-relatedness. Whose but the conscience of Christ-in-me can lead to the love of Christ-in-brown-skinned-you?

Yes, there does exist a South, and in consequence a manifestation of the Living Christ particular to this region of the U. S. A.

From the policy meet at Belmont Abbey the Fathers Bordelon and I headed our Chevrolet west over the Great Smokies, then northward through Kentucky's hills and bluegrass across the Ohio by ferry just up from Cincinnati to nearby Grailville. There we spent last week, the last week of August, conducting a four day institute on "The Mission of the Church Today."

If the South tends toward narrow provinciality, the Grail tends to embrace the whole world: extensively, the world of geographic continents; intensively, the world of woman in all its diverse cultural creations and human concerns. The very breadth and depth of vision of the Grail movement makes these lay apostles difficult for some to understand. Twenty-five years ago five women graduates of the University of Nijmegen launched the movement. Their bishop in Haarlem (Holland) wanted the new concept of the lay apostolate developed in his own diocese. Thence it has spread to the six continents.

Dr. Lydwine van Kersbergen brought the Grail idea to the U. S. in 1940 at the invitation of Cardinal Mundelein. She was one of the original five founders, all deeply indebted for their formation to Father James van Ginneken, a great Jesuit of Nijmegen University who in the 1920's pioneered the possibilities of lay participation in the apostolate. Ten years ago Dr. van Kersbergen established the Grail home base on the present farm site near Loveland, Ohio, under the patronage of Archbishop McNicholas of Cincinnati. By now some fifty American young women have dedicated themselves for life to the nuclear group, and hundreds of others have taken up their tasks in the world prepared by Grail formation in some dozen or more areas ranging from Brooklyn and Detroit to Lafayette, Louisiana, and in missions overseas.

The Grail emphasis is a pervading sense of motherhood. For them the true role of modern day woman cannot be really grasped and thoroughly lived—and consequently woman cannot find happiness—unless she rediscovers the deep meaning of motherhood. Now there is physical motherhood, and that of the spirit. Consequently, the Grail begets a fertile tension between the great ideal of marriage in Christ and the greater ideal of virginity in Christ. The feminine role of creative begetting and nourishing, accepting and giving of self in love underlies either vocation. The young woman must not passively fall into the ruts of modern feminism, which masculinizes woman, remaking her into man's shadow. Man is the aggressor, the conqueror, the specialist. Woman is the universalist; motherhood is an out-pouring, the giving of self: in marriage to beget new children in Christ; in virginity to beget God in all his children and all creation. Either role is dear to the Church.

More than any other group I have encountered in the United States the Grail seeks to christianize our culture: the lively arts and folk customs like song, dance, drama and at the family hearth; the plastic arts and folk crafts like painting, ceramics and sculpture, dress and decor. The Grail community immerse themselves deeply into the world of sign and symbol, those uniquely human elements from which art comes forth. And these signs and symbols must consciously correspond to the realities they represent, the deepest realities like soil and clay, water, food and fiber, sky and fire, animals and, in short, all creation at that level closest to God, before mechanistic man unthinkingly corrupts these raw materials through which God channels life to us. Like new Eves the Grail workers seek the sources of life in that which is freshest from the hand of God. For this reason the surprised visitor may see at Grailville a spinning wheel or a loom, an overall sense of the primitive, of living close to man's natural origins. The ontology of dress and decoration for the human body can best be divined by knowing the feel and substance, touch and stress of raw cotton and wool lovingly transformed into thread and yarn,

warp and woof; patiently dyed and woven into bright
bands of homespun, sewn into clothing to enshrine the
human body which is the temple of the Holy Spirit.

Obviously then the Grail is developing a philosophy
and theology of work, work as love made visible, love
human and divine. And because they return to fundamentals, and because their efforts are still incomplete,
and because they have not answered all the problems
raised by assembly lines and Rosie the Riveter, some
tend to brush off the Grail as retrogressive escapists.
Their formation does begin in a withdrawn atmosphere,
but they do not remain always in the desert across the
Jordan. We encounter Grail workers in the "downtown"
world of Detroit and Brooklyn, on the campuses of
Columbia University and Southwest Louisiana College,
in suburban and slum homes of New Mexico and Cincinnati, and, of course, in missionary clinics and schools
in Africa and Brazil, at the frontiers of Christendom.

This womanly conversation with God's basic creatures,
this communication with the primitive, with the rhythm
of life at its natural fonts, is really a courtship with God—
speaking and listening to Him through His creation. Besides ministering to an atmosphere for cultural growth,
this sense of the sacramentality of nature provides the ideal
exterior setting and interior disposition for living the
Liturgy. The morning Sacrifice opens the day and suffuses
the daily round of work and worship and recreation
through the recurrence of the missal's proper in antiphon
and refrain. The seasonal re-living of Our Lord's Life
through the liturgical year prompts the pulse of joy and
sorrow in the Grail family and community. Is Grailville
a school? Yes, a school for apostolic formation, affiliated
with Catholic University, Washington, as "a community

college." Yes, but then as Father Marvin puts it: "To communicate a truth the Grail not only teaches that truth, they then sing and dance it, write and dramatize it, paint and choral it, symbolize and pray it, taste and eat it."

The historical studies of Christopher Dawson have shown the religion of a people to be the dominant source of that people's culture. Whether conscious of Dawson's studies or not, the Grail begets artistic cultural expression from the matrix of nature's sacramentality and the Liturgy of the supernatural Catholic Faith.

These passing reflexions offer no exhaustive analysis of the Grail movement. It is another outflowering of the Church today evoked by papal emphasis on the apostolate of the *laity* to the *institutions of society*. Among the institutions affected are our own parish and community life. The para-liturgical Thanksgiving and Presentation ceremonies, the Sunday dialogue Mass, the Advent wreathes and baptismal robes—all these Grail influences we deeply prize, but most prized of all is a world vision due in great part to the remarkable Dr. Van Kersbergen and her cohorts.

Back in 1920 Father van Ginneken, their priest-inspirer, wrote these prophetic words: "Would it not be possible for the missions to draw lay people from Europe and America? Or bolder still, could not groups of lay people be sent into mission countries for which they are specifically trained?

"I see in our own time an apostolic laity going forward en masse to the mission fields . . . it will be characteristic of the twentieth century that Catholic missionary bishops from all over the world will invite lay people to mission countries, and in this way the harvest will be reaped in great abundance."

Possibly the outstanding work of the Grail will be their help in awakening the Church in America to the potential of lay missionaries to our two billion human brothers who know not Christ.

Driving homeward we stop a few hours at Gethsemane, the Trappist Monastery. Here is the place that Merton uncovered to the world. How many of us go to see the spot from which he speaks forth rather than the place of silent thunder—in Bishop Sheen's phrase. I wonder if this adulation of Merton rankles what little of the old Adam still lingers in his confreres.

Gethsemane's full up, about to spawn another new foundation. How can this contemplative outburst be happening in activist America? How good of God because we *peregrini gasolini* so engrossed in re-incarnating Christ in the temporal deeply need the prayer and sacrifice of these contemplative counterparts in Our Lord's Whole Body.

4. A Clergy-Centered Press

AT THE MARYHILL CONFERENCE last week we had quite a debate concerning our diocesan paper. The great majority of the clergy favor drastic revision. Our circulation is under three thousand. Our people are largely indifferent to our official Church paper.

We priests have received from the chancery a mimeographed form asking our analysis of our diocesan press. Certainly I feel no special competence in this field, having no familiarity with other diocesan organs, having read no other paper than our own since ordination. Nevertheless the chancery wants an analysis. So mine goes in with a four-page cover letter.

The principal question: "Can you single out any particular reason why our paper does not sell itself to the million Catholics in Louisiana and Mississippi?"

My simple answer: a clergy-centered press. At a Knights of Columbus meeting at Maryhill about two years ago Bishop Greco made a statement to the gathered men which has recurred to me very frequently. He told the men that for some reason the erroneous idea prevails that the Church is to be equated with the hierarchy, clergy and religious. This concept of the Church, our Bishop went on to explain, is wrong. The Church is the hierarchy and laity *together*. To emphasize his point Bishop Greco pointed to the assembled men and said, "You are the Church!" They, the laity, he went on to explain, constituted the Church as much as he the Bishop did, though in a different way and fulfilling a different function.

It is relevant to our Catholic press problems that our Bishop feels the necessity of underlining the position of the laity in the Church. Quoting from my cover letter:

"As Van Noort puts it (translated from page 3 of his theological manual *On the Church of Christ*) the Church is the society of those men who by the profession of the same Faith and participation in the same sacraments, under the apostolic pastors (bishops) and their primate, constitute the kingdom of Christ on earth.

"St. Augustine, quoted in the Catechism of the Council of Trent, page 97, says simply: 'The Church consists of the faithful dispersed throughout the world.' Now, certainly, the Bishop of Hippo is not attempting a complete definition. Van Noort's is more theologically correct. But the point about this quote of Augustine's is his preoccupation with the laity. To him it seemed the more obvious and normal thing to say.

"Van Noort, St. Augustine (and Bishop Greco) are emphasizing the wholeness, the totality of the Church as embracing laity as well as clergy. We are all familiar with the historical reasons why during the past three or four centuries in reaction to the protestant revolt the emphasis upon the distinct status, authority and role of the clergy has been so great, I needn't belabor this point. The great effort being made these past few years to activate the laity shows that we are awakening to the need of more balanced emphasis. We, the clergy, are after all ministers, means to an end. The faithful are in a more precise sense the *causa finalis* as well as the *causa materialis* of the Church than are the clergy. I hope this is sound theology. If not I would like to be corrected.

"The purpose of all of this is to lead to my main point that in our diocesan press there is too great an emphasis upon the clergy. And the counterpart is that there is too little emphasis on the people.

"By way of exemplifying this I have gone through the untidy stack of magazines and papers near my desk and found the issues of January 28th, 21st, 7th (1954) and September 24th (1953). I have totalled up the number of times that there is mentioned on the first page *by name* a member of the hierarchy, a monsignor, a priest, a religious (who is not a priest), and a layman. Here are the results:

	Bishop	Monsignor	Priest	Religious	Layman
Jan. 28	53	3	7	5	6
Jan. 21	7	1	1	0	4
Jan. 7	22	0	10	6	5
Sept. 24	27	3	18	4	8
Totals	109	7	36	15	23

"What are the possible conclusions? Is this as it should be? Possibly our laity do not make news. One sad and perhaps humbling conclusion is that the front page of such a paper is not considered news by our people as they are showing by the fact that they don't read it.

"All of this is raised as a point of discussion. In recent issues front page stories and pictures have told us of the appointment of several new Bishops over the country. My people are quite literate, about half of them have been to college. They have an interest in the Church and the Cause of Christ, but by and large they are not interested 'in a front page way' in who the Bishop of Grand Island, Nebraska, is, where he went to school, what his degrees are, etc.

"They might be interested in knowing that he is the 188th Bishop in the United States, that the Church is growing, that a new diocese has been formed in Podunk, Ohio, because 'X' number of families have moved in around a new industrial area, the birth rate of Catholics is such and such, new schools must be developed, the needs of the people be met, etc.

"Another clue to our clergy-centered attitude: Recently a priest friend of mine was upbraiding our paper because they did not carry in our Alexandria edition all of the clergy changes and appointments of Lafayette and New Orleans. He was thinking of having it serving his needs, he wanted to know where his classmates were, etc. I like to have that same information. But I know in my parish I am only one out of 1300 people who is interested in this information. So I think that a diocesan-wide publication is wasting its space if it carries such stories as news items."

The second question posed by the chancery form: "What about the paper's policy in presenting the Church's teaching on racial and economic problems?"

At the Maryhill conference it was stated that many cancellations had resulted from the paper's handling of the recent sugar cane strike in south Louisiana. If true this is certainly unfortunate. Quoting again from my letter:

"I am not conscious that this has affected the circulation here adversely. . . . It would appear to me that a documentary study of that situation, well prepared, covering several pages, with pictures, and giving all sides of the controversy, giving equal space to a representative of the Sugar League and to a representative of the Union, and an opportunity to the Department of Agriculture of the Federal Government to express their side of it—that such a documentary would be the ideal thing for our Catholic press to undertake. This would interest my people, I know, even at the distance of 300 miles. Again their main source of information during the unfortunate affair was the one column story of TIME magazine. It drew many comments, mostly favorable and to my mind was a better piece of public relations for the Church than many editions of our official organ. Perhaps I am being extravagant but it is something to think over."

Basically what is the Catholic press? And we cannot answer that until we understand more deeply, "What is the Church?"—in the concrete situation of our state and southland, our nation and world, as eternity meeting time at *this* point in space and history.

"Go into the whole world ..."

PERIOD III

❖

IN JOURNEYINGS OFTEN

2 Corinthians 11: 26

What mother experiences when carrying her child affects baby's personality after birth. Once regarded as an old wive's tale this theory of pre-natal experience finds support among some psychologists. While denying for myself scientific competence to judge the theory, it does arrest the imagination when applied to Mary and her Baby. Needless to say in musing over the traits Christ may have acquired from His Mother I chatter in a human way about His human nature. The Divine permits no explaining.

Consider the inclination we Christians have for moving about from place to place. Throughout history we have been on the move in tribal and national migration, crusades and expeditions, voyages and pilgrimages. Our very life we typify as wandering through this vale of tears. We are loco-motive by heritage.

How many of our great saints were great travellers. Our activism shows up even in St. Thomas Aquinas, whose capacity for immanent thought could certainly have satiated and rooted him in one spot. But no; he commutes between Naples, Paris and Cologne; he dies on the road, like so many other holy ones. The first impulse of Vincent de Paul, Loyola and Francis Assisi was to cross the Mediterranean to Islam and Jerusalem. Christopher and the monks of St. Bernard devoted their lives to helping journeyers. And remember St. Martin of Tours; El Greco always painted him on horseback. What world travellers were Boniface, Xavier, Marquette and Mother Cabrini.

All follow the lead of the Apostles, "the sent ones." "Go into the whole world . . ." really caught on, so much so that the whole institution of monasticism came forth to counterpoise this moving around with the monk's distinguishing vow of stability. The Oriental cultures share with us monastic stability, but little of that drive for purposeful setting forth on land and sea. Students of culture might reflect on why the Christianized West invented the locomotive, auto and airplane.

Paging through the Gospels note how often Our Lord went out . . . set forth . . . climbed up . . . passed by . . . arrived . . . entered and departed . . . came to . . . called and was followed. He terms Himself the WAY. The embryonic Church He was then forming apparently has handed down to His ever-growing Mystical Body this same divine unrest, this apostolic itch to reach some goal, some place. His Mother's "Behold the handmaid of the Lord" is followed in the very next verse: "Mary arose and went with haste into the hill country." And consider her trip from Nazareth to Bethlehem just before His birth.

Those psychologists could make quite a case of it all. Anyway I share Paul's "in journeyings often"; and perhaps, too, his "I am speaking foolishly," of the same page of his letter to the Corinthians, number two.

On Letters from Europe

"That I may not seem to terrify you, as it were, by letters."
2 Corinthians 10:9

America is my homeland; Europe is my mother culture. I am a Greco-Judaeo-Christian child of the West. Small wonder I feel so at home in Western Europe. It is not really a return to one's hometown or boyhood haunts. The relation is further removed. Europe evokes memories as would our ancestral home often described to me by parents and grandmother. I would recognize it not by personal flash back but as absorbed from the family album, as imprinted upon the retina of the mind by family memory. So going to Europe is like returning to a place where you have never before been. A return to my ancestral homestead feels familiar in the root sense "of and from and through the family." If America is the tree trunk which sustains me, my spiritual radix is Europe, because America springs forth a virile shoot from European roots.

For all the complaints we affect when touring Europe—the dearth of drinking water in France and of elevators in London, the hinged mattress of the Rhineland and traffic in Naples—we react deep down inside: So this is where we have come from.

With my fellow diocesan priests, Fathers Marvin and Roland Bordelon (they are blood brothers) I spent the summer of 1954 travelling through ten countries of Europe. The phrase "travelling through" is deliberate; covering seven thousand miles from Stockholm to Vesuvius and Devonshire to Salzburg in a few weeks, mostly by auto, carries all the overtones of a hurried glance, like trotting through the Louvre or an hour's perusal in the Vatican Library. We were tourists *par excellence*, "making" as many American Express and Cook's tours as possible in each locale.

Many sophisticates disdain all the implications of the word tourist. It connotes the worse American failings: superficiality, hurry, off-the-cuff impressions, gawking, loose spending. Tourist might well become the century's synonym for Philistine. And for all his help in balancing national budgets the American version of the species takes a lot of criticism abroad. Little can be done about it. The force of fate decrees that a month or two is as much time as most Americans who get there at all will ever spend in Europe. (The military aside; their case is extra-special; they live in artificial oases stamped: Made in the U.S.A.).

And it is only normal that given his six or eight weeks Joe Blow wants to cram in as much as he can. Hence, the hustle and bustle, the urge to see it to say you saw it, and the penchant to spend a pound on a cabbie instead of a shilling for the underground (Londonese for subway). This is a once in a lifetime affair. Much should be excused us.

The priest who goes to Europe on pilgrimage bears (and bares) all the marks of the tourist. The wonder of Lourdes and Rue de Bac, Assisi and St. Peter's can overawe supernatural sensibility as readily as the Louvre and

Pompey and the Alps all heaped together can benumb one's natural powers of absorption by their very force. Indigestion of the mind and spirit results from the rich diet. And, of course, the priest must hurry, too, and greedily gorge himself with all he can possibly get at.

So I make a passing *apologia* for the tourist; appropriately the *apologia* is incidental and on the run. How I would welcome a more leisurely return to my ancestral home; how I would relish, say, a short year in Europe; a sabbatical from the parish—a few months in France and Italy, a few weeks in Bavaria and Ireland. Well, it's nice to dream. The three of us had only eight weeks, which I stretched to twelve weeks through appointment by the U. S. Department of State to attend a UNESCO seminar in Denmark, as you will see in a moment.

Now the Fathers Bordelon and I sought to soften the tourist stigma by calling our jaunt a study-tour. That led our parishioners and friends to conceive our purpose on a more elevated plane than mere gallivanting along the Appian Way. That any subject as complex and kaleidoscopic as Europe might be studied in eight weeks betrays naiveté, stupidity or presumption. We plead guilty of all three. Nevertheless we approached Europe anxious to investigate and understand what little about her that could be understood in a glance so fleeting. Is not our six thousand year accumulation of human knowledge a mere fleeting glance at all reality and Reality Itself? How little we come to know in a life time; a fortiori what can one learn in eight weeks. Still one must make the effort.

In the two years preceding our study-tour we did preparatory home-work. We read Carlton Hayes' *Political and Cultural History of Modern Europe* (according to Christopher Dawson one of the rare American authors used at

Oxford), the books of Michonneau and Godin, selected works of Dawson, Chesterton, Belloc and others. We got suggestions on whom to see and personal references from friends like Father LaFarge, Monsignors Ligutti and Swanstrom, the editors of COMMONWEAL and others. This was the first European visit for my two companions; in 1948 I had spent some six weeks in the D. P. camps of Germany, Austria and Italy with five other priests on a relief and refugee mission for Catholic Relief Services— N. C. W. C.

By correspondence we arranged appointments with some fifty persons with whom we spent most of our time —talking. These conversations provided the real content of the experience: two days with Christopher Dawson in his Devonshire home, Sundays in parishes like Father Langdale's in Eastcote and St. Hyppolyte in Paris, a day with Monsignor Baldelli making rounds of the Holy Father's charity works which he directs, a weekend with Father Schneider, U. S. Catholic Relief Services director in Frankfurt and his counterpart, Father Wilson Kaiser in Berlin; hour upon hour of good conversation with Frank Sheed and Father Hopkins, national Y. C. W. chaplain, in London; with Rachel Donders, International President of the Grail, and her associates in Amsterdam, The Hague, Nijmegen and Bonn; with Father Joe Fichter of Loyola in New Orleans, then a Fullbright scholar at Muenster University; with Archbishop Aloisius Muench of North Dakota, Apostolic Nuncio to Germany, and Patrick Boarman, N. C. W. C. cultural affairs director, headquartered at Bonn; Monsignor Andrew Landi, the able Brooklyn priest who directs N. C. W. C. Catholic Relief Services in Italy; Gunnar Kumlien, Mediterranean correspondent for a Stockholm paper and COMMONWEAL's Roman ear;

the PAX ROMANA leaders at Fribourg, Doctors Sugra-
nyes de Franch, Ducret and McMahon; that man-about-
the-globe Father Albert Leroy, S.J., at Geneva's International Labor Organization; in Paris with Father Poirier
of the family movement and Father Perrot who heads up
the *Mission de France*.

Each of these referred us to friends and co-workers by
the score in homes and schools, Bundestag, bureau and
office.

Then a week at Rennes for the Semaine Sociale, sitting
at the feet of Monsignor Bruno de Solages and other great
masters of socio-political ideology, putting up at the major
seminary with some hundred other priests and laymen
from France and over the world—with never-ending talk
over the fists-full of bread, curlicues of golden butter and
mammoth mugs of *cafe au lait* which breaks the French-
man's morning fast.

We reflected upon ourselves as much as we tour-studied
our mother Europe. By drawing away, stepping outside
yourself, you can from the distance focus upon your own
people and parish, nation and customs with deeper insight.
Europe tells us where we came from and where we might
be going. Cut off from Europe's religious, philosophical,
familial, political, economic and all embracing socio-
cultural roots America becomes a legendary hanging garden, without support in the solid ground from which we
have sprung forth. The U. S. makes much more sense when
related to mother Europe. Without reflecting upon her
we cannot know nor explain ourselves.

My final experience made me see this the clearer. Monsignor F. G. Hochwalt, director of N. C. W. C.'s Department of Education, Washington, requested me via trans-
Atlantic phone to accept nomination by the U. S. Depart-

ment of State to a UNESCO seminar on adult education near Copenhagen. I spent three weeks in one of Denmark's noted folk-schools for community education. Some sixty-five representatives from thirty-two nations rubbed shoulders and minds in discussions, lectures and bull sessions for three weeks on end. Seventeen of the delegations were from the recently or soon to be independent nations of Africa and Asia. Looking at our human family through their eyes led me to focus more clearly upon—in Toynbee's term—our post-Christian West, and enabled me to see America and Europe as the unity which we are; a physical unity now that our technology has changed the three thousand mile Atlantic moat into a three hour broad highway. And breaking bread with Buddhists and Mohammedans, Hindus and sons of Gold Coast chieftains I saw in them all the millions of humans brothers who know not the Christ who died to save the world; I saw in them all the peoples we have failed, with whom we have not shared the Way and Truth and Life. I saw the nations who are scandalized by the way we Western Christians hate one another and I saw our Church KATHOLIKE, our Universal Faith in the profile of narrow self-interest in which three-quarters of the world family see us.

Each weekend I jotted a hurried letter to my spiritual family being tended by our able assistant Father Scherer, with Sunday help from the good Jesuit neighbors of St. John's High School. I wanted my people to taste what I was tasting, to see some vague outline of all the magnificent sights which I saw, to hear some whisper of the wise words which I heard. These letters were reproduced in our mimeographed parish bulletin and read from the pulpit on the Sunday following my having scribbled them. They are reprinted here without change, just as they flowed from my flying pen. They are perforce superficial. Our whole trip skimmed along the surface and these comments skim the whey.

A final word on itinerary that you may more easily follow our wake:

After a gabfestive evening with the AMERICA staff in New York filled with Jesuit victuals, counsel and contacts offered generously by Fathers LaFarge, Masse, Hartnett, Davis and others we flew via Pan-American to London. From Britain we flew to Amsterdam where we rented an Opel Rekord, a German General Motors product, a diminutive Chevrolet. Having criss-crossed Holland for three days we headed west to Muenster, south along the autobahn through the Ruhr, up the Rhine valley to Heidelberg with an overnight stop at Maria Laach Monastery. From Heidelberg schloss we drove to Frankfurt, thence to Berlin for a couple of days and back via plane; on through Wurzburg to Nurnberg south to Munich, east through Bavaria to Salzburg and Berchtesgaden; west up the Inn valley to Innsbruck, up and up through the Brenner Pass down into sunny Italy via Trent into Venice. Padua, Bologna, Florence and Assisi came next in succession all too rapid. From Rome we spoked out into Ostia, Tivoli and Castel Gondolfo, then south to Monte Cassino, on to Naples and Pompey. We hugged the western coast upward through Leghorn, Pisa and Spezia, to Genoa and Milan. Following the fairyland Lago Maggiore we entered Switzerland at Locarno, twisted and turned and climbed St. Gotthard's Pass to arrive at Brunnen for a weekend on Lake Luzerne. Through Bern and Fribourg we reached Geneva, then off to Lyon and down the Rhone valley came Avignon, Aix and Arles, with a look-see at Marseilles.

West now to Carcassonne and Toulouse; a couple of days at Lourdes; north through Bordeaux, Poitiers, Tours and Rennes. A week in Brittany then into Normandy with its hedgerows, war monuments and memories. Mont St. Michel and Lisieux pointed the way to Paris.

After some eight days in Paris and environs we headed for Brussels via Soissons and Rheims. Through Belgium into Holland and back to Amsterdam. The Fathers Bordelon returned home as scheduled; I flew back to Paris to prepare for the seminar, thence via *wagon-lit* to Bonn and Dusseldorf. Finland's airline dropped me at Copenhagen where I stayed the next three weeks broken only by a weekend rail excursion to Stockholm. From Denmark I flew back to New York with a day's stopover in London.

And in the hurry-scurry this I wrote to my people.

June 14, London

My dear People,

A week away from home and time to give you a word about our experience so far.

The flight over was calm. However, instead of flying via Newfoundland, high winds and storm conditions over the North Atlantic forced us to fly via the Azores. Consequently the time required was longer, some seventeen hours in the air in all.

We arrived at London 2:00 P.M. Wednesday. That afternoon we went to Westminster Abbey, a magnificent Gothic structure built by the monks in the thirteen hundreds, the final resting place of Britain's immortals. We had a taxi run us by Buckingham Palace and our great good fortune held out. A crowd gathered at the main gate, and set the stage for our first English joke: We ask the

bobby (cop in America), "Is the Queen coming out?" "No."
Silence. Awkward pause. "Well, then why are all these
people standing in this pouring rain?" "Sir, the Queen is
coming *in!*"

Anyway, we saw the Queen and her husband drive in
shortly, after only two hours in London. The cabbie said
he had been driving for five years and had never seen her.

Thursday morning we offered Mass at the famous Farm
Street Jesuit Church in downtown London called the
Converts' Church because there have been an average of
thirty converts each year for a hundred years. It is the
home of several famous men like Father Martindale and
Father D'Arcy. TIME Magazine wrote it up about six
months ago.

Among the fifty million people of Britain there are
about three million Catholics. Very few people in the
country practice any religion. It's quite appalling. The
Catholic Church is easily the most vigorous religion. More
Catholics at Church on Sunday than the total attending
all non-Catholic churches. True particularly among the
laboring classes. Saturday we visited the Young Christian
Workers who form leader's groups among the factory and
mill unmarried youth till the age of twenty-six. Most boys
and girls leave school at fifteen years to go to work at a
wage of ten to twelve dollars a week to help out the family. Wages are very low compared to ours. People in general do not by any means have our standard of living at
any economic level. They eat less expensive food, very little
meat, have fewer changes of clothes and much rougher
and durable, seldom own a car, using bicycle, subway and
legs for transportation.

Yesterday (Sunday) gave me a good chance to observe
these things. We spent the day at the parish church and

rectory of St. Thomas in a suburban subdivision called Eastcote, very similar to our Broadmoor in every way. Just couldn't keep away from the parish life on Sunday. Father Langdale is the pastor, one of the original great families who kept the Faith through the era of Henry VIII. And a remarkable man by his own right having pioneered the Jocist movement in Britain. He has the Dialogue Mass. I offered the ten o'clock Mass and served as deacon at a Solemn Mass at eleven o'clock. There were about six hundred people at church, many Communions. Father didn't preach as long as we do! In the afternoon he had a Benediction Service at which I spoke a few words telling about our parish and people. We talked for six hours straight in the afternoon, broken, of course, by tea at the proper moment.

Thursday and Friday we spent with the great scholar and writer, Christopher Dawson. That exceeded fondest expectations. Only one difficulty: he was so curious about America and the Faith and parish life that we did too much talking trying to answer his questions. Can't start to tell you all we talked about. Nor can I detail our many conversations with others like Mr. Frank Sheed, author of several books like *Theology and Sanity, Society and Sanity*. He's now getting material for a book on the Newman work on American college campuses to be finished in two years. What a remarkable man! Every Sunday, he, his wife (Maisie Ward), daughter and her husband speak in the public squares like Hyde Park and Tower Hill, telling the people about Christ and His Church to crowds averaging about four hundred and ranging up to twelve hundred.

This morning we went to the Tower where St. Thomas More, Chancellor under Henry VIII, was imprisoned and executed in 1535, together with St. John Fisher, Bishop of Rochester. Thomas More was a great man as writer, statesman, saint and father of eight children.

And we just returned from three hours with the leaders of the Newman Center, in many ways the British proto-type of the COLLEGIUM. They were delighted to hear about our lectures and groups, parish life and hopes for the future. Fortunately one of their great leaders knows something of the U. S., Dr. Ayldware having spent time studying and lecturing at Princeton, Johns Hopkins and M. I. T. More later on this.

Tomorrow at 6:15 A.M. we leave for Amsterdam. Sunday June 20th we fly from Frankfurt to Berlin, a change in our schedule at the request and arrangement of Monsignor Swanstrom of New York, National Director of N. C. W. C. Relief Services. We will be in Berlin two or three days making certain investigations for him relative to refugees and immigration.

Hope all's well at home. Keep praying for us.

In Christ,

FATHER JOE G.

June 20, St. Sebastian's Chapel, Frankfurt

My dear People,

Sunday morning—and again I write from a parish church. One of the most remarkable parishes in the whole world. This is the church for the U. S. Armed Forces and American civilian personnel in Frankfurt, served of course by American chaplains, two of them. The "Pentagon" of Germany (formerly office buildings of Farben Chemical cartels) is directly across the street. The apartments in which the G. I. families live are a block down. This becomes an island of America in the midst of Europe, and feels like home. Five Masses here today, four in the morning, one in the evening. Well attended, about two hundred Communions. I just offered the nine o'clock Mass which the children attend particularly. They said the prayers together much like our St. Joe's school children at Dialogue Mass, and they sang "Come Holy Ghost" and "Lord, I Am Not Worthy." Am now in the parish library and several youngsters have come in for books. The ten o'clock Mass just ended; people are inquiring about baptisms and report cards and Mass intentions. The Catholic Men's Club received Communion in a body and are now walking through to the dining hall for Communion breakfast. In short, it feels like St. Joe's!!!!

Again, this must remain the briefest of summaries. Arrived here last evening, tonight at 8:00 P.M. we fly to Berlin, behind the Iron Curtain, safer than driving through the Russian zone. Msgr. Swanstrom of N. C. W. C. in New York called his office here to arrange our entry into Berlin to make certain observations for him. Among other things he wants us to see the escapees coming through the Iron Curtain which is pretty tightly closed now. Only three thousand last month—lowest rate since the war. So that sad but historic and interesting sight is before us tonight and tomorrow.

Tuesday we flew from London to Amsterdam (the airport is 13 feet BELOW sea level protected by dykes from the North Sea.) Tuesday and Wednesday principally we spent with the Grail Apostolate in Amsterdam, Der Haag, Nijmegen and Tiltenberg. Saw much in the way of parish life and the lay apostolate. Among the most striking: a parish in a Communist area of Amsterdam among the laborers and dock workers. Six priests work as a team to

win the people back to Christ. The Communism of the
ordinary people is motivated by cold economic facts. They
want *three* rooms to live in for their children instead of
one or two rooms, they want better food and clothing, etc.,
etc. The Red vote in this area was forty-five percent in the
last election. The parish has two Grail workers living in a
small flat in the midst of the workers, very unobtrusively.
For instance, to visit them we did not drive to the door
but parked around the corner and singly a distance apart
approached the entrance so the neighbors would not be
aroused. The Grail workers live among them as good
Christian neighbors, visiting the families, calling on the
sick, etc., in order to make a nucleus of friends who will
then influence the others.

Another amazing place is the Russian Institute, a group
of centers conducted by Father Methodius, a refugee from
Lithuania. The whole idea is to gather together escapees
from Russia and behind the Iron Curtain, to form a sense
of community with their own language in sermons, discussion groups, etc., to provide chaplains for their own
Russian way of offering Mass and imparting the Sacraments, and to prepare priests and lay leaders to get back
behind the Iron Curtain to keep the Faith alive and looking to the hoped-for day when the cold war comes to an
end. The Grail workers develop the lay leader angle particularly, among them a Miss Malley from Brooklyn, learning to speak Russian, act Russian, pray and sing Russian!!!
How UNIVERSAL and energetic and all-embracing is
Our Church of Jesus Christ!

Evidence of bomb damage all around. The center of
Muenster of one hundred fifty thousand population was
eighty percent destroyed. But the recovery and rebuilding
since I was here in 1948 is truly an astonishing miracle.

Work, work, work!! En route to Mass at seven o'clock in the morning the brick-layers and concrete mixers are going full blast!!!

I wonder how the brick-layers are doing on our new building? All fine, I am sure. Corpus Christi procession in the streets here this morning, and all the little ones dressed in white carrying flowers before the Blessed Sacrament reminded me of you back home.

In Christ,

FATHER JOE G.

June 27, Innsbruck

My dear People,

It's nine o'clock Sunday morning, the church bells directly across the street are announcing the next Mass, as they have been doing every hour since six—very loudly. I offered Mass at seven-thirty, gave Communion to the people. Church was crowded. The young people's organizations were attending as a group, with banners and very hearty singing. This is a very Catholic city, some twenty-five Catholic churches, only one Protestant.

To back-track a bit:

Berlin last Sunday, Monday and Tuesday, was an aweing experience as expected. Right down the middle of this city of three million eight hundred thousand runs the Iron Curtain. Everyone knows that anything can happen anytime. Daily there are accounts of people disappearing, about a hundred come in from behind the Iron Curtain every day with their stories of woe and hardship; they are screened by the U. S. Army, by the German Government, attempts are made to find work for them, to reunite broken families. Posters with pictures of some twenty to thirty children appear at public places, children looking for their parents. The War Relief Services of the National Catholic Welfare Conference gives out your old clothes from last year's Thanksgiving clothing drive, and helps the worst cases with extra food and medicine. Unemployment in this huge city cut off all around is the big problem. Over two hundred thousand out of work. The government flies these out, distributes them ten and twenty at a time to the towns and villages of Free West Germany who must be responsible for finding shelter and work. And so it goes, trouble and hope, disappointment and daring to hope again.

Highlights: The U. S. Armed Forces EVERYWHERE in evidence. We encounter many more soldiers and airmen here than in Shreveport. Convoys and maneuvers break up traffic almost daily, tanks thunder along the highway right next to us. This is true especially a hundred miles or so along the Iron Curtain.

Tuesday and Wednesday in Nurnberg, old center of Nazi Party activity. Visit the Valka Camp for escapees from countries other than Germany, two thousand persons from thirty-three different countries, mostly Czechoslovakia, Hungary and Ukraine. Living conditions here very, very miserable, since only thirty cents a day allotted for food. NCWC runs a laundry (there are no showers or bathing facilities of any kind) and a kindergarten for one hundred twenty little ones three to six years old. And just like St. Joe's when we went in they all said in unison: "Gut Morgen, Fader!" NCWG supports a chapel here, too, but main effort is to get these poor people out of the country—to U. S., Australia, Canada or Brazil.

Thursday and Friday in Munich: More camps, more

misery. Quote from a twenty-three year old man: "Please excuse me for being alive!" Saturday in Salzburg and Berchtesgaden. Then last evening to this famed university town of Innsbruck tucked away amid the towering Alps. This P.M. to Italy, Venice, then Florence and Rome. Pray for us. Hope all's well. God bless you all.

FATHER JOE G.

July 4, Rome

My dear People,

Since his serious illness last winter Our Holy Father has not been receiving visitors as has been customary heretofore. Only last week did he begin his usual conferences with cardinals. Consequently we did not expect to see him except at the distance when he appears at his office window each day at noon and six P.M. to wave to the three to five thousand persons gathered and impart his blessing. Imagine our surprise last evening to learn that the first audience since his illness was being granted to Archbishop Cushing of Boston and the pilgrims of the Marian Year accompanying him. Through proper connections with Msgr. Landi of NCWC we were permitted to join the group of three hundred plus.

And so at nine-thirty this morning I saw that great man, Pius XII, just eight feet away. He looks remarkably well for his seventy-eight years, cheerful and smiling, his face fuller than when I saw him in 1948. I guess his doctor has put him on a diet to make him gain weight and strength. He extends his fatherly blessing to all of you. How delighted I was to encounter several persons from Shreveport also fortunate enough to make the audience: Mrs. Phil Rosenblath (who has been visiting her daughter and family, Dr. and Mrs. Floyd Penninger, now with the Air Force in England, but really St. Joe parishioners, residing on Charles St.), Miss Salley, Miss Dobson, Miss Zagone and others from Shreveport, Kilgore and East Texas.

We arrived in Rome Thursday evening, having spent two days each at Venice and Florence. These two cities flood the mind and memory with the ideas and culture and civilization of which we are heir. Stops, too, at Padua, Bologna and Assisi. Names and events of overwhelming import pass in review: St. Mark the Evangelist (tomb and Cathedral in Venice of the eleven hundreds), the Republic of Venice lasting from 690 to 1797; Marco Polo's home; St. Anthony's tomb in Padua; the Universities of Padua and Bologna dating from 1220, pioneers in law and medicine; the stout-hearted present day Cardinal Lercaro of Bologna, battling for Christianity in a hot-bed of Communism (we attended his Mass and heard him preach); in Florence the home and inspiration of Dante, Galileo, Michaelangelo, and Machiavelli, who is the father of the philosophy of pragmatic politics. At Assisi, St. Francis, the little poor man and his complete following of Christ, no holds barred, going the whole way.

The last three days I've offered the Sacrifice for you in St. Peter's, just two blocks from our room, this morning at the tomb-altar (i. e. the tomb *is* the altar) of Pope Leo the Great, who in the year 452 over-awed the Hun Chief Attila at the gates of Rome. Yesterday, we visited the Colosseum where Ignatius of Antioch was thrown to the lions in 115 (remember how he wanted to be eaten in order to be with Christ!) and the Circus Maximus and Quo Vadis chapel made famous by the recent movie.

And, of course, the tombs of St. Peter on Vatican Hill where he was crucified upside down and St. Paul, the irrepressible letter writer. And the catacombs, some hundred miles of underground tunnelling where our forefather Christians gathered to worship in those first three centuries when to call yourself a Christian was to risk your neck. Following Christ was no complacent status quo *then* nor can we allow it to be so *now*. Much to say later on Communism, social problems, workers, wages, the role of U. S. and our role.

> From the land of the martyrs,
> greetings in Christ,
> FATHER JOE G.

July 11, Brunnen, Switzerland

My dear People,

Another Sunday and again time out to share a few thoughts and impressions with you. We arrived into the Swiss Alps through St. Gotthard's Pass yesterday evening. After two weeks in Italy we left the Mediterranean Sea at Genoa (birthplace of Columbus), through Milan, with its magnificent Gothic cathedral of the twelve hundreds, then up and up and up into the aweing Alps, covered with fresh fallen snow. And since today is Sunday we're really making it a day of rest, no conferences, no visits, no interviews, no talks.

This morning at eight I offered the Sacrifice in a small chapel nestled at the foot of the mountains overlooking Lake Luzerne. A really famous structure—about 1315 Swiss Declaration of Independence was signed in this little church!!! The chapel was jam-packed, people overflowing out the front door. The pastor was so gracious, the sacristan so courteous, the altar boy (Paul Stein—this is the German-speaking sector of Switzerland) knew his prayers and duties perfectly. You have no idea how it feels to arrive in an absolutely strange town, walk into the church and be received like a long-awaited friend. To be helped into the same green vestments, open the Missal to the same Latin prayers, look up at the same crucifix— say "Introibo ad Altare Dei" and get the same response that the little Mikes and Tommies make back home at St. Joe's. These thoughts preoccupied me during Mass this morning—and when I gave the last blessing the people made the Sign of the Cross, just like you do (and two or three left church a little too early, so it really was just like home.) That's the meaning of the Church KATHOLIKE—The Church Universal.

So much has happened these five weeks since I left you. Two weeks in Italy cram the mind with so much material that at times the mental gears refuse to shift. This afternoon I spent three hours in this hotel room trying to sift impressions and evaluate all we have seen and heard. And during this respite constantly I found myself thinking of St. Joe's—lonesome I really and truly must admit. I almost put in a long distance call to find out how things are getting on. Did the steel windows for the new building come in on time? Rafters up yet? Or still laying bricks? (ought to be through with that, eh, Mr. Building Committee?) And of course, are the pledges coming in on time, because financially we are squeezing a little tight? Checks get through okay, Mr. Finance Committee, because a payment was due last week?

And I'm wondering about polio in Shreveport, whether this is another epidemic year, and whether some of our little ones are stricken, and whether the vaccine is working for the second graders?

And how Father Scherer is making out; the Jesuit priest from St. John's? And about the baseball teams? And the several seriously sick whom I left five weeks ago, are they still with us or gone to God?

Please send me the SUNDAY SOWING to my Paris address so I can catch up with the goings on.

One leaves Italy with so many impressions of such complexity that piecing them together for the present is altogether impossible. As Mr. Gunnar Kumlein (Roman correspondent for Stockholm's greatest newspaper, himself a great Catholic and writer for COMMONWEAL) put it: "There are layers upon layers in Italy." Time has laid down strata upon strata. The Eternal City in all truth!! Any building or architectual work finished since 1700 is of the modern period. When you mention the fourth century, be certain to signify B.C. or A.D.

Why are there so many Communists in Italy? The reasons are complex and have deep roots in history and the stream of ideas of the past four hundred years. But the outstanding factor is economic: Italy has forty-seven million people and very few natural resources. No oil, no gas, no iron, no coal. Most of the farms cling to the mountainsides, terrace upon terrace. Farmers nurse their little plot of land like you do your camelias. Dirt eroded to the bottom of the hill is brought back to the top five hundred feet up in baskets. They work hard, including the women, making hay, cutting wheat with a sickle on hands and knees, ankle deep in water planting rice. They eke out a bare living in the country. Two million unemployed in towns. Of 11,592,000 families 232,000 live in cellars and warehouses, 92,000 families live in caves (actual rock and dirt caves, I saw them); 1,078,000 families live in overcrowded houses with more than three people to each room and 1,032,000 families live in houses with more than two people in each room. 869,000 families NEVER have meat, sugar or milk in their diet and another million have it only about once a week. Cold statistics! Visualize such a situation for yourself. As Monsignor Baldelli put it (he's the Charities Director of the Holy Father; we spent last Wednesday with him): "What Europe needs is 5,000,000 new jobs, or 5,000,000 people must migrate to new countries."

The Communists make the most of this situation. They make their promises. "No water in the village, no medicine for your child, no land to work, twelve hours, six days a week and you make only $18.00 a week?!! Things will be different when we're in power!" That's their approach. And the temptation is a great one. Our Catholic lay leaders are in the thick of the fight. You might have followed the recent Christian Democratic Congress in Naples. TIME Magazine gave it a good coverage. (TIME puts out an overseas edition which we picked up in Milan yesterday) concerning "Militant Christianity." A militant Christianity alone will save Italy and Europe and the world is a good conclusion of this whole experience to date.

The Church acts as the bulwark against the Red tide. Church-organized immediate relief programs have great effect. Again the great role played by the Catholic Church of the U. S. A. Each year we have in our fifteen thousand parishes the Bishops' world relief collections. Well, we have seen this end of the line in action. What good is accomplished! Monsignor Landi, formerly of Brooklyn and he's kept the accent, heads our mission of NCWC in

Italy. We spent a lot of time with him. Again it's a matter of taking the surplus butter, milk, cheese, cotton and wheat of America and getting it to the truly hungry mouths and empty bellies here. With this help of Catholic America some eight hundred thousand slum children seven to twelve years get a month long summer camp. We visited two of these at Ostia directed by the Holy Father's Charity Works (Msgr. Baldelli), one for two hundred little victims of polio, another for five hundred underprivileged children, fifty percent of whom are underweight. And so it goes.

I pass to other things lest I give a distorted view. We visited one of the most active of Rome's one hundred forty-three parishes, the Church of the Nativity; Father Rovigatti is Pastor, and how he impressed us. He has a set-up similar to our block captains. A great sense for the development of lay leaders. The liturgy plays a great role in parish life. Currently this year he has introduced the Community Mass very similar to ours. He was much interested in our Baptismal ceremony, Thanksgiving and Presentation, Advent wreaths, etc. Naturally we discussed church support, so I really bragged about you then!!

Hop, skip and jump: Food and Agriculture Organization of United Nations headquarters in Rome, North American College (we have three seminarians here for our diocese), the great Jesuit University (Gregorian) with twenty-four hundred students for the priesthood from thirty-three countries. Father Arnou of its Social Science Institute, Father Coffey of the Vatican International Radio, the Giunta or Catholic Emigration Bureau of Italy, Mount Vesuvius (to the very top and into the steaming crater), Pompey, and the leaning tower of Pisa. We encountered more Shreveportites: Camille Despot and his mother, who has a son in our parish. Good to see them.

Up at four tomorrow morning and head for Fribourg (only a hundred twenty miles away but about four hours in these mountains) for day with PAX ROMANA, world wide organization of Catholic professors, students, faculties and intellectuals. Then to Geneva on Tuesday and Wednesday with International Catholic Migration Commission, European headquarters of NCWC, and International Labor Organization of U. N. Then Thursday to Lourdes and Mary's great shrine where you'll all be remembered.

In Christ,

FATHER JOE G.

The Shrine of Notre Dame of Lourdes
Southern France, Saturday, July 18th

My dear People,

A few words to you, and many prayers for you, from this most hallowed spot. Ninety-six years ago Mary, Our Lord's Mother, appeared here to a little teen-age shepherdess, Bernadette Soubirous. Ten years ago the best seller novel of Franz Werfel, "The Song of Bernadette," later made into a movie, spread the name and fame of Lourdes to the whole world, challenging non-believers and impelling them to think twice and more again about the great fact of Mary, the Mother of Jesus, and her role in the history of this world and the eternity of Heaven. For two days now we have been absorbing the natural beauty and supernatural splendor of this little town nestled in the foothills of the towering Pyrenees.

Mary has made this place of wilderness a crossroads of the world. About twenty-five thousand pilgrims here now —from Carthage in Africa, Ireland and Germany, America and Spain, France and Italy, Malta and Indo-China. Some six or seven hundred are the halt and the lame, the cancerous and tubercular, lying on wheel chairs and stretchers, bathing in the waters from the spring Bernadette scratched from the earth at Our Lady's feet. You know about the miraculous cures of Lourdes. Doctors the world over, of every faith and of none, come here to examine the sick and the records. The cures are not explicable from natural causes. In some way and according to His Own Wish God touches the earth at Lourdes and softens the pain and burden of His weak human children. The true marvel is the atmosphere of peace and prayer. The flow of Grace is the true fountain, better verified than the flow of water from the grotto's rock. I am sending of this water to our sisters. Yesterday was the 96th Anniversary of Notre Dame's last appearance. We walked, tens of thousands, last evening holding lighted candles, around the mile long plaza fronting the great basilica. For an hour and more the Rosary and Ave Maria, prayers for you and all the world. A humorous touch: by sheerest accident I am marching next to four G. I.'s in civilian clothes down from troops in Germany, who I uncover from the pained remark of the boy from Boston. "Gee whiz, if only the RED SOX could draw crowds like this!!"

Today towards Rennes and the SEMAINE SOCIALE.

In Christ,

FATHER JOE G.

July 25, Paris

My dear People,

Upon arriving here yesterday I found a flood of mail from home—SUNDAY SOWINGS and letters from some five or six families. Was I happy to get all the news!! The bad news, of course, did not make me happy, like Margie Coon, wonderful little mother of four children, having polio; and Earl Deterley's death, father of four children and such a young vigorous man!! How that saddened me, but made me feel close to all of you. My sympathy to these families and to all others who have lost dear ones since my departure as came to my attention from the SOWINGS received yesterday.

I devoured, too, the other parish news: the near-completion of the school (but get those pledges in!), the pending return of our three wonderful Sisters, the surfacing of the parking lot (am delighted with Father Scherer and the Building and Finance Committees), the ups and downs of the ball teams, the progress of the charity drive, the activities of the various organizations. It's so good to feel in touch with my spiritual family. Thanks to all the letter writers and to Father Scherer who keeps things a-humming with your own energetic and creative leadership and cooperation.

Now to tell you about the past week's experiences. The last letter was from Lourdes. I must repeat what an impression that place made upon me. It occurs now and again in life that we pierce beyond the usual in our contact with God. Our usual experience is the ordinary certitude that He exists and cares for us, a product of reasoning and faith. Once in a while we are favored with an awareness of the Presence of God as Someone discernible with the senses—almost! As a *place,* that's what Lourdes is. You must know and feel and act the fact: GOD IS HERE. So Lourdes has been a great grace—for you as well as for me.

Last Sunday we spent at Bordeaux, a great port city on the Atlantic. Many, many American servicemen here, a USO and Army Chapel in the center of town. Had a most pleasant visit with a cousin, friend and former schoolmate: Father Johnny Gremillion, Army Chaplain in charge of this area. Had not seen him for five or more years. Good to spend a couple of hours catching up on the news (Crowley is his home) and getting his impressions on happenings here, within the Armed Forces (moral problems are tremendous) and Europe in general.

Then we drove northward through Poitiers (Charles Martel defeated the Mohammedan army here in 732), overnight at Tours (near the cave dwelling and monastery of St. Martin, an army chaplain about the year 450 during the barbarian invasions), through the chateau country of the Loire valley—home and origin of the French kings, and on to Rennes in the Breton peninsula. Monday through Friday at the SEMAINE SOCIALE, an annual week-long summer school attended by some two thousand Catholic leaders of France, clerical and lay, to study and act on the boiling social problems of France and Europe: economic, management-labor, racial, family, educational, political, cultural. We stayed with a hundred fifty priests at the major seminary, a further advantage in pursuing our inquiry by long and personal conversations (my French is getting good—even I understand it now). The lectures given by the most outstanding deans and profs of France's Universities of Paris, Lille, Toulouse and Fribourg (Switzerland) were brilliant, and increases our hope that these people of such intelligence and capacity will resolve their many difficulties.

In Paris now, through this week. Spent this A.M. in the parish of St. Hippolyte, Community Mass, altar facing the people. An hour's conversation with Father Perrot, Vicar General of the three hundred priests of the *Mission de France,* about which I shall tell you later.

God love and keep you, and keep praying for

FATHER JOE G.

July 31, Paris

My dear People,

The particular news today is good and bad. Bad because it means that I shall not return home before September fifth, a delay of three weeks. Good because of the honor and experience it implies. At the request of the Department of State of the United States government I shall act as their representative at a three week long Seminar on Adult Education sponsored by the UNESCO at Copenhagen, Denmark. This sudden change in plans occurred this week with a flurry of cables and trans-Atlantic phone calls with Monsignor F. G. Hochwalt, Director of the Educational Department of the NCWC (National Catholic Welfare Conference) in Washington. He made the necessary arrangements with our Bishop Greco and the U. S. Government. Already I have begun my briefing with UNESCO international headquarters here in Paris. That swallow of alphabet soup means: *United Nations Educational Scientific and Cultural Organization.*

So between now and August fourteenth I'll be studying and preparing material for this world-wide seminar. Already I've learned that the purpose of UNESCO is "to contribute to peace and security by promoting collaboration among the nations through education, science and culture in order to further universal respect for justice, for the rule of law, and the human rights and fundamental freedoms for all."

> "To realize this purpose UNESCO: 1) collaborates in the work of advancing mutual knowledge and understanding of peoples through all means of mass communication; 2) gives fresh impulse to popular education and to the spread of culture; 3) maintains, increases and diffuses knowledge."

There will be about sixty persons attending the Denmark seminar from thirty-five to forty countries including Iran, India, Ceylon, Africa and most of the European countries this side of the Iron Curtain. Whether some will attend from the Russian side we do not yet know. We will all live together in a school on the outskirts of Copenhagen, have meals together and opportunity for much confabbing outside the regular work meetings. So we should get to know one another—which is so important in this kind of gathering as is obvious. So my address there for your welcome letters:

UNESCO Seminar
Grundtvigs Hojskole Ved Frederiksborg
Hillerod, Denmark

The burden of my extended absence from home falls upon Father Scherer. He will have many decisions to make with Sister Theonilla relative to the opening of school. I know that you will give him every assistance and cooperation. And were it not for my utmost confidence in Father Scherer's ability and judgment, as well as this same confidence shared in him by our Bishop—I would not further delay my return despite the overwhelming importance of this UNESCO Seminar to the Church KATHOLIKE, the world-wide and universal Catholic Church.

But August tenth another big payment will be due on the new building. Please keep those pledges up-to-date and even ahead of time. Maybe the credit union can advance you a bit.

While this new appointment offers the thrill of a challenge and great experience I am saddened to think that it postpones my return home by so long a time. God bless and keep all our loved ones, especially the little ones. And please pray for me, more now than ever, because the responsibility truly begins to grow heavy.

> In Christ Our Lord,
>
> FATHER JOE G.

> August 8, Paris

My dear People,

Since Wednesday past I've been back in Paris, having flown in from Amsterdam. As I explained in last Sunday's letter according to my original plans I was supposed to fly back home with the Fathers Bordelon but all that is now changed because of the UNESCO meeting in Denmark.

The last few days have been spent in study; "homework" in preparation for the UNESCO Seminar. Remember that means United Nations Educational Scientific and Cultural Organization. From the world headquarters here in Paris (near the Arch of Triumph built by Napoleon and resting place of France's Unknown Soldier) I obtained briefing material to peruse and learned that the only other representative from the United States will be a professor from the University of Illinois. These past few days of intense reading and the making of notes in the quiet of one's room have been a great relief after the helter-skelter and rush of this tour up to now. During the past sixty days we spent the night in thirty-one different places, and the effort to absorb all we have seen and heard has been "brain-busting."

This morning, as has been my Sunday custom ever since I left you, was spent visiting parishes. Am always so curious to know what goes on at the Sunday Sacrifice when the People of God gather together. And it reminds me of our own family of families back in Shreveport. Besides there is a great advantage to "sitting in the pews" instead of the sanctuary. How often I've passed judgment on pastoral practices—sometimes pro, more often con—and have been led to think: "Well, now I wonder what the people sitting in the pews at St. Joe's think about such and such?" So even then I'm in school, and learning something, I hope.

This morning, after offering my own Mass here (am staying at a priest's house) I "made" the nine o'clock at St. Severin (Community Mass in Latin by the people, altar facing the people, and a great sense of oneness and solidarity), then ten o'clock at the Cathedral of Notre Dame (a sung High Mass, mediocre choir, about a thousand people amidst architectural grandeur and Gothic beauty beyond compare *BUT* too big and distant and no sense of oneness and participation), then the eleven fifteen Mass at St. Sulpice (sermon also mediocre; mean-

ingful posters and decor around baptismal font, which
presents an idea we must discuss when I return).

Then en route back here, I entered a Communist center, had a most interesting conversation with a couple of
militant leaders about which I well tell you in great detail later in the lectures. Much insight into their thinking. Pray for them; they too are purchased by the Blood
of Christ. And pray, too, for me.

FATHER JOE G.

Hillerod, Denmark
Sunday, August 15th
Feast of the Assumption

My dear People,

Arrived here last night; from Paris, to Bonn, Germany,
on the Rhine River for three days; via Cologne and
Dusseldorf, by railroad and by plane to Denmark. This
is a college and commuters' town of some fifteen thousand about twenty miles out of the capital city of Copenhagen, a huge metropolis of one million population.

The seminar has begun. Some sixty delegates from
over thirty countries. Will tell you about that in a moment. First, as usual I want to tell you about the parish
church, which I visited this morning. There are very few
Catholics in Denmark. The country is dominantly Luth-
eran. Only twenty-five thousand Catholics among the
four million population. Arriving in Copenhagen yesterday I wanted first to make contact with the Church,
to arrange for Mass, announce to the bishop my presence
in the country, etc. I found through the telephone direc-
tory St. Ansgar's Book Store run by a layman, Mr. Sven

Damsholt. (Gee, these names.) He was wondrously help-
ful, showed me around, brought me to the bishop's residence, the local rectory, etc. Catholics here, few as they
might be, are vigorous. Their Faith really means something to them. And, again, what a feeling to arrive in an
absolutely strange land, strange language (many here
speak pretty fair English), and be received like a returning friend!!! That unity and universality which is ours!

The church building here in Hillerod is a rented room
in a non-Catholic home. The pastor, Father Dommans,
spends three days a week here, and the other three days
in a neighboring town twelve miles distant. I offered
Mass at seven o'clock for some of the Catholic delegates
at the seminar—from France, Canada, Spain, Austria,
Italy and Brazil. Naturally, I gave a sermon (20 minutes)
and that on the body of Mary and the Mystical Body of
Christ.

This afternoon I visited one of the Catholic families
where the pastor had been invited for supper. A wonderful family of five blond-headed children, all converts, the
father, Professor Petersen, teaches at the college where
we are staying. The toddling two year old, little Nels,
brought me his ragdoll which we rocked to sleep.

With the proper portion of speeches and ceremony
the seminar opened officially today in plenary session.
Main addresses were by the Danish Minister of Education and by Dr. Luther Evans, Director General of
UNESCO headquartered in Paris. I knew that this big-
shot had been Head of the Library of Congress in Washington, but what a surprise when he starts speaking with
a southern drawl and turns out to be a *TEXAN!* They're
everywhere! You'd think Texas was big and good enuf,

but no! And considering his background he gave quite an intelligent speech.

I received good news about St. Joe's school and the grinding of gears to start the fall activities. Most probably I'll be home September fifth. Till then—

In Christ,

FATHER JOE G.

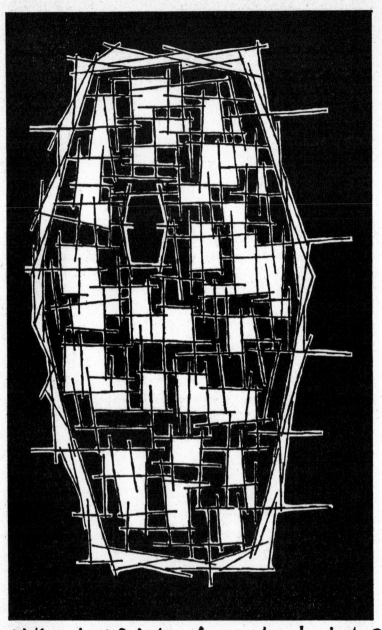

Of these brittle bits who can beget a body?

PERIOD IV

❖

CITIZENS WITH THE SAINTS

Ephesians 2:20

Because of a political census Bethlehem became the birthplace of Jesus. Because of a political caucus Golgatha became the scene of his death. The Jews wanted to crown Christ king to lead them in revolt against Caesar. He refused the role. Ironically Pilate then condemned the King of the Jews, "for everyone who makes himself king sets himself against Caesar." From birth through death Christ's relation with the body politic, Christ's role as Citizen figured prominently. Viewed from the temporal angle political realities captured and killed Him.

Perceiving how citizenship and its aberrations entered so deeply into the first three decades of Our Lord's Life, we should register no surprise that Church and State should somewhat preoccupy Him for twenty-centuries past and until the future consummation of this-world citizenship. Christ lives on: His living Self in Peter and

141

Paul the Roman citizen, in Colosseum and communist martyrs; Christ confronting Theodosius in the person of Ambrose of Milan, Christ confronting Attila in Leo the Great, Henry through Gregory and Mussolini through Pius XI; our own day's Blanchardism, Citizens Councils and Supreme Court decrees—all these tense situations keep arising because Christ is still Citizen today. Because He lives on in those millioned citizens of the world who as baptized laymen form His Mystical Body.

More and more the area of Church and State becomes the arena of the laity. An early portent of papal concern for unparalyzing the laity came with Leo XIII's exhortation to the citizens of France to participate in the Third Republic.

Protestantism and nationalism aided and abetted each other in the shattering explosion which fractured the Christian Commonwealth four hundred years ago. Now that centrifugal urge reverses itself. Today technology pulls the nations of the world nearer and nearer into a planetary neighborhood. Of these brittle bits who can beget a body? Who but the Holy Spirit Who souls the Mystical Body of Christ. A century hence Pius XII might well be best remembered for his insistence on the reality of one human family forming the one nation of the world community, and for his urgings that we prepare for and participate in world citizenship.

How great then the role of Christ the Citizen, in the city of man at ward and world level through four hundred million citizen-laity of the Church KATHOLIKE.

1. Home Again

BACK HOME after thirteen weeks away. It seems even longer. Despite Father Scherer's excellent pinch-hitting, all the events and decisions dammed up awaiting my return envelop me in their flood. Polio victims to be visited, bereaved families needing condolence, broken homes to be reconciled. School opened last week. We got our new fourth sister, Sister Sidonia; thanks be to God and Mother Angelique! The new building looks fine, not quite finished but in use nevertheless. Bills to be paid, loans to be negotiated, pledges to be collected. Committee meetings: building and finance, Mother and Dad's Club officers, Knights of Columbus, scout executive board, Mary's Workers, C. C. D., school faculty.

Projects to be shoved off: the nursery during Sunday Mass for two to six year-olds, Sunday School for public school children, Gabriel Group, Maryhill weekend for young women leaders, the choir to be re-activated after summer doldrums. New families to meet. Salesmen call to sell bread and milk, meat and vegetables, cookies and paper napkins to the cafeteria. More salesmen with the super-duper latest in floor wax and sealer, liquid soap, tissue and all the assorted armory of sweeps and polishers and shiners today's janitor *must* have.

The college crowd says good-bye. Requests for speeches by clubs on "inside Europe." The inquirer's course on *Christ and His Church* must begin soon. The block captains need replacements and extension into the new subdivision which cropped up this summer. Parents from out of the parish make that final fruitless appeal to the supreme-court-pastor to enroll their children in St. Joe's. Meet with the THINK group, talk about the Collegium, plan three Sunday evening lectures reporting on Europe. COMMONWEAL and AMERICA want articles, reports to the Department of State and N. C. W. C. on the UNESCO seminar must be gotten up—written now, verbal later. Details for the entry of two refugee families to be ironed out. A pile of correspondence to be dug into.

Friendship House is under fire again from the city police. With friends from New York and Washington they were taking an "integrated" auto ride. The penalty: over night in jail incommunicado. Will the police keep up this harrassment? Shall we reconcile ourselves to it, struggle back or turn the other cheek? The racial issue has begotten greater tension over the summer. Barely a sign of integration around here, rather the Supreme Court decision will be resisted by every legal device. This summer the state legislature passed laws aimed at continuing forced segregation indefinitely.

And this coming Friday Father Sigur will fly in from Lafayette to conduct the weekend family retreat arranged for by the family group, Bakers, Messmers, Linhares et al during my absence.

Back home! No search for a bed each night. I awaken

in the knowledge that the altar for Mass awaits me right next door. I turn to familiar faces at the Dominus Vobiscum and again feed my people with the Bread of Life and forgive their sins and fret that they need so much more than I can give.

Father Sigur held fifty-five couples galvanized over the weekend. They had one session Friday evening. Then began with Mass at nine in the morning and conferences through 4:00 P.M. on Saturday and Sunday. Breakfast and lunch served here in the cafeteria. Silence and recollection in between as much as home conditions allowed. The babysitter system worked out well.

The distillate of two discussion sessions: What are the dominant attitudes toward marriage today?

> You can get out of marriage if all doesn't go the way you
> dreamed it would.
> Limit the family for economic reasons.
> Marriage is primarily for pleasure.
> Each partner must keep his own individualism.
> Father is the "goat": Dagwoodism.
> A woman past forty must still be a model for *Vanity
> Fair*.
> Love is enough.
> Marriage is underrated in developing the spiritual life.
> Religion is okay if not burdensome and not taken too
> seriously.

The second question: What are the sources of these attitudes toward marriage?

> Attitude of parents.
> Examples of other couples, associates and in the neigh-
> borhood.

Entertainment media, movies, radio, TV.

Printed matter: novels, magazines, comic books, newspapers.

Advertising, whetting appetites for unnecessary material
goods.

Economic pressure, fear of sudden financial stress.

Fads, behavior of public idols.

Poor preparation.

Selfishness.

A good résumé of the pitfalls our young families encounter. At least they alert themselves to combat the
pervading atmosphere so enervating to spiritual strength.
How we need a strong family movement.

While in Copenhagen I received a letter from Miss
Anne Foley, director of our Shreveport Friendship House,
reporting that she and two others had been imprisoned
overnight. After ten days back home I am able to piece
together this second direct attack against Friendship
House by the Shreveport police.

Thomas Wright teaches school in New York. He is a
Catholic, a friend of Friendship House these several
years, in his late thirties. Miss Loretta Butler taught
school in Washington; during the last year she has been
a full-time F. H. staff worker in Washington; the past
month she has been on the staff here in Shreveport on
a temporary basis. Miss Butler is a Negro. One afternoon
she and Miss Foley were riding with Wright in his auto,
he having driven down for a few days while on vacation.
About sundown they stopped on a hill overlooking the
beautiful lake which adjoins our city.

A patrol car approached. Questions were asked. That
Wright's car carried a New York license aggravated the

situation. They were escorted to the city jail, finger-printed and locked up with drunks and derelicts. The police were extremely rude, even crude. Miss Foley who has been a city resident for nine months was not allowed to call anyone, not even permitted to notify her fellow staff workers at the center as to her whereabouts, not allowed to call a lawyer, several of whom she knows personally. Incommunicado—overnight in jail; three persons, all born and reared American citizens, all three college graduates, none of whom was charged or even suspected of any misdemeanor. Their crime was violating the code and custom of the South; their friendship has crossed the Jim Crow line; Negro and white associating as friends and equals. The penalty: disrespect and abuse from those who are sworn to uphold law and order and constitution, the butt of crudity and cursing, a night in jail, release in the morning with this threat from the ranking officer: "If we bring you in again we'll mop up the floor with you!!"

Now a month has passed. Miss Foley discusses the experience in calm tones, even-eyed she looks to the future instead of the past. We could make an issue of such maltreatment, carry it higher up as we had done last May. "But is that what the Lord wants?" Anne wonders, "Maybe jail, the fear and embarrassment, are what He wants us to undergo. Maybe that's part of our vocation. Should we complain at an opportunity to turn the other cheek?"

With this she cools the fire of my indignation. Without intending it a whit she shames me. How would I react to such an offense against my person? In a manner less like Christ I woefully fear. This poses a problem. Obviously the police attack only the lay workers; they will not lay a finger on me, the chaplain, the priest. But *I* am the Other Christ, Christ Priest *and* Victim. Can I allow the staff to continue as victims while I remain secure, a mere spectator? Can I ask them to suffer that from which I am immune?

And worse yet: when will the screws tighten on our Negro friends? When will attendance at Friendship House begin carrying automatic intimidations, gradually becoming starkly bare threats of jobs that might be lost and eviction notices and loan cancellations, hanging heavily over patient heads for centuries bowed in passive acquiescence? To how much can we subject them?

Already mid-October. School in high gear. Parish and community activities in full momentum. Father Scherer returns tomorrow from a well-earned visit home with his folks near Pittsburgh. How gladly will I transfer his share of the load to his willing shoulders.

Each of the three Sunday evening conferences on Europe drew over one hundred fifty persons, of whom a score or more were not Catholics. I eschew the mere travelog, although necessary to some degree. Preparation for these six hours of lecture have forced me to try and make sense out of the summer's multitudinous experiences. I mimeographed a three page outline for my "students." I quote from the kernel sections of the outline on page 149.

Despite this honest effort I feel such inadequacy trying to communicate to my people a particle of what I saw and felt, heard and pondered through the past summer. If I could expand these six hours to a six semester study we might do a bit better. Most of us have so little background in European history, ancient and modern; our roots are so thin and brittle. I studied no European his-

Some Factors in Diagnosis of Europe:

1. Geography
2. Economic Reality
   e. g. natural resources,
       Rhine River
3. Economic Theory
4. Political Theory
5. Social Theory
   —class and classless
   society
6. Nationalism
7. History
8. Cultural Heritage
9. Idealism
   —a cause greater than
   self
10. War
11. Moral Degradation
    —failure of hope
12. Changing World
    Pattern

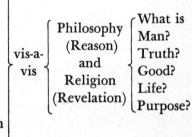

vis-a-vis { Philosophy (Reason) and Religion (Revelation) } { What is Man? Truth? Good? Life? Purpose? }

Some sources in this Study of Europe:

A. Historical Monuments.
   e. g. Tower of London, ruins around St. Paul's, Patton in Normandy, Colosseum, Notre Dame.
B. Historical Documents.
   e. g. Magna Carta, Vatican Manuscripts, Record of 855 Polish Priests Killed at Dachau, Marx' *Kapital*.
C. Current Media and Publications.
   e. g. Radio, News Reels, Papers (Communist *L'Humanité* of Paris), Billboards, Foder's Modern Guide (reading as we drove in rented auto).
D. People—by far most important source: conversations, lectures, bull sessions.

tory since boyhood days in high school. Church history
in the seminary was too narrowly ecclesiastical to be dignified as history at all. No relations were established between Christ's Mystical Body and the body of society. It
were as though the Divine Word had "incarnated" ecto-
plasm, as though Christ lived on in a sealed vacuum instead of enfleshing a world of three dimensional humans
—working, voting, stealing, legislating, marrying, con-
tracting, hating, loving, cheating, renting, borrowing, ex-
torting, exploring, researching, hiring human beings.

Two or three readings, pen in hand, of Carlton Hayes'
Political and Cultural History of Modern Europe, constant study of the works of Maritain, Barbara Ward,
Arnold Toynbee and Christopher Dawson have helped
to fill this sad gap in my seminary studies. The social encyclicals, Cardinal Suhard and his school, the universal
range of Pius Twelfth's allocutions to butchers, bankers,
bakers, astronomers and treaty makers have guided my
continuing effort to understand the what and the how,
the when and the why. But alas! There is so much to
know, so much of the past to explore, so many intangibles
to foresee, so many tangled strands to plait into the
religio bond that binds creature man to His Creator
God.

We can know so little and at such a price of search
and persistent toil. How sad those errors which set us
back, especially the error of the Enlightenment which
crowned Reason a god, and forgot about humility and
love and all the wisdom refined by our ancestors and
offered us in heritage handed down.

Bishop Greco dedicates our new school building. Our
debt now totals about one hundred twenty-five thousand

dollars. Since our souls inform bodies with five senses, two feet and a stomach we must have brick, steel, concrete, heat and light, desks—and now air-conditioning. In the simplest equation this means money. And spending money which will be at hand only at a future date equals debt—a sign of vigor and confidence, the bankers exude optimistically.

Father Maydieu, O. P., director of CERF publications, Paris, plans a book on the Church in the U. S. A. He wants me to do the chapter on Louisiana; others will treat of New England, the Mid-West, the Bible-belt South, the West. Father Maydieu says in his letter that the regional divergencies in the huge expanse of our country greatly impressed him when he visited here a few months ago. Other chapters will relate the Church to education, parish life, labor-management, race, literary and cultural life in America.

This volume is one of several projected by CERF in conjunction with FIDES Publishers, which will attempt to explain the various national Catholic communities to each other. Probably similar volumes will be written on the Church in France, Germany, Britain, Ireland, Italy, Spain and Latin America. The purpose is to interpret to each other our particularities of history, emphasis and socio-cultural impact. We deeply need such communication horizontally, nation to nation, Catholic people with Catholic people, as distinct from official vertical communication to the Eternal City, then out into the various provinces tinctured with that official impress. We are brothers, not merely sons of the same Holy Father; we must speak to one another directly, not merely through him.

I have just noticed that the nations listed form the Atlantic Community, the Christian West vis-a-vis the world's other cultures. This Western Community is fast becoming conscious of itself, as our mother nations became self-conscious in the sixteen and seventeen hundreds, dissolving the city-state structure. The posture of the Church in the Atlantic Community reflecting inward must now be much different from the posture of the Church during these recent centuries within the bounds of the several countries taken separately. Taken one by one the Church might not loom large in the life of each and every country. But taken as the unity, physical and spiritual, toward which the West now progresses the Church becomes the common sky and sun which shelters and enlightens all who inhabit the Atlantic *mare nostrum,* its coasts and rivers, valleys and seas. In trying to understand our Western past, asking the questions: How and why did we come to be? Who made us? the answer which explains most (but not everything) is the Church KATHOLIKE.

How necessary then that we perceive the Church as the pervading reality of the Western world instead of fostering a continued fragmentization in the strait-jacket of *passé* parochial states. The flow of Catholic consciousness must cross-current national particularities. We are the soul of our society; this society, though held physically one by the taut scaffolding of treaties and codes and pacts, cannot become truly at-one-with-itself unless the soul inspirits the whole with this unifying consciousness. To be conscious of the whole members must be in touch, aware of one another. Hence, the CERF-FIDES series in part fill a need for intensifying this trans-Atlantic conversation.

Then another challenge arises which we have barely recognized. Danielou, Considine, Foucauld et al open our eyes a wee bit. Having looked inward and reflected on our religio-socio-cultural unity we must look outward and examine our posture vis-a-vis the rest of the human family now dwelling in one global neighborhood. Even before we can properly mature our Western unity, we must answer Suhard's: "Who shall unite the world?"

Belloc and Christopher Dawson have helped us to deepen this insight. But where do we stand looking outward, vis-a-vis the Buddhists, Hindus, Moslems and others of cultural loyalty measured by millenia, now subjected to the might of matter our Western world begot? Toynbee poses the question ably and offers a response which I do not as yet fully understand. The final four volumes of his *Study of History* are now appearing. Something to chew on for a life time. At this moment in history when our Greco-Judaeo-Christian at-one-ness at last fuses together our national particularities we must overcome our Western separateness to realize our at-one-ness with all that is true and good among other cultures created by children of the same Father and brethren of the same God-Man Christ.

All Saints' Day is a grand catch-all to glorify the glorious. I wonder if some non-canonized saints are higher in heaven than some officially canonized ones. Don't see why not. I bet Mamma's mansion is a sky-scraper penthouse.

All Souls' and All Saints' underline the Communion of Saints. These feasts extend "no man is an island" through the door of death and birth into the past and future. My God, how cramped in the non-believer must feel, stifled with the walls of this-world. How much neurosis results from cosmic claustrophobia? How I'd hate to be squeezed in by the range of a telescope and seventy candles on a birthday cake, super-market manufactured, untouched by human hands.

Back home in my bayou boyhood I loved to explore: a strange palmetto thicket, a new path through the cypress swamps, a trail freshly blazed by the wood-cutters, a newly dug drainage canal. During the youthfulness of heaven I hope God will permit me boyhood excursions to explore the Milky Way and along the wake of comet tails. Will we always have to travel with the speed of thought? Here on earth we strive constantly to go faster, faster. Maybe *the* tourist problem in heaven will be how to slow down to the dawdle pace one needs to explore an uncharted galaxy or spiral nebula just a-borning. All Souls' Day witnesses to our union with the Church suffering; All Saints' Day to our union with the Church triumphant. What about an All Men's Day witnessing to our union in the Church militant—formal participants and potential recruits, AWOL's and all the People of God—which means all living humans because Christ's Blood marks all in It's power of what can come to be.

Finally got reports on the UNESCO seminar off to the Department of State and the National Catholic Welfare Conference. Am planning the personal conferences for mid-November, trekking on to New York, Cincinnati, South Bend, Notre Dame, and Chicago. The necessity of remaining here for the Diocesan Teacher's Institute and returning for the annual Thanksgiving ceremony squeezes my trip down to ten days.

Father Knaebel's funeral this November morning. His soul left his body lying on the rectory floor, in the octave of All Saints'.

He established the work of the Holy Childhood which gives thousands participation in the apostolate of his confreres of the Congregation of the Holy Spirit. He spent ten years a missioner in Africa. His last years here have been difficult. Always sickly he had to find space and teachers, desks and books for four hundred ninety little ones, sometimes eighty to the classroom. Always strapped for money. These poor have so little. Like so many other priests working among our Negroes, to beg he was not ashamed. If he felt shame he swallowed it as his people swallow the indignities heaped upon them.

It was my privilege to preach the sermon. Sixteen thousand times he offered the Sacrifice of the Mass. Unlike myself and so many other pastors of "good" parishes of affluent people, Father Knaebel like Christ was not only priest-offerer but priest-victim as well. He felt keenly the rebuffs and discrimination, the helpless discouragement suffered constantly by his people. He cared for the Negro and dedicated his life to their wellbeing forty some years ago when interracial justice was only an idea in the mind of God and Father LaFarge. It's so easy for me to jump on the bandwagon now moving along and to forget what these pioneers had to suffer.

I paraphrase the offertory prayer:

Receive, O Holy Father, almighty and eternal God, this body broken and spent, this soul tired and exhausted, which your unworthy servant, Father Knaebel, offered unto Thee, his living and true God, for his own countless sins, transgressions and failings; for all here present and for all faithful Christians, living and dead: that it may avail both him and us unto salvation in life everlasting. Amen.

Emcee the groundbreaking ceremony for the new Catholic hospital. To cost six million dollars, one and a half pledged by the public drive, same sum from U. S. government through the Hill-Burton Act, and the remnant half becomes the Sisters' debt.

Just about all the city's big shots on the platform, and most of them talk. Only one goes overtime so the silver shovel bites into the dirt within the hour. Interesting shovel, it was used to break the ground for the Grand Coulee dam.

Off for Washington at 7:00 A.M. as a hitch-hiker—in the superconvair of United Gas Company. Mr. McGowen, president of this largest natural gas company in the world, and several of his top executives are headed for the capital and New York. After a cup of coffee they huddle around a table scrutinizing blueprints and briefs, reviewing arguments coming up before the Federal Power Commission, examining the prospectus for financing another pipe line, discussing tideland leases and the petrochemical plant now a-building near Pensacola. The great Mississippi slips by ten thousand feet below us, at one sweep of the eye we glimpse three TVA dams, over on the horizon is the Oak Ridge atomic installations, valleys of autumn gold and bronze undulate under the azure canopy of the Great Smokies, we drop low over the Potomac near Mount Vernon, Washington's obelisk and the capitol dome loom larger, we touch again mother earth.

What marvels are these great corporations. From them

issue forth the marvels of our technical age. We hear much about their faults, and these we can easily discern because these are human creations. Having taken into account the danger of power concentrates and the tension arising from the application of due restraint, once we have acknowledged the tendency toward impersonal relations between an executive and his five or ten thousand employees, once we have critized exploitation of natural resources and deplored the helplessness of the non-organized individuals who must deal with a powerful business on a fanciful man-to-man basis, I still marvel at the modern corporation. In our industrial society we depend upon General Motors and General Electric, General Rubber and General Foods and all their numerous associates for the wherewithal to keep alive. The Church mediates between God and man administering the supernatural goods of Redemption; these great institutions, manager and worker, mediate between bountiful Creator and needful creatures, administering the goods of creation. We have a well developed theology of the supernatural; we need a better developed theology of the natural.

Properly, we have placed great emphasis upon the supernatural in our theology; we need now to emphasize further the implications of the natural.

2. A Look at the World

How do you go about making a report to the Department of State? I have never done that before. They have sent me no outline, no questionnaire, no schema. Are they really interested in my reactions to the UNESCO Seminar, or is this invitation to confer with six or eight department people at 3:00 P.M. on a wet November day only protocol courtesy?

Anyway, what can I possibly tell that they do not already know? Why should I cram their archives with more data? Undoubtedly they already have more than humans can digest. Because even the Department of State is composed of humans, humans of merely human intelligence, humans capable of only so much comprehension, humans with limited powers of prophecy, with more hindsight than foresight. We tend to magnify the power of our human institutions by the same mechanical equation that we magnify the lens of a telescope. An institution composed of twenty thousand people is not necessarily twenty thousand times more perceptive than one single person. How correlate all the minute scraps of information gathered from a global network of a hundred listening posts each with a dozen ears? What memo of a memo of a memo of a memo can brief John Foster Dulles on the status quo? Who will brief the briefers and sift the sifters and check the memory of the memorandeurs?

Yet we constantly speak of the Department of State and (similar social organs) as if it were some sublimated species of superman possessed of a single intellect and will similar in quality to that of the human person, and equal in capacity to the manifold tasks with which charged. Two heads might be better than one but twenty thousand minds do not shed intellectual light to the twenty thousandth mind power. News articles and columnists announce, "The Department of State thinks . . . remembers . . . forgets . . . plans . . . regrets . . . projects . . . envisions"; learned treatises in *Harper's* and *New York Times* and *Atlantic*, books by the score, analyze the policy and mind of the State Department. We get the impression that it's possible to go to Washington and interview some keen-eyed, close-mouthed Ivy League product of prodigious mental and executive range, a really old guy who appears outwardly a vigorous steel gray fifty despite his fresh memory of posting George Washington on "foreign entanglements" and egging on the Monroe Doctrine. Political cartoons contribute to these images. Again the restrictions of the power of articulate expression. We are so woefully walled in; the windows of the senses through which we contact the world and each other are such small apertures, so often misted in or the casement closed and clogged with mud.

Anyway I made my report, swelling U. S. Department of State archives, providing further micro-excitation to a fibrillous antennule of that organ of our body politic which should see all, hear all, know all and say little, even under the duress of Congressional investigation.

Probably my earth-shaking observations got sidetracked into the nearest ganglion bureau, mayhap continental commuter Dulles never quoted my report in some miles high secret session winging over the ocean. Nevertheless it was pleasant and pride-glowing to sit at the head of a tolerably long oak table, see the eight or ten assistants to sub-department under-directors finger my five pages report mimeographed at government expense and bearing code number URS (54) 12, and comment knowingly before their polite eyes and professionally cocked ears. And this is what I said, give and take a little here and there, with occasional meandering far afield for the presumed benefit of present company.

Professor Herman Erickson of the University of Illinois and I were the two U. S. participants accredited to this seminar. Upon parting we decided to make separate reports. Since he was going on to Sweden on a Fullbright scholarship, and I was immediately returning to the United States, we would have no opportunity to work up a joint report.

The Seminar took place in Grundtvigs Folk School located some two kilometers out of Hillerod, Denmark, a commuters' and market town near Copenhagen. Grundtvigs is one of the more famous of Denmark's sixty unique folk schools for continuing the education of adults. The physical set-up of the small college, having meals, recreations, walks and bull sessions together, created excellent atmosphere for the participants to come to know one another on rather close terms during the three week period. This experience of communal life among some sixty-five persons from thirty-two different countries is a benefit of inestimable value which no report can properly

evaluate. A genuine spirit of human camaraderie and em-
pathy did in fact develop, disturbed by few conflicts.

The official languages were English and French, the
former heavily predominant. The participating countries
were told on invitation to select only persons who could
speak either language. Fortunately I am able to handle
both. I understand French quite well from bayou boyhood memory, although speaking with difficulty through
lack of practice. For plenary sessions we used a simultane-
ous translation system with individual earphones and all
the cumbersome paraphernalia. This worked out quite
well. When we divided into groups the translator spoke
after each person had had his say. This method consumed
much time, slowed the train of thought and tended to
divide the groups into those who spoke French and the
English speaking. But listening to both language versions
greatly facilitated my note taking.

Besides my constant awareness of the difficulty we humans have communicating our thoughts (how I wish someone would perfect telepathy) several other linguistic points
linger on: that of the six persons in the whole gathering
who spoke only one language four of these were from
France, that English has quite replaced French as the
lingua franca of the world, that some African countries
like the Cameroons or Gold Coast might have ten or
twenty diverse tongues within their narrow boundaries
and must rely upon English for nation-wide communications, that relative neighbors like India, the Philippines
and Indonesia likewise resort to English in their inter-
changes. The British Empire might transform itself into
a voluntary Commonwealth, but however tenuous the
political and economic ties a cultural empire will remain

to remember Victoria. This universal reality of English gives us a great advantage in the cold war.

This was the fifth of a series of UNESCO seminars on adult education during the past four years. Rural areas received especial emphasis in this one. Before arriving we received reports of the four previous sessions and a brief outline of the material proposed for this one. I had spent one week in Paris conferring with Mr. Harry Dawes, director of UNESCO's adult education section, and in private preparatory study. Subject matter and participants were divided into three groups:

> Group I —Special Conditions and Needs of Rural Communities.
> > Chairman: Professor Amlan Datta of India.
> Group II —Programmes, Methods and Techniques.
> > Chairman: M. Jean Nazet of France.
> Group III—Organizations in the Field of Adult Education.
> > Chairman: Mr. E. L. Harris of Britain.

After meeting on the first day at Hillerod Professor Erickson and I agreed that he would choose Group III on *Organizations* and I would select Group II on *Programmes, Methods and Techniques.* Through reports to and discussions in plenary sessions each evening we retained close interrelation among the groups. This intermeshing was further helped by innumerable off-the-cuff tête-à-têtes during meal and recreation periods. The degree to which the business of the seminar filled the conversation of non-work periods provided a good measure of the participants' serious absorption in the problems at hand.

Our group further divided our material into literacy, fundamental education, vocational and professional training, and complementary or cultural education. Since the so-called underdeveloped nations of Asia and Africa composed about half the representation, we tended to spend much time on literacy and fundamental education, a necessary emphasis under the circumstances.

Only now do I realize that well over one billion of the world's people are illiterate and worse yet this illiteracy is concentrated into the eighty and ninety percent majority of some forty countries. Fundamental education endeavors to reach those who have attended no formal school whatsoever as well as those who received too little schooling to make a lasting impression. Fundamental education directs itself to sociological groups forming the structure of society—the family, the village, the region. It offers an active education which can be applied immediately in the areas of citizenship, sanitation, family and personal hygiene, community living: how to mark a ballot, village drainage, why baby's drinking water ought to be boiled, the principles of credit union and co-op, how to follow directions in using insecticides. My sixty pages of closely scribbled notes plus fat mimeographed summaries tell about heartening and more often heart-breaking efforts made under depressing conditions to enlighten minds and form national consciousness in those two simultaneously awakening continents, Africa and Asia. I will not repeat the accounts detailed to us personally by principals of hinterland schools, administrators of development projects, supervisors of bookmobile and health teams, and educational directors of labor unions in India, the Sahara, Indonesia and the other nascent nations.

But we cannot too often repeat these facts of life: over one and a half billion people, better than 60 percent of the world's population, live in the underdeveloped areas of the world. Seventy percent are illiterate. Their per capita income averages less than one hundred dollars a year; in the U. S. it is seventeen hundred dollars. Their life expectancy is thirty years. India has a hundred million malaria cases each year. And so on, fact after dreary fact. We can no longer ignore these facts. Our Western technology, planes, radio, cinema, television, have made of the world a neighborhood. In 1776 when John Adams wanted to confer with Benjamin Franklin he travelled three hard days by stage to Philadelphia, and Thomas Jefferson joined them by two days at horse-killing pace up from Virginia. Now President Eisenhower can reach Premier Nehru within a few seconds by wireless, or meet him face to face within a few hours in the Columbine.

And so we must interest ourselves in what goes on in India and everywhere else. We have no choice in the matter, any more than our suburban parishioners can ignore the slums of our city's Negro ghetto. Mr. V. B. Karnick directs regional social education on the outskirts of Bombay. He had attended a Jesuit school while remaining Hindu. We hit it off well, usually sat together in our group, a friendship began. He shared much with me. Ninety percent of India's population dwell in villages, most of which are school-less. How arouse initial interest in these remote areas. The educational department has organized the *mela*; *mela* means fair, a centuries old community tradition bringing much delight to the Indian villagers. But the *mela* is different now.

Four big motor trucks arrive in the village. The trucks disgorge electric lights, loudspeaker, music, a footlight stage. Young and oldsters crowd around with glee. Talent and music competitions win prizes worth nine American dollars. Displays and exhibits county fair-wise contrast how-to-do-it with how-not. How to keep the village well cleaned, how to prevent erosion, how to drain a stagnant mosquito breeding pool. There are lectures, discussions and a portable library. At the end of the three day stand a squad of teachers moves in with the adults in the evening, organize a library of a hundred simple books and initiate the literacy school which is carried on by resident primary school teachers when the introductory team moves on.

In country after country, valley after valley, oasis after oasis this herculean effort goes on. They employ every possible technique. Indonesia has reduced illiteracy from 90 to 70 percent in eight years. The centuries old traditions of the people are transformed into vehicles for the new learning. The chronicler and songster, comparable to our feudal day troubadour and mime singer, now wanders from village to village with a novel repertoire. Using the five tunes basic to all Javanese music, the heritage of the ages and universally known, he puts across a lesson in latter day lyrics, like:

> "If we want the best from our soil,
> And a proper reward for our toil,
> Our rice must be planted in rows
> With manure to make sure it grows;
> We must pick the best seeds
> And hoe out the weeds—
> But that every good farmer knows."

We all like to play Atlas now and again. It is human—and Christian—to assume the weight of the world. "I was hungry and you gave Me to eat; I was thirsty and you gave Me to drink; naked and you covered Me; sick and you visited Me." How does the West, a West still going through the motions of being Christian, feed and clothe and nurse a billion human brothers except through Relief Services, Point IV, FAO, WHO? We quickly tire of these "give away" programs. We coin cute epithets like "globaloney" to deride them. But what else are we to do, we having so much and they having so little? What a fool the Samaritan appears to be in the eyes of the Pharisee.

And to compound the ills of our weary world even in the peaceful setting of this seminar certain inter-group stresses and strains appeared repeatedly, witnessing to rancor and deep distrust beneath the suave exterior. I have had little direct experience in foreign affairs especially as affecting non-Western peoples. Previously I have done some work in Mexico (migrant workers and rural rehabilitation in 1951 and 1952 with Monsignor Ligutti and the National Catholic Rural Life Conference) and in Germany and Austria (relief, refugees and migration in 1948 with the National Catholic Welfare Conference). Despite the paucity of experience I record the following situations which impressed me profoundly, wearing ridges in my brain by cropping up constantly in our exchanges. (I quote directly from my written report to the State Department):

1. The tide of nationalism arising in Asia and Africa.
2. The revolt of colonial peoples against the imperialism of the West.
3. The refusal of non-Caucasians to remain in a subject or inferior position vis-a-vis the white race.
4. The growing solidarity of the Arab peoples and *their* nationalism in particular.
5. The bond of Islamism between the Arab and the non-Arabian (e. g. Indonesian) Mohammedans.
6. The bitterness of the conflict between Israel and the Arab states.
7. The world-wide interest in the U. S. Negro.

"And possibly the greatest reality of all is the degree and speed at which Asia and Africa are being Europeanized or Westernized, imitating or transplanting our institutions —governmental, educational, communications, industrial economic, labor organizations, technology, etc., and all this goes on unabashedly exteriorly while inwardly they seem somewhat apologetic or ashamed that they must be imitators of another culture. The inherent instability of peoples suddenly independent but with no long term growth and preparation for self-government struck me very forcibly. With equal force I perceived the utter impossibility that these peoples in this epoch remain as colonial subjects. Many of the participants from these areas gave indication of an appreciation of the dilemma facing them (again by conversation and private discussion rather than public statement). They realize well that their people *must* obtain their freedom for which they are *not ready*. We could discern at times in consequence a frantic search for the means by which a people can be made politically and socially mature in the shortest possible period."

What attitudes did I encounter relative to the United States?

One of the first questions asked almost invariably concerned the progress of the Negro in the U. S. All knew quite a bit about the subject, probably more about this than any other facet of our national life. All knew about the Supreme Court decision of May 17, 1954 on integration in education. We engaged in many personal conversations on the subject. The fact that I was born in the plantation South, that my grandfather had fought in the Confederate Army, etc., and despite this background engaged myself in desegregation activity seemed to intrigue them no end. We might formulate their questions as follows. I again quote my report directly.

1. Can the United States become truly democratic politically, economically and socially?
2. Can the U. S. Negro acquire the education and other cultural development necessary for equal status and total integration into all phases of life?
3. Will the whites of the U. S. *permit* the Negro to become their equal?
4. If the white man will permit this, to what extent will he help and accelerate the Negro's attainment of total equality and integration?

"I make a brief summary of the background of these questions (other than historical and cultural) especially on the part of the non-white underdeveloped nations who have very recently obtained their independence from Western nations, or who are striving for this independence. And I was struck by the degree to which the presently or formerly colonial peoples make 'common cause' among themselves although they might live thousands of miles apart. For example, the struggles of Tunisians against France, of the Mau Mau against the British, and the successful issue of the Indonesian struggle against Holland form an ideological unity in the mind of the delegate from Jordan or India. Returning to the four questions above, the answers given here have great personal impact upon the people asking them. This is not a question of mere long-range sympathy. The 'cause' of the U. S. Negro partakes the 'cause' of all non-Whites throughout the world.

"They are most anxious to hear an affirmative response because the U. S. is regarded as something of a test case. If a thorough-going democracy can become a reality in the United States then it can happen elsewhere. If, on the other hand, the United States with all its advantages of natural resources, geography and historical development *cannot* become a truly democratic society, then the ideal of democracy cannot be made operative in less-favored countries. Some other way of life must be sought. And most of these presently and formerly colonial peoples are *seeking*; they have not yet set their compass for the future."

To phrase the test case in other terms: if the United States cannot solve its race problem with a mere minority of 10 percent Negro, how then can this same nation assume leadership of a world with its own race problem, a minority 25 percent white? If the white U. S. will not treat with equality and respect its own Negro citizens, how can the colored three-fourths of the world be expected to come to terms with the remnant Caucasian quarter?

The participants wanted to believe in the integrity and good faith of the United States. Still in their eyes we are identified with our mother Europe. Britain, France, Belgium and Holland have held sway over two continents and a billion people for three centuries. Xenophobia repels the U. S. too. Memories of even the best colonialism include bitter memories which die hard.

The seminar included no iron curtain countries. Among the participants I found no inkling of pro-Communist sympathy. Despite our shortcomings these nascent nations seem to believe that we of the West offer the best simulacre of what they would like to become. A final problem: there exists the tendency to regard democratic self-government as a mere series of techniques (secret ballot, mass literacy, mass communications, etc.) and little appreciation of the fundamental truth of man's dignity which is the centuries-refined product of our Greco-Judaeo-Christian heritage.

I concluded my report to the Department of State with
three recommendations:

1. The United States should be represented at all such international gatherings as well as at the regional seminars now being planned by UNESCO. The absence of
   United States representatives will always be noted by
   all. While other nations might indulge the luxury of
   abstention we cannot do so.
2. Negroes should form part of the United States delega-
   gations whenever and wherever possible. Negroes should
   should be members of as many diplomatic missions
   (permanent and ad hoc) as possible. One Negro Information Officer in an African embassy conveys more
   than I or printed pamphlets ever could. Delegates from
   Africa told me of such U. S. Negro Information Officers
   and of what it means to them to see the U. S. represented by a Negro.
3. The exchange program of students, professors and citizens should be continued and intensified. At least four
   of the participants had been to the United States on
   such exchanges. Their insight into our nation, its
   strength and weakness, good and evil, their over-all
   sympathy for and identification with us, were most
   heartening.

How sophomorish is much criticism of our foreign
policy. Ultimately does foreign policy aim at conforming
the will of the world to our will or merely establishing a
modus vivendi by suasion and threat, ideals and economics? We of the U. S. compose a mere six percent of the
world's people. Eighty other nations have national poli-
cies of their own. Why be surprised that their wills do not
conform to our national policy?

God, too, wants our human wills to conform with His

Will. But we are in habitual rebellion. Still He doesn't resort to force; He only uses Grace; He leaves us free.

Some would have the Department of State perform feats which even God Almighty does not attempt. We humans are so limited even in the conjoined strength of our U. S. industrial might. The failures of our foreign policy remind us of our creaturehood. We are not masters of our own destiny. God directs His world.

Then to the National Catholic Welfare Conference to talk things over with Monsignor Hochwalt, director of the educational department. Some propose that the Church have nothing to do with UNESCO. What might my experience contribute to this discussion? In the written report to N.C.W.C. I confined myself to three points.

First, concerning the over-all attitude of the seminar toward religion and the Church: such information about UNESCO as I had previously acquired prepared me for the rationalist-secularist *esprit* which was actually encountered. After all, the mental genes of Julian Huxley begot offspring in great part to Huxley's own image and likeness. But mutation can and does occur, with greater facility in a moral person. UNESCO can and is and must be reoriented, even by shock treatment if necessary. I must register that the Huxley *esprit* was not nearly so vehement as expected. At no time did a spirit of irreligion overtly manifest itself.

Despite the absence of positive acts against the Faith there did crop up now and again an "active indifference" toward religion, an attitude of resignedly admitting its existence as a cultural phenomenon which deserved an italicized footnote in the pursuit of erudite scholarship. Relativism prevailed in most educational theory. Any system of absolutes was by passed. Dr. Luther Evans, UNESCO's Texas born Director General who flew in from Paris to deliver the inaugural address, distinctly stressed the absence of absolutes as a thesis basic to UNESCO's conception and operation.

The second point regards Catholic participation. Eight participants from Austria, Brazil, Canada, France, Italy and Spain identified themselves to the seminar as Catholics by word and act. I would even classify them apostolic laymen. They spoke readily and with conviction about the work of the Church in their respective nations both in formal sessions and in conversation. Without forcing situations or arousing animosity they witnessed to the Faith by demonstrating professional competence and making valuable contributions to the seminar. All eight attended Sunday Mass under circumstances which required extra initiative because local arrangements did not envision church-going in its schedule. Two of them are full time Jocist leaders in their own countries. Four or five came to daily Mass with me, requiring a taxi or a two-kilometer walk (always the former for this sore footed American). I suspect that some four or five participants from France and Italy were "croyant, non pratiquant," i.e. non-practical Catholics.

Finally, the conclusions of my written report (I quote directly):

"Over and above the usual reasons for maintaining our presence in such conferences in the U. S. and Western Europe to check and counterbalance the secularist-rationalist persuasion, the world-wide gathering presents another very important motive. Present there are representatives from the underdeveloped, recently or soon-to-be independent, nations of Asia, Africa and Oceania. These are the non-Christian hundreds of millions among whom our Catholic missionaries strive. The degree and speed of their Westernization is astonishing. They imitate the U. S. and Europe in political structure, economic development, educational institutions, mass communications, etc., etc. Seventeen of the thirty-two nations represented at this seminar fall within this undeveloped, missionary category. I found that most of the participants (school principals, college deans, labor union leaders, etc.) had never before left their native land, and had never personally come into the West and encountered Western civilization face-to-face. They are shaping the future.

"It is to my mind most important that in this first experience they should come into contact with the Catholic Faith in both its religious and cultural manifestations, and not merely with the secular aspects of our culture. And this contact will come about only if Catholics are present in the flesh at these UN and other international get-togethers. How else will they come to know our educational system, our social doctrine and Catholic labor leaders, our work among the Negroes—and race is among the greatest of their problems vis-a-vis the "Christian" West.

"For these and other reasons which space will not permit me to detail I recommend that far from undertaking a sanitary boycott to the 'God-less' UN and all its works, we rather redouble our determination to participate in every way possible."

The Word did not become Flesh by boycotting the world. That's what Pius Twelfth keeps saying every day to butchers, bankers, bakers, astronomers and treaty makers.

3. First Week of Advent

M. JACQUES MARITAIN told me last week I should keep a journal.

How typically good of the great man to offer such encouragement. I wonder if he ever feels tempted to forsake a book once begun. How good to know that such a man counsels the setting down of my knothole exits and entrances. If I persevere in this undertaking M. Maritain will shoulder much of the credit or the blame. His words urge me on. The start of Advent is a fine time for new beginnings with new resolve.

His suggestion came spontaneously about midway our discussion. I had not asked a single leading question. He was not trapped by the trend of conversation. Imagine trapping Maritain!

We spent over an hour together in the living room of his home on Linden Lane. Some days before he had received my letter requesting an appointment, introducing myself as his unseen student who sat at his feet reading his books and pondering long over his thought. His *True Humanism* stands high among the dozen or so volumes that have most influenced me. What a pity never to have seen the man who commits such wisdom to paper where all may partake. And he living only fifty miles from New York. Would he give me even a few minutes to say thank you? My letter contained too a ten page memorandum about the collegium we dream and talk about. A special delivery envelope awaited me Monday at the Mayflower Hotel in Washington and the note signed by his secretary Miss Sobolevitch said M. Maritain waxed enthusiastic over the collegium idea. This coming Thursday afternoon would be fine. Call up from New York in the morning to assure that his health would permit the visit. (He has had heart trouble for some months). And take the three o'clock train from Penn Station. Change at Princeton Junction for a couple of miles on what proved to be quite a Toonerville trolley. And so it was done.

We talked: in French and English, he soon choosing the latter as he perceived my difficulty with French. We talked about the Church in the U. S. and the world, about parish life and its thin diet, about the intellectual apostolate and how the collegium approach at the very bottom of the ladder dove-tailed with what he and his colleagues are doing at the top echelon. He expressed sorrow that Dean Hugh Taylor was absent from the campus because he would be most interested in our experiments. He will hand over the memorandum to Dean Taylor after Mass Sunday. They will talk it over; obviously he and the Dean of Princeton's Graduate School are close friends. Is Sunday morning coffee a standing date between them? He asked about the THINK groups. He recalled his own fruitful participation in a similar group in Paris decades ago; Father Garrigou-Lagrange was *their* priest participant! We talked about his books, his present study of Hegel (pointing to his upstairs study), his most recent *Approaches to God*, volume one of the World Perspectives series on whose board of editors he serves with J. Robert Oppenheimer, Niels Bohr, Hu Shih, Robert MacIver and S. Radhakrishnan.

M. Maritain expressed pleasure at having been asked to contribute the first volume of what he expects to prove a significant set of books: "written by the most conscious and responsible minds of today . . . to offer new vistas in terms of world and human development . . . from the broad perspective of the world community, not from the Judaeo-Christian, Western, or Eastern viewpoint alone." (quote from editor Ruth Nanda Anshen's introduction.) To the classical five proofs of the existence of God M. Maritain has added a sixth. He wondered what I thought about his daring to introduce another to the "ways through which the intellect is led to the certitude of His existence." And he wondered what "they" will think about it.

I wonder whom he means by "they." A man of the mind, a man like M. Maritain lives in his thoughts. The truths he propounds are projections of himself to a degree we mere men cannot understand or appreciate. Truth is so precious to such a thinker, perhaps more precious than he is to himself. He is contacted, penetrated, understood, judged, personalized in the idea he expresses. Like God the Father Who sees his Idea-Son rebuffed and rejected, men like Maritain must suffer deeply at seeing an idea, a great truth reviled and cast aside.

And so we talked, he and I. Most of the time he sat in a straight chair secluded in a corner. It seemed odd that he should seek that corner of the spacious room. Maybe it was warmer there; he had a muffler around his neck. But rather I believe that sitting in a corner may reflect a characteristic self-effacement. He must have realized that I had come filled with devout admiration: a pilgrim to a living shrine. Perhaps he strove to appear unimpressive. With that humility which marks the sage and the saint he sought to avoid dominating the scene—even his own living room. So he sat in a corner. Again maybe he felt a draught; it was snowing out.

We had wine and cookies. Then he called a cab and I rode back to the station.

Princeton's campus properly impressed me. Dour, almost foreboding, those grey stone eminences. The November fog sombred them still more. Why should a university be gay and slaphappy? Especially one which shelters Einstein and Oppenheimer and other great minds of our age who have exposed the epidermal layers of matter's mystery. I always approach a university with a sense of awe. Someone well said recently that the university is *the* masterpiece produced by our Western world.

But just for now I must leave Princeton and Maritain and all the other great places and people I saw during the last fortnight. I am back home, back in my rectory and at my desk, back among my people given me by God to watch and feed, to teach and love. I do a little of each but not enough. And it's past six on Sunday evening so I must run over to Church, turn on the lights for seven o'clock Mass, and maybe spend some minutes with the Christ whose shoes I try so foolishly to fill.

Canonical visitation by Monsignor Vandegaer, our dean. I did not know he was coming, so I had no time to tidy things up. Best that way. Three hundred and fifty questions about the ins and outs of parish and people, church and school and rectory: Is there a credence table covered with a white cloth? Are the Bishop's letters read to the people? What provision is made for the burial of the poor?

Do you carry fire insurance on contents of buildings? Amount? A sample of the points of inquiry. In this way Mother Church counters the frailties of us pastors, not permitting our negligence to proceed too far, checking up now and then on the shepherds.

Monsignor demonstrated his priestly qualities by accentuating the care of the tabernacle (he opened and inspected the ciboria to assure Our Lord decent surroundings), the cleanliness of the corporals on which He lies during the Sacrifice, and the condition of the baptismal font through which we enter Christ's Mystical Body, the font which is the womb of Mother Church.

Monsignor stayed for dinner. Someone had brought us wild duck. But he didn't stay long because people kept coming in to ask about non-Catholic bridesmaids at a wedding, roofing the new scout hut, an approaching goiter operation and so on. Rectory traffic; a crossroads 'tween time and eternity.

Ten P.M. as I write this. Just came in from the Monday night lecture on CHRIST AND HIS CHURCH. The crowd has held up well these eight weeks, about forty-five tonight, twelve to fifteen non-Catholic inquirers. Some will come into the Church; some will not. Why? What makes the difference? God's Grace? Is it not offered to all? Some cooperate, some don't. Free will? What's free will? How little we know. How little we comprehend. Understanding how little we comprehend is so fundamental to understanding man and God and life. Science theorizes that we can understand only what we comprehend. What an error. Human knowledge merely touches truth with the tip of the fingers. The mind enfolds, comprehends so little.

Last week and the week before I listened to several truly

great men and some not so great—Toynbee, Vishinsky (two days before his death), the Senators in Washington embroiled in the McCarthy censure; and conversed with the great and the near great—Maritain, LaFarge, Simon and others. How little they know, even they, and how little they understand. How much less they comprehend. I resist the temptation to call too many things a mystery and pall over our dim intelligence with an easy word. And now and then a piercing insight spears through the pall and we know that we can know—and that's so fundamental to knowing at all and living at all.

Forty hours devotion began this morning. Only a hundred or so at the six-thirty High Mass. Hard for mothers of small children to get away from home and kitchen so early in the morning. But I wonder why we don't have more of the dads. We have coffee and rolls for them in the cafeteria so they can receive Our Lord's Body, have a bite and go directly to work. Anyway, they don't come. We could scarcely beg any harder. Of course, it's easy to expect too much.

Adoration and worship men find difficult. To reach out for God directly seems to strain a man. Last night eight or ten Knights of Columbus sorted and packed old clothes until ten o'clock for shipment to war-sufferers overseas through N. C. W. C. That sort of thing men understand and put out for. "I was naked and you clothed me!" That's crystal clear. They act for the suffering Christ, they strive to keep Him warm. Does the American pragmatic spirit enter in? The patently useful, the immediate beneficial becoming the only norm? So the emphasis becomes *doing things* for your fellowman for the sake of God. That seems much easier than doing something for God simply and directly. Just being, existing for God simply and directly is harder still. It's got to involve action, and action toward a perceptible end. And the noisier the action the better. On the other hand, St. Thomas says that the excellence of action is proportioned to its inwardness. The more immanent the act, the more its object is withdrawn from outside goals, the higher the nature of the act. Life is self-activity: the more self-contained the self-activity the more noble the life. The Trinity gives us a wee glimpse of the most exalted Life: God knowing and loving His own Truth and Goodness. The most exalted human life is likewise knowing and loving God's Truth and Goodness.

To most men God Himself as the end of living, God as the purpose of being is barely perceptible. We dearly need to see the Unseen. Until we see Him we won't get up at six A.M. to listen to a tentative choir singing words we can't understand and a hoarse celebrant intoning litanies beseeching the ear of God to hear us and the hand of God to deliver us. The Unseen remains the Unheard and the Untouched. Men will send shoes to Korea to shod the barefoot Christ and blankets to Berlin to swaddle the Baby Christ. But battling sleep-laden lids to admire the *Unseen* and heart to heart talk with the *Unheard* that's another thing. The crux of the priest's role: convincing man that He Whom man does not see sees, and He Whom man does not hear hears.

Despite it all the men will turn out handsomely for the all-night adoration. Is there some romantic appeal to spending an hour with Christ from two to three A.M.? Does the memory of Gethsemane move them? Anyway they will be there. Aside from the Redemption what wisdom and goodness of God to send His only-begotten Son to be seen and heard by man.

How do I make Him seen *here?* How do I make Him heard *now?*

This afternoon Charlie Ducros' crew erected the basketball goals. Father Scherer's pleased as punch. I watch him scramble with some thirty pint-sized players, and I remember high school dreams of snagging the ball and dribbling ferociously down court, outmaneuvering center and guards, leaping gracefully (who me?) to the goal for the winning shot amid the plaudits of the high school crowd. Ah, for a word of gruff praise from the coach and a smile of sweet praise from the girls. That was the dream of life. How much of life consists of dreams. And how dreams change.

Way down deep we are what we want. How do I root well and deep my want for God and how infect my people with this holy contagion?

Father Denny preached the Holy Hour. His usual style full of heart and touching stories. And he has plenty of both. I've heard him now for ten years and he still springs a new story on me now and then like the one tonight about the six millionaires of the roaring twenties who had more money than the U. S. Treasury. In the decorous hush of the sanctuary I feel that story lose its wallop because today's U. S. Treasury is in deficit. Are the people thinking this same thing? He should have said "—than all the gold in Fort Knox." But that's hackneyed to death by now.

Anyway Father Denny went over. He always goes over. And it's not his thundering voice (he disdains the microphone), or his three hundred plus pounds of poise and presence. It's his big heart. He feels for people. And his constant theme is that Christ feels for people, too. However little people feel for Christ, they like to feel that Christ feels for them.

After the Holy Hour tonight Father Denny and I took in the tail-end of Dr. George Mitchell's talk over at Friendship House. Doc made the most of the rich possibilities of his subject: *Education in the South, Past, Present and Future.* As executive director of the Southern Regional Council he knows the issue in all its sad complexity. About fifty Negroes and twenty whites present. Among new faces brought in by this national figure was Rev. Anderson of the Free Christian School. Also another minister who wanted to know whether white ministers exercised sufficient effort toward integration. Both rather astonished at the well mixed gathering.

Doc takes a hopeful, not-too-long-term view of the education picture, a longer-term view of total integration. A good meeting all in all. Southern Regional Council now has operating funds. Two hundred forty thousand dollars from some foundation. Will get details from Doc at lunch tomorrow.

All night adoration by the men of the Parish.

And tomorrow is the eleventh anniversary of my ordination.

A letter from Dr. Hugh Taylor, Dean of Princeton's Graduate School. M. Maritain talked with him last Sunday and gave him the Collegium material.

Eleven years ago I dared to undertake the impossible: become Another Christ.

You could present good evidence that the man who presumes to seek the priesthood is shot clear through and through with pride and ignorance: ignorance of what continuing Christ really means; pride that he could to any degree live up to the ideal of bringing God to man and man to God. To some extent I go along with the ignorance argument, but with the pride question *no*. The aspirant to the priesthood demonstrates humility. By reason of the very height of the ideal he sets for himself he knows that in the eyes of men and God he will never attain it, and since meanness is relative to the norm of comparison, in his own eyes he becomes less worthy by the year, further and further from his Model. As he perceives Christ more clearly, Christ appears higher and dearer, and the distance lengthens between Creator and creature. God is All, man is nothing. That's the shattering Truth. When I shatter my pretence to something-ness then God draws close.

What ever possessed me to aim so high? At the time I did not realize how high I aimed. Saving ignorance. Would I do it again?

Would I do it again? Would I do it again? Theorizing about the future makes much more sense than theorizing about the past. If finite man exercises little control over what's coming how much less can he undo what's done. The acts of man in the present set the past in solid concrete. The future is plastic, malleable, subject to the impress of man's limited will. But once the ictus of the present sets its seal the die is cast. What's done is done. What's passed is past and irrevocable. The present perdures. The present perdures like eternity. "Who are You, God?" "I am Who am!" God could only answer Moses in the present tense.

Christ alone reconciles time and eternity. The priest tells man: Christ will judge your ever-present eternity by your irrevocable past, your past is what you presently make of your formless future. So the priest speaks to man, and speaks the same words to himself.

Would I do it again? Would I lie again supine on the Catholic University chapel floor? Would I offer again my empty hands and empty heart to give my nothingness to Him Who is all and has need of nothing? Yes, I would. To Him Who has need of nothing I offer again my creature nothingness which He needs. Anyway He says he does.

Dr. Mitchell and Larry Pausback here for lunch after lectures at Centenary College: the Mississippi Delta Negroes are countering the Citizens Councils (no KKK as yet!) with economic boycotts of their own. Neither white nor colored teachers can take initiative in the education impasse; both are bound by their very position. Church groups must play major role, especially women. The Protestant sects brought into existence by the Civil War have taken strong pro-integration positions. White and Negro must be brought together within normal economic, professional, civic and religious areas of society.

Father Scherer preached a good Advent sermon today. John the Baptist contradicts the people so at last they pay some attention. No one likes to be contradicted. John contradicts the whole worldly world. The worldly world says: I'm *it*. John says: World, without Him your're zero. The world acts surprised at being contradicted. Everybody after all is saying: I'm it; everybody's doing it; and everybody makes a majority and the majority is always right. So when a voice in the wilderness contradicts the majority some pay some attention for a while.

The priest must repeat: World, your zero——!

The priest being in the world and derived of the world sometimes he also says: I'm *it*——!

The priest stretches in the tension of the world's *itness* and *zeroness*. Sometimes the rack breaks him.

Bishop Greco blesses the new St. Theresa's School in the afternoon. Well-planned, clean-cut, like a schoolboy's shining morning face. The sacrifice our people make to support our Catholic schools never ceases to astound me. Two hundred fifteen thousand dollars!

Then the Jesuit fathers invite us over for the annual dinner honoring St. Francis Xavier. Conversation with Bishop Glennie of Ceylon in town on his periodic begging tour. He reconfirms the accelerated anti-Western feeling in Ceylon and India. American missionaries are allowed by sufferance. "Don't complain; you have no right to be here anyway." He endeavors might and main to develop a native clergy. The three Ceylonese Bishops must constantly intervene with the government for the Western Bishops who no longer have any standing. "They're not anti-Christian but anti-West."

As the Department of State official observed *re* my UNESCO Seminar report last month, this Eastern revolt against the West is as important a factor as Communism itself in world affairs.

Has Christianity become identified irrevocably with the political imperialism, economic colonialism and racial domination against which Africa and Asia now declare their independence? How awful if the Christ Saviour of these billion and a half people seem to block their 1776. Should Christianity share the blame for the failings of a post-Christian, this-world man-centered humanistic West? Can the city of God ignore the City of Man? Has it? And has the City of Man ignored the City of God?

How can we Christians avoid the blame? My friend Shafig of Jordan insisted with me at Copenhagen that the Mohammedan thinks of the Westerner first and foremost as a Christian. Do the Buddhist and Hindu react identically?

At Notre Dame University a couple of weeks ago I heard Professor Arnold Toynbee decry the exclusiveness of the claims of Christianity as inevitably dividing the one world. Would he have us jettison that which we die for, that which has made us what little we are that we still care to be? God forbid. The pressure will increase to have us dilute our Christ-given deposit of Faith. Toynbee is a person to reckon with. Christopher Dawson said last June: "Arnold is a cultural relativist." Culture *is* somewhat relative, relative to the root-truths (or myths) of its human creators. Now Toynbee seems to say that our Christian root-truths are relative.

I must get to work on the last four volumes of his monumental *Study of History.* His first six volumes indicate that he is among the great philosophers of history, returning the human caravan to the Heavenward course set by Augustine and veered from by Gibbon. But now! What exclusive claims of Christianity would he have us resurvey and deed over to our Hindu and Moslem brothers? that Christ is Divine? that He established the Church? His Presence in the Eucharist? His redeeming death and final judgment? Do these truths stub good Buddha's toes?

Or does Toynbee mean that we must emphasize our common ground and over-arching sky: children of One

Father, all in His image, all dignified with immortality, all bound to justice and love, now living in one world neighborhood? Well and good.

Or does Toynbee mean merely that we must recast our exclusive Western cultural molds: architecture, clothing, outlook and emphasis, language and literature, esthetics and manners? The other cultures contain many values of which we can partake? Agreed.

What does Toynbee mean? I must study him carefully. He is a man to reckon with. His *Study of History* shall beget a Toynbee literature as the *Summa* begot a Thomistic literature. Then we shall have commentaries on the the commentators for decades, maybe centuries to come.

I fear that Toynbee seeks a dilution and denial of Catholic dogma specifically. He was anything but coy before a dominantly Catholic audience on the Notre Dame campus. Probably he threw quite a few people for a loop. The priest who chaired the session deflated the tension with a paraphrase of the radio and TV station safeguard: "The opinions expressed by the speaker are not necessarily the opinions of the management."

Father Marvin in over-night, weighted with his fresh responsibility as editor of our new diocesan paper. What is the role of the Catholic press and of the official organ of the Diocese in particular? Before we could theorize, now he must act. Inform and interpret. Tell God's People about God. And the People of God here about the People of God there. Develop a sense of belonging, upbuilding the Christian community, arouse consciousness and conscience. The paper participates in the teaching magisteruim. The Bishop breaks to his people the bread of life which is the Word of God. Editor and staff break it into more digestible bits and passes the bread around. The Catholic press views the contingent changing world through the lens of the Absolute All-seeing Eye. Necessary, but not easy. Like everything else we must go on trying. Now here's something fresh to thresh out for the next few years.

Father Marvin wants a column on the liturgy and the spiritual life of the people. Maybe Father Louis can do it. He's willing to make a try. Another column from a couple about home and family—a homey, down-to-earth *raconte* of Mary's teething and Johnny's broken collarbones, pungent with the smell of dirty diapers and Lysol and burning autumn leaves; maybe Tom and Lena Belle can do this one. They live it, but can they write it? We'll ask them.

And a third column on "stuff." God and His World, Christ and Man, Church and Society and all their comings and goings, tensions, tears and tears, rebellions and reconciliations. I am supposed to try this. Maybe the Lafayette edition, too. And, of course, very shortly Monsignor Matthew Smith, the TIME-sung Lord of the Catholic press, will perceive my genius and circulate me over the U. S. A. with his 796,000 *Register* copies every week!

Charlie Ducros treats Father Marvin and myself to lunch at the Petroleum Club with Leonard Warren. Charlie tells us about his latest love, his mass spectrometer. It dissects the molecular structure of hydrocarbons by running the molecules (or ions?) through a hundred eighty degree racetrack. Bombarded with some kind of electrons the ethane, methane, propane, et cetera makeup is revealed, subjected to quantitative analysis and now man knows something he never knew before and can learn even more about the innards of the earth. And very incidentally this gismo finds more oil and gas!

How complex are the simple things like simple dirt and air, clay and rock. Interlocking solar systems, twisting tornadoes, roaring Niagara whirlpools churn relentlessly in every mote and clod of God's good earth.

4. The Marian Year Ends

MARY CONCEIVED without stain. "Full of grace," Gabriel phrased it. The Marian Year comes to an end. I have come much closer to Mary these twelve months. The motto says, "Through Mary to Jesus." Somehow this has not applied to me. It's the other way around. Christ has shown me His Mother; Christ in Heaven and Christ on earth, His Mystical Body the Church.

One of the stings of my life is that I have never felt close to Mary. And all along I have known that I have been missing something. A hollow place in my heart kept saying so over and over again.

Perhaps the fault has been in my juridic approach to the Church and the means of salvation. Peter and the Apostles, the Pope and Bishops! That stark reality of nineteen hundred years, that "constitutional" fact has dominated my masculine mind. Peter and Pope possess authoritative power and legal sanction. "As the Father has sent me, I also send you. . . . Going, therefore teach all nations . . . to observe all I have commanded you." The Church's foundation charter stands as firm and clear to me as "We the people of the United States . . . hold these truths to be self-evident: that we are endowed by our Creator with certain inalienable rights." In fact the legal sanction of the juridic Church is directly from the God-Man and not indirectly from God through men as is the legal sanction of the United States of America.

This direct historic authority of the Church handed down through twenty centuries of successor-bishops has filled and satisfied my mind. The prerogatives of Mary seemed poetic by comparison. But I have undergone a change of mentality this past year, a change for which I have begged: "Son, show me your Mother." And now I see her much more clearly.

During retreat last year the change began. I recall our discussions of the place and power of Mary, discussions brought on by meal-time reading about her appearances these past few years. LaSallette, Lourdes, Fatima, Rue du Bac. Did they really happen? What does all this mean? Who sets policy in the Court of Christ? What cabinet meeting decision sends her back to earth? How are the Bernadettes and Francescas chosen? Why so often to these little ones?

Mary travels more than John Foster Dulles. Ambassadress to the battlefields of earth. What are her credentials? What is her role in the whole universe of God and man and angels? What power hers as next to Pius XII and Bishop Greco?

These and many more questions moved me to entreat the Lord of Heaven and of earth "Son, show me your Mother!" And so He has. Lourdes meant much this summer past. Who lingers there with open heart and bowed head comes to know within himself that here the Mother of Heaven touches mother earth and brings with her the touch of God.

This Marian Year Christ has taught me much about

His Mother and has shown me too how much more there is to know.

This evening our Bishop dedicated the new Church of the Holy Rosary. *Locus terribilis,* the House of God! I chant the litany answered by some dozen priests. Peter and Paul, Stephen, Francis and Dominic, all ye cherubim and seraphim, lend me your ears. Herald loud down the halls of Heaven that on earth the Lord finds a new dwelling place. The Creator of Mars and Jupiter and Halley's comet has moved into a new neighborhood. Michael, Gabriel, Raphael, dispatch a squad or two of angels to stand guard before this flat table-top altar, to perform "Salute arms!" before this tabernacle wherein dwells the King of Kings at 1755 Corbitt St. Driving north down Linwood Ave., tell the corporal of the guard to turn left at the stoplight; opposite Caddo Heights Grammar School a massive cross of concrete sets against the sky and marks the church. Enter and adore.

How much exists real as concrete which our eyes of flesh fail to see!

Hurry back to St. Joe's for evening Mass. Filled to overflowing. Toddlers and chatter aplenty—to celebrate the conception of Mary. And so ends the Marian Year. The end nears, too, for Pius XII, Pius the Great, seriously sick for several weeks. We pray for him. But I find it hard to ask God to keep on earth a few more carefilled days a man whose destiny is the Face of God and the Peace he sought and did not find on the face of the whole wide world.

This morning the current Gabriel Group held their final meeting. I discuss the greatness of the trust of God entrusting to man the seed of life. I impart to the expectant mothers the blessing of Mother Church. To them a most interesting point: that parents in the marriage act perform an act which is not merely permitted, not only good in a natural sense, but also supernatural and meritorious, gaining for father and mother additional supernatural grace. Among the eight mothers there numbered thirty-five children and some of them still quite young.

Just hanging diapers in the backyard is their act in the apostolate! The waving diapers become banners flapping forth the greatness of God the Father entrusting to man the seed of life, semaphores signalling between Heaven and earth, and carrying the evangel over backyard fences via clothesline telegraph.

Luncheon with the Knights downtown. Their Friday gathering works out well. Committees meet, inter-council business settled, programs progress without taking them away from home. And a good sea-food plate for $1.12. Mine free, of course; Joe Cumella treats me every time. Why do people spoil us priests to such a shameful degree? Do we ever think we're half as good as people seem to think we are?

I finally answer Dean Taylor and Jacques Maritain. The Dean of the Graduate School of Princeton University writes:

"M. Maritain handed me on Sunday last, at his home, your precious document *re Collegium*. I cannot tell you how happy I was to receive it. You have been very much on my mind since the publication of your communication in the *Commonweal* last November. I was not among those who wrote to you but I was probably among those who interiorly most applauded your effort."

He goes on to recount how my letter fired his concern for the continuing intellectual life of graduates particularly in areas of unusual concentration by reason of industrial development and scientific research.

"Out of those thoughts three communities suggested themselves to me: Wilmington, Delaware, around the huge chemical research industry; Summit, New Jersey, around the Bell Telephone laboratories; and Schenectady, New York, around the laboratories of the General Electric Company. There must be others in great number but of which I am less personally aware."

As president of PAX ROMANA MIIC (Mouvement International des Intellectuels Catholique) Dean Taylor initiated discussion of the subject in Wilmington. An interested nucleus led to classes in philosophy taught by Father Henri Foltz. Other groups now discussing Church and State will lead "to an integrated study of contemporary problems of the Church and which we hope will capture broad participation of the Catholic professional men. . . . And might even develop into a " 'night university' in the coming years."

Plans are afoot to tackle Summit and Schenectady through Father William Rooney of Catholic University.

The men here devour Taylor's letter. It truly astonishes them. They begin to realize that we may have come upon something of first importance and not just "another good project." We discuss the *movement* quality which must be preserved and in my response to Dean Taylor (copy to M. Maritain) I stress the *movement* aspect, quoting last June's letter from Christopher Dawson:

> "I believe that there are immense possibilities for the development of a movement of this kind at present, above all in the United States. But that makes it all the more important for those who are concerned to have personal contacts and discussions. I feel that the greatest danger at this stage is that the movement should become institutionalized and popularized before it has matured. It is one of the evils of our present mechanized civilization that the spiritual seed is never allowed time to mature. As soon as the first leaves appear we expect the flower, and the flowers are picked so quickly that there is no chance of any fruit. Nature and grace are alike in that they both need time to grow."

We puzzle over where to go from here. The whole gang must get together for a session soon.

Almost a year has passed since we opened Friendship House; twelve months of forums, staff meetings, days of recollection, surveys, feeding the hungry and clothing the ragged, loving the hated and forgiving the vengeful. The begging letter the staff sent out this week offers a review of what these remarkable young Christians stand for.

The tension mounts even as Christmas approaches. This letter to friends and well-wishers barely indicates what Mary, Larry and Diane must undergo to continue bearing witness that Christ's Birth makes a difference 1955 years later:

Santa Claus has been around for almost a month now, songsters have been carolling their good cheer, shopping areas are festive with holly and ivy, toys and usual bright decorations. Christmas has been openly declared in business places and hidden away in closets, and that's all well and good.

It seems though that the Christ, the Son of God, came —according to the Bible at least—for even greater reasons. He came to tell us of the need to keep His Word. His Word was of justice, peace, mercy, and the greatest of all the commands that He gave us was to love one another.

His desire for this was so great that just before His agony and death He prayed to His Father "that all may be one, even as Thou, Father, in Me and I in Thee," and in the same prayer: "That the love with which Thou hast loved Me may be in them, and I in them." So at Christmas we especially remember that Christ came to bring peace and justice and love. We remember not only our common origin and our common goal—but we remember this more important oneness which Christ desired for us. That we should live together on earth with a love for each other so great that it makes us one—as Christ is with God.

We believe in the oneness of the human race and the dignity which Christ has given it. We do not believe that just sitting back and believing this will change the existing patterns of living which make it easy for people to be unjust to other people . . . which sometimes makes it impossible not to.

Since February of 1954, when Friendship House first came to Shreveport, we have been having weekly forums. Together, all of us, Negro and white, have heard speakers and discussed race, slum clearance, segregation in education, legal rights, the importance of voting. We have, on the lighter side, enjoyed record sessions, "trips" to Mexico and Germany, movies. Altogether there have been about 40 of these forums. Some 500 people have attended one or more. It has been our hope that in meeting together and beginning to understand these problems, which belong to all of us, we would get from them good for our own understanding and development. We would also get a sense of the unity which exists among us and realize the whole city's need for this unity. This we must work for.

This unity will not be achieved without changing the unbrotherly customs and attitudes which are the driving force for the injustices worked upon many of the citizens of Shreveport. Unmannerly treatment of Negroes in stores, newspapers—even in churches. Unequal opportunities for housing, employment. Jim Crow trollies, theaters. Laws which command segregation.

We at Friendship House expect to be here during 1955 to work with you on all of these problems. When we presented a report on the year's activities, Bishop Greco graciously reaffirmed his desire that Friendship House continue and grow. So we are asking you to make it possible for us to be here, not only by letting us share with you in the work of making Shreveport a more Christian city but by providing the necessary funds to maintain the House.

It will cost between thirteen hundred and sixteen hundred dollars to maintain Friendship House for the next six months. This includes rent, gas, light, and water, paper and postage for notices and announcements and correspondence, books and pamphlets and reference materials. Also food for three staffworkers and rent for the one who doesn't live at the House. Staffworkers work full time with no salary other than room, board, and six dollars for incidental expenses.

Christ, whose Birth we celebrate, whose word was justice and love, had this to say: "Everyone who comes to me and hears my words and acts upon them, I will show you what he is like: he is like a man building a house, who dug deep and laid a foundation upon rock. And when a flood came, the stream broke against that house and could not shake it." This is the house we would build—a house that includes all of Shreveport—eventually the world.

The whole universe is a womb-....

---❖---

FOR BUILDING UP
THE BODY OF CHRIST

Ephesians 4:11

Christ came on earth to return all creation to God from Whom we came. This return to God is not a matter of mere book accounting, nor a question of making a delivery by motor freight. All being must re-enter God out of Whom we first issued forth. We humans re-enter God through Jesus Christ, and non-rational existence returns to the Creator through Christ in us.

By work man perfects the raw universe, refining the ores and tilling the soil and spanning the seas. By work nature feels the impress of God's Mind and Will imaged through the mind and will and touch of working man. By work man exercises dominion over animal and plant, earth and rock and air, a dominion God-given and perpetuated in the faculties of man's skill and sinew. By *work man draws forth good from creatures and tastes fleetingly the savor of God's sweetness, for all that is beautiful in the universe and all that soothes the desire of man is from God and calls us back to Him.*

But only through and with and in Christ can we return with all the universe to Him from Whom we came. That's why Paul is so anxious about "building up the Body of Christ." Yes, Mary did this once during the nine months between Gabriel's Ave and the angelic choir's Gloria. From her pure body Mary nourished and built up His physical Body of flesh and bone, joints and cells. That marvelous physical Body was born on Christmas Day. Since then another Body has been conceived and in process of growth, Christ's Mystical Body. That development will continue until the end of time.

The whole universe is a womb and history records the billion yeared period of gestation, until we who are Christ are born into eternity. The Last Day is the Day of Christ's Nativity.

1. The Nativity

CUB SCOUT CHRISTMAS PARTY. And right smack on an ember day with a real live Santa, a tree and all the trimmings. Oh, well, we cannot effect changes too suddenly. And what changes do we want? How reconcile the pros and cons of Santa Claus?

The Cub Pack get-togethers have become grand family affairs. Mom and dad and all the little ones, about a hundred fifty in all. A bit hectic but worth the while. Jim Rohmik and Pete Ruesler work hard as cub-masters and get things done smooth as silk. No worry at all to me. And the den mothers! They *are* great! We hear a lot of supercilious banter about scouting but they *do* offer something wholesome; certainly not a total answer, but a good natural basis to build on.

How much time and effort should the parish spend supplying good natural needs like recreation and social life? Some pastoral theologians would throw out the athletic and social aspects of C. Y. O., scouts, etc. But shouldn't the parish help provide a wholesome human natural life upon which the supernatural can engraft itself? Especially if laymen supply the time and leadership for this natural life without depriving the priest's time unduly from his supernatural ministrations. Providing this natural social life is in part the vocation of the laymen in the parish.

An hour with Frank Dunn who is home overnight from the polio ward. His progress has slowed down considerably; now the long pull sets in. Heat therapy, massage, muscle stretching become his Job's lot. He will need all of his admirable patience and long-suffering. Fortunately from his wheel-chair he can resume some of his work, poring over blueprints and specifications and price-lists. Mrs. Dunn holds up courageously with the three little girls. The papers say that Dr. Salk expresses renewed confidence in the effectiveness of his polio serum.

God grant it! Man strives and sometimes succeeds but victory over human ills comes only with the resurrection. And we are so loathe truly to believe.

Tom Abraham and Father Louis over to consult with Father Scherer for a city-wide forum on labor relations some time in February. Tom to contact Bourg, State Federation Secretary; Paul Barker, State Counsel; and Father Lou Twomey of Loyola. This has possibilities.

The Bishop expressed concern Thursday night to the Serra men about our forgetfulness of social justice.

Graham Greene's play THE LIVING ROOM has closed on Broadway after a freshet run of twenty-one days. I am not surprised. America has little stomach for tragedy. Leaving the theater last month (I saw the second performance) was like stumbling from a meal of leaden worms. We all taste suffering and evil, sin and guilt at

some time or other; we disguise the sad savour with
catchup and alcohol. America will not soon exchange
eight full courses of unrelieved anguish for our drive-in
snack of hamburger and coke. If someone would force
feed us with unhappy endings, unrelieved and undis-
guised, we regurgitate. Greene's fame led twenty-one
diminishing herds to the water trough but he could not
make them drink. And the other horses heard about it.
But there's something deeper here.

Even TIME magazine raises an eyebrow. London
packed the house for thirty-eight weeks. Now this same
play "in which an adulterous triangle destroys itself in
the helpless presence of a paralyzed priest, against a background a bigoted neurosis" runs dry in three weeks on
Broadway. (In its juicy litany did TIME forget suicide?)
Do we have here a clue to the difference in the British
and American character?

COMMONWEAL expresses concern over the reaction
of the New York critics. If critic and audience do not go
for Greene's handling of a theme, that's one thing; but
the reason they adduce, that's another. "Sin? Suffering?
Salvation? What, most of them (critics) asked, is all the
fuss about?" These are not realities; they went out of
style with dragons and witches when Queen Victoria was
cutting teeth.

From the reviews COMMONWEAL (TIME-quoted):
"gained the impression of a culture not merely secular-
ized but somehow de-intellectualized, a culture stripped
of even passing acquaintance with the fundamental concerns which had made it great. Brooks Atkinson, for example, confessed in his (New York) Times review . . .
that a dialogue on sin between a psychiatrist and a priest
was quite beyond him. And he wondered what all the

play's gloominess, all its brooding over guilt, was about.
. . . After all, Mr. Atkinson implied, religion is meant to
make people 'happy'.

"What has religion to do with suffering? What is guilt?
What is sin? What is the problem of evil? Graham Greene
may or may not have dealt successfully with these questions in *The Living Room*, but the fact that the majority of New York reviewers could not see that the questions are real is a depressing sign of what our culture has
come to. We have been fed such a diet of peace of mind
and peace of soul, and been provided with so many
guides to confident living, that we apparently can no
longer grasp the meaning of spiritual anguish or pain in
our drama. . . . And so there will be no Living Room on
Broadway; there will be only Solid Gold Cadillacs. . . ."

Since our civilization began in Athens drama has reflected our inner being. Here then is excellent confirmation of Toynbee's contention that our Western culture is
now post-Christian. So very "post" that the interpreters
of drama-reflection of ourselves have forgotten that Christ
came to ransom our *sin* at the price of *suffering* to obtain
our *salvation*. How ill equipped the critic who would
comment on Graham Greene without understanding
that Greene really believes in Christ—this Christ of sin,
suffering and salvation. Mr. Atkinson does not have to
believe such pietistic drivel but he should remember in
the future that Greene and a few other people do so believe. Barbara Bel Geddes made me feel that she believed in sin and guilt, too, for that spate upon the stage;
that is why I felt leaden worms in my stomach. That's
why she's a good actress.

Of course Mr. Atkinson never heard confessions on
Christmas eve. But he must have heard of *Job* and *Ham*-

let, Everyman and *Oedipus Rex*. *The Living Room* is often re-enacted midst every parish flock; Barbara Bel Geddes frequently rings the rectory bell seeking a way out; and but rarely the priest in life's drama is paralyzed as well.

Now I do admit that Greene's treatment of religion is depressing, heavy, joyless, a belly full of writhing leaden worms. His is not the whole picture. Besides sin, suffering and guilt religion offers the catalyst of grace, the catharsis of sorrow and penance, the balm of mercy and forgiveness, everlasting hope. But no critic can expect Greene to trot out the *Summa Theologica* onto the stage in three short acts. A play dissects a sample sliver from the tissue of life. Greene has done this. Onto the laboratory screen he has projected his micro-slides labelled sin, suffering and guilt, and the sophisticated specialists of Broadway do not even recognize the testing tissue scalpelled from the Greco-Judaeo-Christian body which gave us birth.   *

Christmas parties for all the little ones at school.

The sixth graders re-enact the Nativity with shepherds, kings, angels and all the extras.

No Santa Claus this year—neither in person nor in decoration. The debate on banning the old man goes on.

Ed Williams was killed in an auto collision last night, right around the corner, five blocks from his home. Fortunately they reached me immediately. Gave him conditional absolution, then I was able to spend some hours with the distraught mother and dad, family and friends.

Sudden death emphasizes death. The sudden death of a fine eighteen-year-old youth highlights death still more.

Pitiful to see his friends, and they are many, groping to understand what death is. Most of them have never till now looked death in the face. Boys and girls, former classmates, freshmen at Tulane, Washington and Lee, St. Louis U. and Randolph Macon, came hand in hand; teary-eyed they stand around knowing not what to do or what to say; good, big-hearted youngsters, they want to rise to the occasion and find all the pat sayings and easy clichés flat and unsatisfying. So they stand downcast, hurting deep inside, hurting like mother hurts.

And I am about as useless as they. No flow of words can wash away a mother's grief. Her own flow of tears provides a more healing balm. Only God and time can assuage this wound; the scar remains till the resurrection —like the scars in Christ's hands and feet.

Mr. Brooks Atkinson thinks religion must make people "happy." Rather, must it make some sense and derive some value out of suffering. Suffering lies around like an undiscovered and unrefined ore. A fatuous fallacy of scientism is its pretense at doing away with suffering. And it further confounds the issue by rendering suffering less understandable and valueless. It removes the "whys and wherefores" of suffering, and man's wondrous dignity resides in his asking "why?"

A sadness thrice compounded: this morning with Ed's mother and dad to select the coffin, the plot at the cemetery, and in the afternoon worst of all to view their boy's body, to touch his cold forehead and numb hands.

Stabat Mater dolorosa . . . stood the mournful mother weeping.

Why not have a funeral on Christmas eve?

What incongruity between the green encircled crêche

and the somber steel casket side by side in Church? between the angel's "glad tidings of great joy" and the muffled sobs of a loving mother?

Death makes sense of the Nativity; Christ's Birth gives meaning to death. Christ is born into this world in order that Ed can be born into the next.

But the human heart does not keep step with the human head. Mary, your Child is born to earth, with you we rejoice! Mother, your Edward is born to Heaven, accept our sympathy.

Confessions from three to nine P.M. Sum up all the self-accusation, sorrow and reconciliation that goes on this day in all the fifteen thousand churches of the nation, in all the four hundred thousand churches of the world. More peace in more hearts than on any other day of the year. Tensions between East and West perdure but the Prince of Peace wins out in another way.

Midnight Mass. The choir does very well. Father Scherer preaches a good sermon comparing Christ to light coming through the tinted glass who is Mary, taking her human form while remaining the Divine Light. But again the poverty of human expression. Father compared the stainless Mary to stained glass.

Our speech and eyes and ears are windows in the fortress wall isolating the shell of self; through them we flow into the life and love of God and one another; but how small these apertures, and even these we drape in selfish folds and deflect with leaden shields what weak communion radiates from our nuclear ego. *Me* and *mine* are victors still, despite the Birth of Christ.

People feel closer to Christ on the Day of His Nativity than at any other season of the year. More assist at the Sacrifice, Catholic and non-Catholic than on any other feast. His Babyhood attracts them. Who can resist a baby?

Finite man constantly strives to embrace the universe, to comprehend and enfold the whole of reality with his limited mind and will. At Christmas God reduces Himself to manageable proportions; man *can* embrace a Baby, though that Baby be the All.

2. Epiphany at Work

THE SERRA CLUB's annual banquet at the Shreve Hotel complete with Bishop, flowers and ladies in their Christmas finery. Roger Corregan, President of Gulf Gas and Electric, at our table; surprised to find that five hundred of their total twelve hundred employees are in organized labor. Had no idea the percentage would be so high. Must get to know him better and seek his ideas on the future of management-labor relations. Does the rash of "right-to-work" bills indicate that the forward momentum of the labor movement has halted? Indefinitely? Will the "enlightened" corporation render further organization unprofitable to the worker? Has rugged individualism died a corporate death?

The corporation possesses such power, affects so many people so completely with such constancy that its "philosophy" is paramount in our society. A decade ago we thought that labor and capital as articulate institutions would become equal partners in the economy. But now this trend seems arrested and reversed. The corporation seems to be winning again the confidence of its workers and public. Is this because the corporation begins to think of itself as a public or representative body? "Public" in the sense of partaking in Lincoln's "of the people, by the people and for the people?" "Public" and still distinct from government as such?

Will a "tertium quid" arise from the struggle of private and state enterprise? In the seventeenth century, government to Louis XIV was a private affair: *"L'état c'est moi!"* And not merely a witty epigram. Then government became a closed corporation of the Lords Temporal and Spiritual in Britain.

George Mitchell was telling us last week that about 1790 William Cobbett was imprisoned for listening and reporting to the people via his news sheet the debates in the British Parliament. Parliamentary discussion was not the business of the whole people. Parliamentary government was a closed affair.

The same held true till very recently of the "private business" of corporations. Now more and more of their inner-workings are known to the public forcibly via tax reports, anti-trust and labor contract hearings, and voluntarily for public relations. The time may come when the Cobbetts of today as A. P., U. P., and I. N. S. reporters will attend the meetings of the board of directors of General Motors just as they now attend the sessions of Congress and Senate committees.

For this "tertium quid" we must invent a new adjective. From "pro populo" I submit "propop." What an explosive sound!

Governor Kennon opens the new Youree Drive Expressway linking our Broadmoor area to downtown in seven minutes. The assembly of citizens and politicians, big and small time, bow their heads while I pray:

Great God, we beseech You, hear us!

Father of us all, Creator of this Earth and all its ores, Maker then of this steel and concrete which through the co-creating ingenuity, labor and sweat and engineering skill of man have become this great highroad linking city to city, office and work and home—

To us your human children you have given dominion over all these your creatures.

We thank You for inspiring in our civic and community, state and national leaders a God-given sense of duty and creativeness—

A creative genius God-like in its impressive scope and magnitude, lowering the hills and filling the valleys, refashioning the face of the Earth—

So that our citizens and fathers of families through this increased facility of transport and communication, commerce and industry may the better fulfil their duty to family and little ones, friend and fellow citizen.

For all these great goods and concepts, Father of all, we thank You. Through Christ Our Lord.

Amen.

Here is the City of Man at work, the kingdom of this world at its best—refashioning the face of the earth; completing, perfecting the raw creation of God.

This project required the intermeshing effort of many social groupings: governmental bodies, city, county, state and national; levee board, highway commission, street department, drainage district; real estate board, assessment team, expropriation court; engineers, architects, contractors, corporations, steel mills and labor unions, chamber of commerce, newspapers, civic clubs pressuring and cajoling. Thousands of heads and hearts and hands must work as one to lay an eight lane concrete band two and a half miles long. How evaluate these herculean heavings, these bulldozing exertions of the human society as builder? Man engirdles the earth with couplings of steel, spans river and ocean, pierces strata and stratosphere, eyes the spiraling nebulae and whirling galaxy, deflects the electron from its appointed course, begets heat to boil the sea. Man searches and discovers, experiments and refines, remakes the physical face of the earth. Shall we write-off all these strivings, shall we snub all these attainments with an Augustinian fiddle-dee-dee?

Did Augustine's dichotomy dig too deep a ditch between the temporal and the spiritual? The pressures of his day, the rottenness of pagan Rome, the bestial violence of barbarian band, seemingly begot a pessimism unfathomable. The City of God and the City of Man became irreconcilable. *Quid hoc ad aeternitatem?* So what toward eternity? Does Augustine really answer: It profits nothing! Nary a thing! Or have his commentators changed his voice? It it possible that all the corporate sweat and struggle of human society cause not a ripple on the shores of eternity? That God doesn't give a hang? Cardinal Suhard following Leo and the Piuses will not have it that way. Not as long as they speak for the Divine Word Who Himself became Flesh, sweating, striving, stinking Flesh, which sweated, strove and stank like the rest of us humans. The society of man on earth forms a continuum with the cherubim and seraphim, somehow, some way.

Did Augustine give us a bum steer? Perhaps he reacted too violently against the goody-goody Pelagians who did not see the gaping wounds of man's stricken nature. Augustine saw them all too well. God's Will, God's healing grace must effect the cure. And as the offertory prayer of the Mass puts it *mirabilius reformasti,* the repair job came off even more wonderfully than the pristine creation.

If God's grace can repair the individual nature of man, cannot man's social nature and the community man creates be repaired, enobled as well? Can it be—shouldn't it be? Luther denied that grace really and truly repaired man's wounds and elevated his nature. Shall we anathematize Luther's teaching concerning individual man and embrace his heresy concerning social man?

The devil would have the Church withdraw to the pinnacle of the temple and stay there. Certainly he knew that Christ had more sense than to throw Himself down. Satan's real hope may have been that Christ would remain on the pinnacle haughtily withdrawn from the temporal disorder below. Leo and the Piuses espied this less obvious temptation but we have been awfully slow in rejecting it completely. Pinnacles are so exhilarating and quiet.

Another year ends in a few hours.

We know so little about life, possess so little being ourselves that God feeds us existence with a baby nipple drop by drop. Droplets of seconds and hours and years. If the wave of Being Itself flooded upon us we would fall flat like Paul did that day near Damascus. Thank God for life, yes. But for now thank God for life in time, for spoon-feeding us lest our nothingness dissolve in the floodtide of His All.

The year of Our Lord 1954 comes to an end. Has it been the year of Our Lord? Pastor and people ask ourselves during the watch hour. Some of His life-giving elixir we have vomited, spewed back into His Face.

Circumcision; Christ's *suffering* for our *sin* and *salvation* begins.

I guess the cutting hurt, so I imagine that Christ cried. His redeeming blood and baby tears began to flow. And these few drops of red and shiver of pain suffice to wash away the sins and dirt of all mankind past and to come. But Christ is so thorough, so thoroughly human and thoroughly divine. He must needs say: It is consummated. The consummation begins today.

An afternoon watching the Sugar and Rose Bowl games over at the Sampsons.

TV is amazing. Most impressive view: the Gillette cartoon hero shaving himself in three strokes. Disney's jerks perform such superhuman feats! like shaving in three strokes! Man will not resign himself to his limitations. He burns with a restless stirring, striving for the unlimited, the infinite. Cartoons can portray man doing what a mere man cannot do. That's why they're so popular. They free man from his creaturehood. They endow man with quasi-divine attributes.

TV is wonderful, once or twice a year.

Father Paul Goubeau from Lafayette surprises me arriving about seven P.M. We talk for hours. He wants to come into our diocese. Even back in Seminary days he wanted to be a diocesan priest but only the Society of the Divine Word was taking Negroes then. Will I speak to the Bishop on his behalf? Gladly, and if I know Bishop Greco he will gladly welcome him.

His own superiors are glad to cooperate.

To Maryhill for Eucharistic Day. This monthly gathering of all our priests has brought great blessings upon our diocese. Leave here at eight A.M. to make the ten thirty Holy Hour and meditation. Then a conference of bishop and priests, laying plans, launching programs, bestirring projects, until one o'clock dinner. Followed by meetings of consultors, marriage court, diocesan committees and other groups. Back home the hundred and twenty-five miles by six o'clock.

We plan another priest's institute on the C. C. D. for March.

Tonight the THINK group talk things over. We decide on a four or five month series of gatherings, every other week as usual. The group spirit is still very vigorous. The UN and integration dominate the evening. We decide to begin bimonthly gatherings of pastor and people to chew over today's issues, to relate man and society to God, time to eternity. A seed that can grow. We will call these confabs soirees, just evenings together.

Weekly staff meeting at Friendship House two to four thirty this Tuesday afternoon. Afterwards to St. Anne's Home for sister's confessions and conference. Then over to Dr. Louverture's to meet Dr. Wilson from Mound Bayou, the famous all-Negro town in the Mississippi plantation country near Greenville.

Dr. Wilson and his colleague Dr. Redding have sparked the courage of their voiceless people. As a state wide rallying point they organized the Southern Regional Leadership Council, broader in scope than the NAACP and with more local initiative to forestall the rebel cry against "Northern agitators." The NAACP fights the legal battles of great national consequence. The home-grown Council while aiding and abetting these court struggles exerts itself on the community and state level where local custom and administrative procedure carries on the discriminatory code of the South.

At first Dr. Wilson hesitates before me the stranger, the white man. Although I am Louverture's friend it takes a while before restraint gives way to confidence. After an hour and more I have heard today's great drama summarized by one who plays a leading role. Leading and heroic. The struggle to vote, to work, to study, to ride, to borrow money, to buy a home—to live with dignity, and without servility, without fear. He cites cases, names names, recounts threats. What the mayor said, what the sheriff thought, what the banker did, what the governor did not do.

Dr. Wilson neither looks nor acts the role of the prophet liberating his people. Mosaic thunder and fumings would not fit this humble figure. Not once does he raise his voice, not once does he point a finger of accusation. He knows what he is up against. This man without illusions is immune to disillusion. Should I compare him to Gandhi—threatening no violence, fulminating no ultimatums, invoking no battle-cries—but endowed with a patience and persistence ineluctable, irresistible; grinding, grinding, grinding like the mills of the gods. These are the men who move mountains.

"I ask myself," he says, " 'What are you doing here? Why don't you leave? Why do you put up with all this humiliation, with all this indignity?' I want to leave. Sometimes I just can't stand it any longer. I could leave. Good openings await me elsewhere. But I stay on. For some reason I stay."

These men are the heroes of our time.

The three magi with camel and retinue appear at the crib this morning. The little toddlers come and feast their eyes. The camel fascinates them, bedecked in red and green; the queerly clad kings absorb their attention. And there's the Babe, arms outstretched. The toddlers know not the what and the wherefore, the whence and the why of Epiphany. This manifestation of God made Man, this lifting of the veil, this revelation to the Gentiles means about as little to us grown-ups.

We are a superficial people, our powers of apprehension overwhelmed by multitudinous sense impressions, our keenness to spiritual reality blunted. Matter seems almost victorious with a finality overwhelming as a Mississippi flood. "God made man . . . the Light to enlighten the Gentiles" moves our innards like "Mary had a little lamb, little lamb, little lamb!" We see about as little in this manifestation as the children see. We see surface and shape, color and form. Substance we do not see.

"In Him was life, and the life was the light of men. And the light shines in the darkness; and the darkness grasped it not." Still we hold up the light—that's Epiphany.

To Centenary College this morning to speak to the convocation of students and faculty. At the Dean's invitation I tell them about the UNESCO Seminar of the past fall at Copenhagen. They listen attentively; more attention than I expected from the hard backless gym stands.

The world interests these thousand youngsters. Afro-Asia vis-à-vis the West, world wide racial tensions interlock with our own local racial realities. I spare no punches. "We must have complete integration. *When* and *how* we might discuss, but not the goal—that is definite. We must work for the Negro's total equality." After forty minutes the applause is loud, long and sincere. As yet Centenary has no Negro students.

3. The Parish Is Christ

EXECUTIVE BOARD MEETING of Confraternity of Christian Doctrine this afternoon in the rectory. The block captains, center and soirees, Lenten mission, Presentation ceremony and daily missals preoccupy us.

The block captain system does not work a hundred percent but is hugely worthwhile at seventy-five percent effectiveness. Worthwhile from two points of view: the good the block captains do for the parish, the good they do to themselves. What pastor can say, "I know mine and mine know me." Even with our small parish, of fifteen hundred souls—very small relative to the gargantuas of New Orleans and Chicago, even with our small parish of five hundred families I cannot say, "I know mine . . ." much as I would like to. How visit the homes that minimum once a year? Six to eight in the evening are the ideal hours for these visits, when husband and children are home. A daytime visit with wife and infants alone is not a family visit. Then about fifty percent of our families are mixed marriages. Visiting the non-Catholic wife alone is out of place; visiting the Catholic wife in the absence of the non-Catholic husband means you do not get to know him. Besides, the children are off at school, and mother is washing, scrubbing, vacuuming, ironing, lounging.

So six to eight in the evening is the time for visiting and blessing home and family. The family is at table in the kitchen. The kitchen provides the very best place to get acquainted, the most important, most-lived-in-room of the house—and I hit pot-luck now and then. I try to avoid pre-arranged meals by invitation: too formal, too much trouble for the missus, the pastor becomes identified with stiffly starched napkins, shining silver, gleaming crystal and succulent steaks; I don't see the family as they really live—on hamburgers and potato chips gulped down unseen in the TV twilight.

So six to eight in the evening I call on my flock. BUT— that's the very hour at which most people call on me, after work to arrange marriage plans, husband and wife to talk over a problem, non-Catholics to discuss the Faith. And that's the very time we have all our meetings and meetings and meetings, as well as Mass and confession and Way of the Cross and other devotions.

So try as I might I do not visit my people enough. Besides I don't try very hard; I am lazy. Even when free I stay home and read. I do not know mine and mine do not know me—not well enough anyway. Over half the adults are active in organizations; I see them there. Ninety percent of the children attend our elementary school; instructions, nursery, scouts, C.Y.O., socials and athletics for the others. I stand at the front of Church before and after Mass. Introduce myself to newcomers, glower grinningly at the late arrivals, chew the fat on the front walk, inquire about backaches and cancer and nervous breakdowns, facetiously ask early departees if they feel faint, wave at non-Catholic husbands in waiting autos, meeting visiting mothers-in-law, bless St. Christopher medals. And Father Scherer does the same.

All good and fine. But too seldom do I see the family at home where life is really lived. Usually the family visit means trouble or sorrow: death, a fuss, desertion, drink, a marriage case, an unbaptized baby, Communion to the sick, a problem child, misery of some sort or other.

Too seldom do I see the family at home where life is really lived. It hurts to hear my folks say: "Our pastor has never set foot in our house." And the people are so good and understanding that they imply no mean rebuke, no accusing complaint. It's an invitation, it's a welcome, it's a compliment that they want me to be part of the family. Their homes are open to their pastor, their father in God. And on the whole they well realize the demands of being father to fifteen hundred children. Their numerous children make demands which they too find it impossible to fill.

Still my conscience rebukes me constantly. I should visit my people, I should and I try and I fail. I assuage my guilt by thinking about Christ: how few of His spiritual family did He know in a human way. How restricted the geographic scope of His personal ministry. So He sent out Apostles. I sent out block captains. The Apostles didn't succeed a hundred percent. Neither do the block captains.

And of course the great difference: Christ loved. Can a pastor, a mere human really love his people? What mere human can love fifteen hundred persons, really love them? Or five and ten thousand in the really large parish of Detroit and Boston? The mere human cannot love so many people. Christ living and loving in that human can. But how make this theological truth a pastoral reality except by letting Christ take over all the way? Such Saint Pastors seem so few and very far between. Christ lives in me, loves through me, only by fits and starts, and to such slight degree. How relieved I am to reflect that Christ does not depend on me individually but as a member of the much greater Whole. Christ lives and loves in His Mystical Body, His Church. The Church is Christ living and loving here, today.

How then relate pastor and parish to the whole Church, to this living, loving Christ? We begin a new year. We take inventory. We examine our consciences. Who am I? Who are my people? What is a priest, a pastor, a parish?

I am pastor of St. Joseph's Parish. A parish of the Universal Church of Christ—the Church KATHOLIKE.

I must see our parish in the setting of the whole world, I must see the world in the setting of the whole of time and of history which is time's unfolding, and I must see time's unfolding between the two immeasurable termini which is the One Eternity, the Beginning and the End.

To see our parish in any other, any narrower, vision is not really to see it at all, but only its fragment, its shadow. And to see our parish as fragment is to be a pastor in fragment and in part. To be a partial pastor is to fail to fulfil myself in my vocation and to fail Christ. I fail to complete myself if I fail to enable my people to discover who they are, and so they never find the meaning of their life. And not to know the meaning of life, to perceive purpose but dimly is to live a life that is something less than human, to frustrate what could have been, to stunt and shatter the masterpiece of the One Artist. The man who knows not the meaning of life does not know himself; that man who does not know himself is unconscious, cocooned by chronic amnesia.

Our parish must awaken man to the full life of full

consciousness, to the deep realization of the innards of his being. Who shall tell man that he came forth from the Eternal God? And who shall bridge time's stretching chasm till man enter again into his destined Eternity? Who shall bind his wounds and direct his feet along the twists and turns of the Faustian way? Who shall lift him when he falls and wipe his brow and make strong his creature frailty? No one shall so serve man between the nothing from which he comes and the All to which he goes save Him Who joins together time and eternity, the God-Man Christ. And this God-Man lives on in the four dimensions of time and space through His Mystical Body the Church. In the *hic* of this geographical area and in the *nunc* of this day's unfolding the Church is St. Joseph's Parish.

What is a parish? What is our parish? The nature of our parish is a mystery as the Church of which it is a part is a mystery. Christ's Mystical Body, our limping language avows. The concept of mystery is not a cloak to cover the eyes. The foreknowledge that a truth is a mystery helps greatly in grasping that truth. We approach that truth with reverence aware of our limitations. We search beneath the surface. We probe deeply knowing the while that truth's totality will not unfold to us alone, and that each fold will likely reveal another fold within its depth. Mystery guards us against the facile foolery of the Philistine. Precious mystery, master of time, making time bearable by lending savor to the search for the True which gives time meaning. Precious mystery which weds time with Eternity through the continuum of human wonder. Death alone answers the final why. The Beatific Vision is that utter unfolding of the mystery we begin unraveling in this world. Little Audrey's "Why, Daddy?" is man's first cry for God, the

same unquenchable thirst which rended the restless, quest-
ing Augustine.

A parish means many things. The sound of the word
conjures many concepts to the mind. The mystery's over-
lapping layers unfold. A church cross-crowned; the tabernacle, vigil-light, beckoning man to the waiting Light
watchful there; the altar, the crucifix and the Sacrifice;
the table of Communion; the pulpit and the word of God;
the confessional and the Alter Christus on his seat of particular judgments this side of death; the *congregatio*, the
People of God on the Lord's Day conjoining their minds
and wills and bodies in the Great Offering: kneeling, sitting, standing, speaking, singing, bowing as one, the One
Body of the One Spirit.

A parish means many things. Ann and John made one
in Christ. The school: May (O Mary we crown thee with
blossoms today.), the pep rallies (Ole Sacred Heart she
ain't what she usta be.), First Friday assembly line confessions, and still the personal touch (I shot a spitball, but
missed.), the PTA bazaar and its bellyaches, homework
and puppy love, and Sister's serenity. The bitter with the
sweet: the drinking party, the family quarrel and the miscellany of human hates. Mrs. Murray's mite and Father's
fretful Sunday fuming on the giving of the green.

A parish means all this and more. A mystery still because
the parish exists for and by and through that Mystery
which eye hath not seen and the like of which hath not
entered into the heart of man. A parish embodies this
Mystery *here and now* on this planet earth, attaches an
address and a phone number, pulls the Mystery out of the
haze of Plato's universal and Aquinas' Pure Act into the
flesh and blood of Joe Smith, 464 Patton Avenue, Shreveport, Louisiana, U. S. A.

Joe Smith at seven in the morning. Joe Smith with his Schick-nicked face and petulant voice and pregnant wife. Joe Smith with *his* yawning youngsters gulping rice crispies at and on and off the breakfast table (excepting Jimmy in bed with the mumps and months-old Mike masked in the grisly green of the squashed spinach Mommy's spooning down his gagging gullet from the Gerber's tin with the Good Housekeeping label—and of course being only in her second month Mommy's got morning sickness). Joe Smith with *his* bills to pay and *his* bus to catch and *his* clock to punch and *his* work to do.

This Joe Smith made to the image and likeness of God? How will he ever know? Who will tell him, convince him? How open *his* tired T-Veed eyes to That which eye hath not seen? How will a Pierced Heart on a Cross on a skulled hill across an ocean and two seas, back over time's ticking through nineteen hundred years, how will that Heart pierce his heart with a warmth that hath not entered into the heart of man? How shall the True penetrate *this* mind imprisoned by popular puns, enslaved by slogans, benumbed betimes with whiskey's wooze.

Only Christ can do all this. On our burnt-out cinder mother earth and till it burns again Christ lives on through and by and in His Mystical Body the Church. And to the people living within the boundaries of *this* brushy bayou, *this* river, *this* city street and *this* county line the Church is our parish. Our parish is Christ. A logical conclusion to this compound syllogism? Logical, yes, but theological?

Theology tells man the secrets of God. Two centuries ago in the flush of the anthropocentric humanism we call the Enlightenment Alexander Pope wrote:

"Know then thyself, presume not God to scan,
  The proper study of mankind is Man."

Pope erred. He erred with an earth-shaking error. He said that man must not seek the secrets of God. Did he not know that only God can tell us the secret of man? And the study of those secrets, those mysteries, is theology.

"The proper study of man is man," says the earth-bound humanist. He would encase the human mind with the horizons of this world. He would deny history, for history records man forever pushing back the borders that would bind him, man refusing to be socked in by the fog of the merely finite. Moses asks: "Who are you God?" John the Baptist: "Are You the Christ or shall we look for another?" Christ: "Who do men say that the Son of Man is?" Caiphas: "I adjure you by the living God that you tell us if thou art the Christ, the Son of God." Pilate: "What is Truth?" Paul: "Oh, the depth of the riches of the wisdom and of the knowledge of God! How incomprehensible are his judgments and how unsearchable his ways! For who has known the mind of the Lord."

Alexander Pope to the contrary notwithstanding, man will ask his questions and man pursues his quest. Man will not be sated by bread alone. Our parish is Christ arousing these questions and lifting the veil, Christ whetting the appetite and breaking the bread. Small wonder the parish is a mystery as the Church is a mystery and Christ is a mystery. And the mind of man strives to clarify and the Holy Spirit strives to illumine man's darkness: Theology.

The question "Who is Christ?" preoccupied theologians during the first five centuries of His existence here on earth. The Docetae and their many relations would have only his appearance, not his punctured Flesh and ruptured side and heaving lungs, only a shadow but no human bulk to block off the light, only an Alice-in-Wonderland phantasm like the Cheshire's smile minus the cat. The Arians and their numerous kin would have the Son a mere human stripped of the Divine, merely HOMOI (like unto) the Substance of the Father.

In 325 Athanasius and the Church Universal at Nicaea explained to the Joe Smiths of Constantine's day and our day what had been true before the daystar came to be: that Christ is HOMOU (equal to) the Substance of the Father. Christ Consubstantial, "the only-begotten Son of God . . . of One being . . . with the Father" our Joe Smith credoes with his family and neighbors at the nine o'clock community Sacrifice—a dialogue Mass—each Sunday morning from his Stedman missal, page 25.

The Whoness and Whatness of Christ walking about Galilee for thirty-three years became less a mystery (and yet a Mystery still) during those fifteen centuries before Trent and the revolt that convoked that Council. The Protestant Revolt attacked the Church—the whoness and whatness, the nature and essence of the continuation of the Way, the Truth, and the Life through time and space.

Nicaea had explained that Christ is "the only-begotten Son of God." Trent made clear that the Church (One, Holy, Catholic and Apostolic, whose visible head on earth is the successor of Peter as Bishop of Rome and Vicar of Christ) is the only-begotten Church of Christ.

Since Trent we have received from the Rock of Truth an ever-deepening understanding of the whoness and whatness of the only-begotten Church of Christ. And pressed on by this century's historic events our Holy Fathers have brought emphasis and growing clarity to the concept of the Mystical Body of Christ. We now see the Church more clearly as Christ. Christ dwelling in the souls of men, yes; and Christ dwelling in the bodies of men as His temples, yes. But more than that. We see the truth that humans, body-and-soul and body-and-soul and body-and-soul, in the thousands and millions, are bound together in One, by a Bond far more than the moral bond of common purpose and common pursuit. Bound together in One by a Life which is more, far more than created grace and creature charity. Bound together in one Body so that the body-and-soul named Joe and the body-and-soul named Bill and the body-and-soul named Jane are principled and life-given and united and souled by One Soul (as truly my own left hand and right foot and optic-nerve are principled and life-given and united and souled by one soul) which One Soul is the Holy Spirit, the same Holy Spirit of personified Love Who binds in Unity the Father and the Son.

We see that we who are the Church are Christ. And Christ here on earth is we who are the Church.

We can perhaps paraphrase the Nicene Creed's "God of God, light of light, true God of true God. Begotten, not made; consubstantial with the Father. . . ." Is not the Church "Christ of Christ, light of light, true Christ of true Christ. Begotten, not made (insofar as divine with the Divinity of Christ and her Soul, the Holy Spirit); consubstantial with the Son . . . ?"

Yes, the Church is divine with the Divinity of Christ, transcendental as Suhard so ably tells. But the Church is human, too, human with the Humanity of Christ, immanent in the gripes and groans of this world's travail.

Is not the Church also Christ made man and crucified and suffering? Some would have the Church only as the already resurrected Christ, triumphant, glorious! His wounds no longer bleeding, the thorns nothing but a memory. Some would keep Christ in His tabernacle and expose Him only to mount Him in the monstrance for their Sunday incense. But the Church is not only Christ on Sunday. The Monday morning Christ is here nailing boards and sweating human sweat, healing Samaritan wounds and leper scabs, confounding wordy legalists and prodding professors, calling Zacheus from his lofty penthouse in the sycamore to right his wrongs of usury and such, facing up to Caesar and the might of matter of his day. How could such a Son of such a Father Who "so loved the world" retreat from the world He came to save? How could He call it quits after only *one* Good Friday and *one* Golgotha when all nations and all the sand of time must still flow through the narrow neck of history's hourglass before His final "It is consummated!" at the consummation of the world?

From the great treasury which is the deposit of Faith all this wealth of truth unfolds. One fold of the mystery reveals the deeper Mystery still to be pursued even this side of death. And so we continue the quest.

Our great Shepherd Pius XII has told us much, especially in the encyclical *Mystici Corporis* of 1942. Many have commented. Much has been written. Theological studies, university lectures and theses, spiritual conferences, popular books, TV programs, discussion groups, pamphlets, magazine articles, each add their ray of light. Clergy and laymen rub their minds together in apostolic groups and staff meetings and executive boards. Emmanuel Cardinal Suhard writes his pastorals. Translations cross-current across the seas and mountain barriers. New vistas open before the eye. The hierarchy, the living magistry teaches. Even pastors begin to think, to ask questions and expostulate.

The world over we must each see that our parish is Christ. And this must become a conscious vision. But our

one parish alone is not Christ, not if cut off from the rest
of His Body. If the member becomes engrossed exceed-
ingly in itself, if the branch would compassionate and minister but to itself, if the limb lives not for the whole Body
—then that member grows to canker, that member would
shatter the Body and break Christ's bones which even
Pilate's soldiers never did in the first crucifixion on that
first good Friday.

So since our parishes constitute our Christ we *must* each
see our parish in the setting of the whole world; we must
see the world in the setting of the whole of time and of
history which is time's unfolding; we must see time's unfolding between the two immeasurable termini which is
the One Eternity, the Beginning and the End; and we
must consciously conjoin our parishes, the People of God,
into the Eternal One, the Alpha and the Omega, the One
Christus-Pontifex Who bridges the gap.

4. Pastor and People

MONEY. Finances. Building fund. Pledges.

About fifty men gathered after nine o'clock Mass this morning to get pledge cards and instructions for winding up our annual building fund drive. The angel in man is anchored in matter, the Holy Spirit touches man through matter, which means brick and steel, glass and cement, which means money.

Our people are good about money. On the whole they do their share. The regular Sunday collection runs about five hundred dollars now. The extra-curricular building fund will total about twenty-five thousand dollars this year. The special collections run about five thousand dollars more. Add the organizations' budgets and benefits to reach a total of about sixty thousand dollars a year exclusive of school tuition. And for some seven hundred adults sixty thousand dollars is quite good to very good. Anyway, I feel no impulse to rake the people over the coals about money.

Rather, we must create an atmosphere regarding money: "The parish life is an extension of your family life. The church and school and playgrounds are an extension of your own home. You're paying installments on your house and lot, on your furniture and auto and washing machine. Similarly you're paying installments on this the House of God which is your House, too. All this is 'ours' with Christ and in Him and through Him. So we have responsibilities—responsibilities which we sometimes forget and put off and must be reminded of."

Our January first report to the Bishop shows an estimated gross value in real estate, property and furnishings of $309,949.59. An indebtedness of $127,689.78. A net value of $182,259.81. This net value has accrued in six years at the rate then of some thirty thousand dollars a year. So we're doing all right financially.

But to keep doing all right we must always try to do better.

Good talk last night at the Youngs.

John and Margaret tell about their "up East" jaunt over the holidays. Yale's Graduate School of Drama asked them up to speak to their faculty and students. Then several days in New York with John Gassner et al. These two are tops in American community theater; how fortunate we are to have them direct our Shreveport Little Theatre.

John and Margaret recoil from the intellectual iciness encountered at Yale and Columbia. All so, so technically perfect, *savoir-faire* and *savoir-dire* fill the cup, but joy runneth not over. Gassner peers about the Columbia Faculty Club: "More brains per square inch in this room than anywhere in the world but no joyousness." Wasteland desert in the midst of gardens, palms and pot plants; loneliness on Times Square.

A grand confab with William Dunham. The collegium would fill his need and he could contribute much. Here's a thirty-year-old Tulane University graduate who is still growing, seeking, probing, maturing.

Via F. S. C. Northrop and Bertrand Russell he has discovered Aristotle and Thomas Aquinas. It surprised him to find that the Church had developed a philosophical system centuries ago, then based revelation and theology upon this structure of natural truth known by unaided human reason, a system of truth to which even Russell had to make a passing nod. He inquires about the seminary course of studies. The prerequisite philosophy astonishes him. We go into a few fundamental metaphysical concepts: potency and act, being, the transcendentals *bonum* and *verum*.

Dunham finds it difficult to *read* philosophy. Russell puts him to sleep. I observe: philosophy must be talked, mind must rub against mind, akin to dialectics, one mind challenges the other, butts against mental inertia, opens vistas; small wonder that some of the most enduring philosophy comes to us as Dialogues, conversations among several of Plato's friends.

Then we launch into natural law. Dunham and Fred Cunningham frequently tie into that increasingly popular subject. At Tulane University hardly more than the vaguest concept of natural law came up in jurisprudence. Utility and precedence of the gospel according to Holmes prevailed. Dunham has become more aware of the substance and importance of natural law in the ten years since graduation. He has noted reference cropping up here and there in public utterances and legal articles.

Soon we must read and discuss Lippmann's THE PUBLIC PHILOSOPHY which according to reviewers and *Atlantic Monthly* prepublication articles presents a thesis embracing the concept of natural law. By coincidence I received today a note from Governor Shivers of Texas enclosing the requested copy of his recent Birmingham speech. I quote:

"As John Adams once told the people: You have rights antecedent to all earthly governments; rights that cannot be repealed or restrained by human laws; rights derived from the Great Legislator of the Universe.' . . . Our American Constitution represents the first effort of mankind to give permanence to man's inalienable rights by expressly denying the central government absolute power. . . .

"It took nearly eighteen hundred years for the human race to bring forth on this continent a truly progressive system, embodying the principles of the Christian ethic—a system which made the individual supreme to earthly government and effectively protected the individual against the supremacy of the central government."

Good statements from Governor Shivers; it's good to see him sinking the foundation of practical politics so deep into the past from which we have come and the eternity toward which we are going. As to be expected he then applies these principles to the states' rights controversy. Whether or not his conclusions are valid, he begins from excellent premises. In their public utterances President Eisenhower and Secretary Dulles repeatedly ground their political philosophy on some aspect of the natural law.

And closer to home: When Hodding Carter, Pulitzer Prize winner of the Greenville (Mississippi) paper, spoke to the Caddo Parish Bar Association here a couple of months ago, he too invoked the same principles in speaking of the Supreme Court decision on segregation. That decision did not surprise him because the constitutional rights being interpreted are inalienable rights derived from man's Creator, and because the Christian ethic still influences us. He expressly repudiated the thesis that "Law is Law" based on precedent or legislative fiat without regard for our deeper philosophy and religious heritage. Must get to know Carter better. Soon I must accept his invitation to visit him and talk things over—things general and things specific—but especially things general.

Too few people think and talk about things general, the abstract universals which unify all the concrete objects and happenings which compose life. The universal alone supplies the needed conjunctive, conjoining concrete fact to concrete fact. Because the universal concept is of the spirit it can penetrate into the matter of the concrete fact and relate it to another concrete fact. The universal idea causes the concrete entities to compenetrate one another. Otherwise the concretes can only touch each other's surface; my pen and this paper "know" each other only through my mind. The material (concrete entity) divides reality, the spiritual (universal idea) unites all being.

Our technological civilization emphasizes the world of three-dimensioned matter, the concrete event, the single act. The spirit, the flow, the relation, the universal principle, we tend to ignore this world of reality. So we must concern ourselves with things universal. Hodding Carter seems to live in both worlds.

Father Don Hessler drove in last night about seven. From Maryknoll headquarters on the Hudson en route to his mission in the jungles of Bacalar, Yucatan. Driving a three-quarter ton GM truck, pulling a canvas-covered trailer bulging with clothing, lanterns, books, farm implements, plows and harrows, axes, saws, hypodermic needles and an outboard motor. St. Boniface and Alcuin brought substantially these same instruments of civilization with them into the heart of Europe. That combine made the West. Twelve hundred years later that same Voice calls Father Hessler from the air-conditioned ease of twentieth century U. S. A. into the stinking, steaming jungle to tell an earth-grubbing tribal chief that he is a child of God.

By eight o'clock Father Hessler is telling the ladies of Mary's Workers (by coincidence assembled for quarterly meeting) about his arrival in Yucatan five years ago to find his church abandoned for a century, enfolded boa constrictor-wise by the living jungle, with huge trees down the center aisle, trunks pushing through the crumbling roof; about his forty thousand parishioners scattered in some eight settlements over eight thousand square miles, only a couple of high school graduates among them; about digging their water reservoir and facing it with masonry so now the people can drink without infection and wash the dirt from the children's bottoms and ease their feverish aches; and about the tractor and the field and seeds and fertilizer, clinic, midwives and many other things.

By nine o'clock we have transferred to the men's group, by coincidence gathered for their fortnightly gabbing.

By midnight we have heard a wondrous account of a wonderful man and his people, God's People. Father Don Hessler has an especial interest in the participation of lay people in the missionary apostolate. Some six or seven lay missionaries have been with him for several years—doctor, nurse, midwife (infant mortality is 50 percent), engineer, craftsman, farmer. He emphasizes the two couples, one with several children. They teach Christian family life by the living of it.

This the priest and sister cannot do. The families teach

the universality of the Church and her tender care for the whole life of man in a way the celibate cannot. The Yucatan Indian seeing only priests and sisters as missionaries inclines to conclude that the Church wants all to become priest and sister—that all American Catholics must be priests and sisters—they never see any other kind.

On that first Sunday following her arrival Mrs. Smith could not speak a word of Mexican dialect. After Mass the women stood stiffly apart staring at her baby. The urge to communicate filled the alien white woman and the bronze-skinned mothers as well. But no word did they know to bridge the gap. Mrs. Smith approached the group smilingly, extended the babe in her arms. An Indian mother embraced the child, cuddled him; a wreath of smiles and spontaneous joy filled the crowd; the infant was passed from mother to mother. The months-old, toothless missionary spoke eloquently of things that words fail to convey. He brought LOVE itself and not merely words about love.

Bishop Lane, the Superior General of Maryknoll, recently spent some time with Father Hessler. What about lay missionaries? What can they do? How does it work out? Single or with families? Can children be brought into that wilderness and survive, grow and flourish? How finance these efforts? All these and other questions Father Hessler attempts to answer. He spent seven years in China, three of them in a Jap concentration camp. Now in tropical heat and jungle. Christ must live in him.

This morning after offering the children's Mass he spoke to them. What a blessing to our parish to have him as a guest! What a favor to know such a man of God and have him open our myopic eyes to the grandeur of the Church KATHOLIKE, to pierce the tin can curtain of parish boundaries and local concerns and the petty parochialism of *our* debt and *our* school, *our* altar and *our* sins, *our* Eucharist and *our* salvation! How dead is the little finger which would set up its own circulatory and nerve system, *sans* heart, *sans* head and soon *sans* everything.

Via the afternoon train to Avoyelles reading Kirk's *The Conservative Mind*. Is human thought an enduring reality? What is the force of idea on society's structure? Do concurring ideas form a stream which, flowing over man's mental physiognomy, leaves its trace in grooves and patterns of thought and behavior? Certainly each generation does not begin *tabula rasa*. An essential of culture is its pass-on-able-ness, its tradition-ability. How much we inherit from our fathers, how much we pass on to our sons. How make progress if each generation jettisons the past and must re-discover for itself the alphabet, the wheel, calculus, Aristotle's Unmoved Mover and the cotton gin.

Kirk's conservative emphasizes the stable content in the cultural stream of political and socio-economic theory. Kirk's liberal (fittingly the words mean a dozen things, and a different dozen to Disraeli, Herbert Spencer and FDR) would dam the old stream to allow new springs to appear; the new eddies and currents are so new and so recent and so modern and *therefore* so good.

Where but in God is there life without polarities and where are there polarities without tensions? Healthy tensions between conservative and liberal, traditional and new-created, authority and freedom, the individual and community. On this earth a living society will always be in tension. Social tension is a symptom of a vigorous social body. What human body is always only moving or always only resting, always only speaking or always only listening, always only obeying or always only commanding, always only alone or always only in the crowd. A true social and political philosophy must be a philosophy of tensions. It cannot be static.

Yesterday we spent the whole day at the student center of Southwestern College at Lafayette. Monsignor DeBlanc hosted this grand get-together of priest-friends come apart to talk things over, rub our minds together, exchange experiences and inspiration. Separated by hundreds of miles we seldom see each other, and when we do chance together at a CCD workshop, canon law institute or K. of C. Convention, what little opportunity for chewing things out amidst the hustle and bustle of programs and panels and myriads of other people.

Hence a deliberate withdrawal even for a single day among a dozen brother priests and so seldom as once a year does for us immense good. Michonneau develops the idea of sabbatical withdrawal and the priestly team, the sense of community which can result. Recalling the unity of the apostles, Christ's Last Supper exhortations, the community-sense of the first Christians recounted in the Acts of the Apostles, later development of the monastery, religious brotherhoods and cathedral chapters, no doubt we diocesan clergy have become lone rangers by comparison.

How few priests have sufficient gifts and grace from God to indulge the luxury of lone-wolfing. We lose something by cutting ourselves off from our fellow priests. The flow of grace of state is not only vertical downward from our bishop, but also horizontal priest to priest. This sense of brotherly solidarity we especially need in attacking social problems like industrial and race relations and in activating the lay apostolate. How easily the most gifted and most zealous can go off on a tangent with meteor's brilliance, soon to thud his head into some unforeseen obstacle or to zoom off into space so far from his companions as to destroy the gravity pull of leadership. Of small use the beacon so distant as to be invisible.

The group of priests who work together exercise a salutary check and balance. My idea had better be a good idea to undergo the hammering of other sacerdotal minds. And if it survives the rhubarb, it exits a tempered product and no longer mine but ours. Besides how can one priest possess all the specialized knowledge and experience required to return Christ into our complex society. The priestly team grinds away that prideful importance and self-sufficiency to which we are so inclined. It's humbling and good for the soul, and best of all it prepares us for similar discussion and exchanges with that paralyzed lower echelon of the Church's apostolic army—the laity. If we will not submit our ideas and whims, projects and visions to the judgment of our brother priests, how much less will we enroll the laity as true participants, co-workers in the apostolate.

So we get together periodically to talk things over, share each other's burdens, joys and sorrows. Pastors, superintendents of schools, CCD directors, Newman Club chaplains, editors, chancery officials—a motley baker's dozen bound by the Priesthood, friendship and a community of interest. A community of interest in: the integration of the Negro into the total life of society, management and labor, philosophies of education and law, Catholic school development (vocations, lay teachers), Church and state, Catholics on secular college campuses, the liturgy, family life, the role of the layman and his formation, which variety of interest we distinguish by the ignoble name "stuff."

My Priesthood derives from Christ. "You are a Priest forever according to the order of Melchisedech." My Priesthood needs no renewal; it is a substantial enduring reality. But the human person in which my Priesthood adheres, this frail human person finds strength and renewal in these *Alteri Christi* who are my friends and brothers. I return to my parish and my people renewed and refreshed.

An evening of recollection here in our church and center sponsored by Friendship House given by Father Evanstock, C. S. Sp. Some twenty make the sessions which I close with Benediction. Again white and colored have met as children of God and brothers of Christ. They go home tonight and to work in the morning loving God with a wee bit more of their whole strength and loving their neighbor with some greater fraction of their own self love.

After Saturday night confessions I fulfilled my speaking appointment at Bert Golding's home. He had gathered about twenty-five friends, mostly fellow Unitarians. I would like to know exactly what the Unitarian creed is. I wonder how they would react to the Catholic explanation of the Trinity. Probably they would grasp the point of *that* kind of Persons being three and still only one God. How hard it is to understand that God actually loves man to the extent of becoming one of us. This Divine Love surpasses comprehension. Maybe the Unitarians try to comprehend too much.

On another occasion we'll go into these things but for tonight we talked about the world racial problems, the usual take-off from my UNESCO seminar experience in

Copenhagen. An intelligent group, good questions and several questions that became coherent speeches.

The Goldings have two bright boys and another baby on the way. They and their co-religionists have been from the beginning among the staunchest supporters of Friendship House. May the *God*-Man love them.

School faculty meeting this afternoon. Planning the parent and teacher conferences, setting up the Lenten school schedule and of course Father Hessler will get the gravy from the mite boxes.

Now in the second year of trial, the parent and teacher conferences have proved out to become a permanent feature. A bit hard on the teachers but they're convinced the effort is worth-while. We divide the year into four nine week periods at the end of which tests and reports are given. Instead of merely handing the child his own report card to be signed at home, the parents are invited to a conference at which they discuss with teacher the child's progress. Mothers alone dominate but some couples come together. They then take the report home and discuss with the child his school status.

We have been having some difficulty with discipline, rowdiness, talking back. Many of the youngsters have the run of their own homes. Concepts of authority have grown deplorably lax. Respect for parents degenerates. The teacher takes the parent's place and becomes likewise the object of the child's vindictive pettiness. Things are not coming apart at the seams but we do need some overhauling of our discipline. Maybe some sort of correction hall could be its backbone. But what about parental authority? How can the teacher as the parent's delegate exercise more authority than the parent who is the source of teacher authority?

Respect for lay teachers in particular adds complications. Next year we will have only four sisters and seven lay teachers. We must gear our school system so that a half religious and half lay faculty becomes normal. Such a ratio would delight me.

Annual choir dinner tonight at the Caddo Hotel. Twenty-six turn out for a good meal, a couple of speeches, a lot of banter and a sing around the piano. Someone had the foresight to mimeograph twenty old timers like *Harvest Moon* and current hit paraders I never heard of.

The choir plays an official role in the liturgy of the parish, a role comparable to that of the ministers in the Mass. You cannot have a High Mass without a choir. The choir is the Voice of God's People, praising Him, thanking Him, beseeching Him. Much less is the choir a conglomerate of twenty individuals each singing out in his own name. The choir's prime function is not to entertain the congregation, nor to create a mood, nor to stimulate devotion, nor to provide a background for someone's private prayers. The choir speaks for the parish as Moses, the prophets and the psalmists spoke out for the chosen people. So the choir sings out with the finest sounds of the finest talents God has given His children. Theirs is a solemn, public and official function comparable in these qualities to the function of the priest. That's why the best choir is the whole congregation. They then become the voice of the whole people in a real sense. But we have not reached that point yet.

Mr. Paul O'Brien was invested a Knight Commander of St. Gregory by Bishop Greco this evening. An affair of impressive dignity, well-attended by Mr. Paul's many non-Catholic friends, white and colored. The Bishop explains that the recipient was recommended for this papal honor because he brings the light of Christ's justice into society at large and uses his great talents for the upbuilding of the whole community. All recognize Mr. Paul's courageous championing of the rights of the Negro. A delegation of fifteen or more from the Negro Chamber of Commerce give mute testimony of their appreciation just by sitting in church.

Another victory for that peace which is the work of justice. But we still have far to go.

Today we take another timid step forward. We open the parish center and begin the Sunday soirées. Another effort at answering: What is the parish? Who are the People of God? What is the life of Christ in His Mystical Body? What relation between parish and community?

We are probing, looking, trying to find what we need from Christ's storehouse of the old and the new. Direct quotes from today's *Sunday Sowing* can best indicate what we have in mind, insofar as we have anything at all clearly in mind. Here are the choppy phrases our people read today in the parish bulletin, undoubtedly further obscured by my sermon:

> They marvelled at the words of Grace that came from the mouth of Jesus.
> —St. Luke in today's Communion prayer.

GRACE brings Truth to the mind
    and Love to the will and warmth to the heart.

All these gifts of True Life flow from the Person of Our Lord.

Today Jesus Christ continues to live in time and space through His Mystical Body, His Church.

Today our minds are enlightened, our will strengthened, our hearts softened by Christ living with us, speaking to us in His Church.

And in a particular way we hear the Church and partake of Christ's life through our Parish.

OUR PARISH IS A FAMILY OF FAMILIES IN CHRIST.

—we live in the same neighborhood around this House of God where Christ dwells in our midst night and day.

—we gather as the People of God each Sunday to offer the Sacrifice and our selfish selves.

—we worship God not merely as private individuals but as a Community of God's children, publicly professing our thanks and praise, our weakness and our love.

—in serving God together we serve and strengthen each other; in serving each other, in bearing one another's burdens we serve God Who dwells within us by Grace.

—we bring Christ into our family and home, play and business, work and world from which He is so often exiled.

OUR PARISH is many things because it not only is a living thing but a LIFE.

—Church and School, Prayer and Sacrifice, Youth Activities and Athletics, Credit Union and Blood Bank, Choir and Ceremonies, Clubs and Societies, Friendship and Love and Service, Family and Children, Work and Play, our whole City and Community and Missions over the world—Time and Eternity meet here in St. Joseph's.

TODAY we officially open a new phase of our Parish Life— our Parish Center.

—What is the Parish Center?—sort of a Parish LIVING
ROOM. Physically: a room fifty feet by twenty-eight
feet in the new building directly back of the Church,
well-furnished by Mary's Workers and other benefac-
tors. Nature and Purpose: further means by which
Christ can speak to us bringing TRUTH to our
MINDS, LOVE to our WILLS, WARMTH to our
HEARTS.

More specifically for example:

—Father Scherer's Series on CHRIST AND HIS
CHURCH on Monday evenings.

—Meetings of officers and boards and organizations,
where policy is formed and disagreements chewed over,
and great men like Father Hessler the Maryknoll Missionary speak to us.

—the Parish Library with books and magazines to browse
through, seated in comfortable chairs and quiet, open
till 9:00 P. M. every evening.

—and new things to come like the SOIRÉES which begin
tonight at 8 o'clock.

WHAT'S A SOIRÉE?

Literally the French word *soirée* means evening.

So—an evening together, Pastor and People.

To strive together to understand more deeply God and
Man, Human Life and Love, the World and History,
Society and its Institutions.

Today through the lens of Eternity.

The broadest of scopes united under the God-Man
Christ, in Whom we live and move and have our
being.

No pat formulas, nor capsule recipes, nor five easy lessons, but the patient long-term upbuilding of a LIFE
together in Christ.

Continuing our little efforts and spirit of the Sunday
night and group gatherings of the past few years.

Conducted by your Pastor with the assistance of panels
and discussion leaders in the future.

Tonight at eight o'clock and every second Sunday till
Easter.

TONIGHT: RECALLING THE PAST AND EXPLOR-
ING THE FUTURE.

—we look forward to further recounting by Father G.
of the European Study Tour, comment on develop-
ments since then, Foreign Affairs, the United Nations,
Philosophy of Communism, Conservatism and Liberal-
ism in the U. S. and the West, the Revolution of the
East against the West, the World Racial Problem,
Segregation and Integration, the Welfare State, Educational Theory, Christ vs. Socrates, Labor-Management
Teamwork, the Common Good, Men-in-Braces, Science
and Scientism, the Arts, Literature and Drama, the
Lay Apostolate, Parish and Community, looking behind today's headlines and commentators.

—all from the viewpoint of Him Who is the Way and the
Truth and the Life.

—What else would you like to discuss?

—everybody welcome, invite your friends, eight to nine-
thirty P. M., coffee for all.

End quote from the *Sunday Sowing*.

About thirty-five turned out for the initial soirée. Successful? Who can measure such things except by their
fruits. And of necessity any fruit is a long way off. So we
keep trying——.

Annual clergy retreat coming up next week. Four days
away from telephone and doorbell, four days without
meetings and talks, four days free of the problems and
aches and pains of others, four days in which I am ex-

pected to be selfishly solicitous for my own soul's welfare
to the exclusion of every other care. The difficulty about
the annual retreat is that it comes but once a year. Naturally we parish priests are free to take more time off
for our own spiritual good but few of us ever do. Besides
inertia, habit and laziness we seem afflicted with some
type of pride which pretends that all would go to pot if
we took time-out from people and parish to draw closer
to God.

All the writers on pastoral spirituality from Christ to
Michonneau exhort us to withdraw frequently from the
busy shores of Genesereth to climb some way up the
foothills of Mount Thabor. Michonneau insists on a
weekly sabbatical, a day alone for pondering and prayer,
the prayer of silence and just being with Him Who is. To
what extent am I a victim of activism because I want to
impress men who see and hear me more than I want to be
impressed by God Whom I do not see and hear?

About a hundred fifty cram-packed Friendship House
last evening to hear and see and meet Bishop John
Wright of Worcester. How good of the man to share
with us way down here his precious time and more
precious talent. What encouragement he gives to our
staff and associates. His talk was spiritual in content, an
analysis of and exhortation to the very virtues most
needed these tense days. He avoided fixing blame and
fulminated no threats. It was a charitable talk, and yet he
pulled no punches. And despite the range of the Bishop's
gifts of the mind he still reached the people.

Back in the rectory (Father Roland had come up for
the occasion) we talk into the wee hours. Then in the
morning he offered Mass for our school children, acced-

ing to my request he spoke to them. Tonight he speaks
in Dallas, then tomorrow Fort Worth. We shall hear
much of this gifted man for decades to come.

New England has been the Athens of America, the
brains of a nation of brawn. It is good to see the Church
in New England providing a parallel intellectual vision
to our Mystical Body uniquely American in our brick
and mortar emphasis.

Father James Courtney, S.J., arrives to preach the week
long mission; Ash Wednesday through the week end to
next Wednesday; really the first week of Lent. As Father
Scherer explained in the SOWING last Sunday we have
the mission for everybody; all should come because we
all need Christ's light and grace and strength.

I hope the people buy the hundred fifty daily missals
the altar society ladies are selling amidst the rosaries,
crucifixes and holy odds-and-ends in the vestibule. Getting a hundred fifty daily missals into use would make
the mission a grand success.

I have decided to preach a six- or seven-minute sermon
every day during Lent, usually a homily on the Mass of
the day. The CCD board advised advancing the first
Mass to 6:15 so we can have the sermon at the proper
spot after the Gospel and still finish in plenty time for
mother to get breakfast and dad to get to work. In that
way we should get many of the families represented at
the Sacrifice each day. I wonder how long before we can
offer daily evening Mass, and what effect would it have?

The soirée on segregation and integration went
smoothly last evening. No one lost control of temper or
emotion. About eighty people took part. So many

wanted to speak up and ask questions that by popular demand we will have a second session the coming Sunday.

Riley Fell opened up with the legal and historical aspects, all about Plessy vs. Ferguson et al., through the acts of our state legislature, down to the present conflict of Supreme Court vs. state legislature. Dr. Holoubek gave the anthropological side, the oneness of the human family from the viewpoint of science and medicine. I presented Catholic teaching: one God our Father, one Christ Our Redeemer, one Mystical Body, our call to justice and love and Christian perfection. Vic Martzell commented on the difficulties of integration. Harry Johnson moderated and refereed; about twenty-five others joined in pro and con, and mostly on the fence.

Few *want* desegregation, a goodly number believe it is on the way; a few will die hard, most will go along one way or the other. What a time for leaders!

The Evangeline Quartet went over big in last night's première down to Alexandria *coram episcopo*. The dramatic reading *à la* Charles Laughton of Longfellow's epic poem came right across to engross the audience for two self-forgetting hours. Most appropriate for this year's bicentennial celebration of the exile of the Acadians from Nova Scotia and their heart-breaking odyssey to our Louisiana bayous. The four thousand who reached here in 1755 and shortly thereafter now number some four hundred thousand descendants; we are the hundred fold increase promised by Our Lord in the gospel.

Mary Pickels conceived the idea as a collegium production and whipped it into shape. She had seen the original platform reading of Shaw's *Don Juan in Hell* here in Shreveport en route to Broadway. This Charles

Laughton and Paul Gregory success gave the medium status; Gregory treated us to *John Brown's Body* with Tyrone Power, Raymond Massey and Anne Baxter last spring.

Mary found abundant talent in a United Gas office manager, city policeman and a Barksdale accountant: Joe Sullivan, Del Johnson and Pete Braud. Housewife Beulah Griffin and oil well engineer Ray Meleton handled sound and lighting effects to whip up a truly home-grown production. Now we plan the Shreveport appearance and maybe hit the road again.

Pericles Alexander, Shreveport *Times* drama critic, wonders about the adaptability of this genre for other community groups. In his daily column "On With the Show" he asks: "Can this medium be used effectively by amateurs? What types of literature are adaptable to this means of presentation? Will people receive literature fed to them in this manner? Will it be another avenue to assist in the cultural growth of a city? What details of technique are required for the different types of material which might be offered through this medium?"

We are perusing coming possibilities. One stands out: selections from Old and New Testament telling the story of the Fall and Redemption, direct quotes from Genesis, the Prophets David, Isaias, Ezechiel et al., the Gospels and Acts, Paul and John—grafted with transitional material, both original and from the greats like Augustine, Dante, Milton and T. S. Eliot.

To my mind the dramatic reading by reason of its spareness of setting, sameness of costume and restriction of movement requires more imaginative creation from the audience, inducing greater emotional participation and identification-of-self by the listening-me than does

the usual drama. That's not Mary playing the role of
Evangeline, nor Pete Braud enacting Benedict Bellfon-
taine. Their voice, eyes and gesture hypnotize me into
becoming for the moment who and what they tell of.

--abounding life of the Church in the U.S.a.,

PERIOD VI

❖

COMPLETE THE DOING

ALSO...CARRY IT THROUGH

2 Corinthians 8:11

Once humans have settled "to be or not to be," and if so why, we next puzzle over "to do or not to do," and if so how. We American humans tend to emphasize the doing and the how rather than the being and the why. The United States is adjudged activist by the world's thinkers. And much of the world is adjudged thinkist by us American activists.

In the realm of Christian life this simplification finds support. The Church in America has been marked by frontier bustle; we have been brick and mortar builders. Whom do we study for theory and ideology? Who plumbs the relation between absolute truth and passing realities? Which thinkers nourish us with great ideas? I glance at

257

my book shelves and see Maritain, Dawson, Suhard, Gilson, and of course the great popes of our century. Even when we want to think about how to do a thing, when we need to theorize about action we resort to Cardijn, Godin and Michonneau. Mother Europe feeds us still.

Thanks to these thinkers our American apostolate becomes less instinctive and more fully reasoned out. European visitors remark upon this abounding life of the Church in the U. S. A., a youthful zest charged with get up and go. We must continue and rejoice in our bustling parishes, bursting classrooms, building drives, social action and charity services overflowing to millions in thirty-five countries over the seas. As Europe feeds us fare for the mind perhaps we can reciprocate by transfusing some of our optimistic blood to energize our brooding motherland so often near despair.

And maybe the Church in the U. S. A. verges now upon a more balanced maturity. Bishop John Wright, Fathers Courtney Murray and Tracy Ellis, among others, hold the ear of thousands in their plea for a heightened and deepened intellectual apostolate. Under Cardinal Stritch's paternal care Chicago becomes a crossroads of the world in all things apostolic. There the Cana and Christian Family Movements, the Adult Education Centers and numerous other flowerings cross-pollinate European thought with American action to beget hardy homegrown plants.

To all these worthies we are profoundly indebted for our provincial experiments in the "why's of to be" and the "how's of to do."

1. Rectory Weekend Traffic

THIS MORNING, Monday morning, I received in the mails a manila envelope containing the May, 1955, issue of the American Bar Association *Journal*. A scribbled note was enclosed:

Father: Thought you would find this article interesting. It is a new twist in the justification of O. W. Holmes.

LEONARD

The marked article was "Nature, Man and Law: The True Natural Law," by George W. Goble, professor of law at the University of Illinois. In a bold-face paragraph the *Journal* summarized Professor Goble's thesis:

The subject of the natural law and the judicial philosophy of Mr. Justice Holmes have been the theme of several articles in the *Journal* in recent years. Professor Goble here shows that our knowledge of science and the history of the moral evolution of man refute the idea that "natural law" in the classical sense exists; that is, that the idea of classical "natural law" itself is unnatural and wholly man-made; he also shows that Holmes in his opinions was influenced by deep moral beliefs . . . (page 403).

Leonard, who mailed me the *Journal* and penned the note, is a parishioner, a convert of four years, now in his middle thirties, father of five children, alumnus of the school of law of our State university, partner in a top law firm. He had read the article pen in hand. Blue-ink brackets, underscorings and marginal notes enlivened the pages. Underscored was:

"Whatever it was that caused Xenophon's [hypothetical caveman in Professor Goble's illustrative parable] first moral judgment, there was no law that coerced man's conscience to respect this judgment, until experience demonstrated that the judgment was good . . . (p. 407).

"Within limits, man has power to make laws which govern his own behavior. These laws deal with what he ought to do rather than simply with what he does. . . ." (p. 476).

And there was a marginal query in Leonard's blue-ink scribble. "What makes a man think he 'ought to do' something other than what his animal instincts dictate?"

What response does a pastor make when his parishioners begin asking such questions? Who in this 7-per-cent-Catholic city of 160,000 will discuss with lawyer Leonard the 49 footnotes quoting Bertrand Russell, Dr. John Wu, Lecomte du Nouy, Aristotle, Cicero, Roscoe Pound and Georgetown Law School's Father Francis E. Lucey? How many of the twenty Catholic lawyers in town are asking similar questions? How many non-Catholics?

Should I preach a ten-minute sermon on the natural law, devastating Holmes and all his cohorts with clever clerical satire? Should I give Leonard a pamphlet to read, or Maritain's *Man and the State,* or Lippmann's *The Public Philosophy?* Can he without help read and ruminate and digest such intellectual fare?

Or should we simply burn the American Bar Association *Journal* and tell Leonard to say the family rosary and forget all this silly rationalistic bickering about so obvious a thing as the truth?

Yesterday was Sunday. After the seven o'clock Mass, Charles Ducros came in for a cup of coffee and to bring me up to date on his latest business venture in Mexico, whence he returned the day before. This parishioner, also in his thirties, is primarily a petroleum technologist, founder and president of a million-dollar geological company, servicing Shell and Gulf and Standard and other oil companies with his own patented exploration and production techniques. A gifted executive and financier, he is now branching into other fields opening up in Latin America.

He possesses a great social conscience. By some natural instinct or Christian grace his heart goes out to the little man, especially to the Mexican campesino, or peasant. He follows the migrant-worker problem through personal contact and high governmental connections. He looks to the development of a hefty middle class in Latin America as a stabilizing influence.

He hungers for the Christian social principles, for an international social justice in which to root his own life and undertakings. He needs the universal sweep and groundwork depth of the papal teaching to synthesize the findings of his laboratory researchers, feeding geological data into his mass spectrometer, with the social and familial implications of irrigation on the Pacific slope of Mexico's Sierra Madre.

How does a pastor answer all his questions and arouse him to others still? By what means can a parish communicate to him the meaning of work, the joy of creativeness, an acceptable cosmogony, the reality and primacy of the spiritual (all his college studies were non-Catholic and narrowly scientific), the responsibility of wealth, a truly Christian world view?

Then after the nine o'clock Mass yesterday morning Mr. Mann dropped in for a cup of coffee and a between-Masses chat. He occupies a top executive position in a local bank. We talked about the violent, months-long telephone strike and the negotiations for a guaranteed annual wage in the auto industry.

Smoothing the ribbons of his daily missal he wondered "how the Church could be so sympathetic to unionism and socialism." He recounted instances of woeful irresponsibility on the part of union leaders. He deplored the AFL-CIO amalgamation as a dangerous blow to free enterprise. What power this united labor front would now direct toward the organization of workers in our region!

I countered with a brief restatement of basic principles, already vaguely known to him but too easily suffocated in his country-club and chamber-of-commerce atmosphere. He listened respectfully, readily admitting that we live in an era of change, that we must continually re-examine our business and economic structures and subject them to the test of eternal realities.

He does not condemn the Church's social teaching. He would dearly like to understand it better. "It is so difficult," he said, "for a man immersed in business to view his mundane affairs through the lens of God's eternity. Still it's the only sensible view, life being what it is."

This morning, Monday morning, the phone rang. Judge Baker is in town. This former parishioner moved to a neighboring city when appointed Federal District Judge some years ago. He will preside over the court here during the coming month. Would I have dinner with him some evening this week?

What will we talk about? Old times: the Catholic Men's Club, of which he was first president; our choir, of which his wife was once a member; our growing school, which his son formerly attended; our mutual friends like lawyer Leonard. He will share what he can in conscience recount about his court experiences, since I gave the invocation at his formal investiture two years ago.

Inevitably we will discuss the Supreme Court decision on May 17, 1954 directing that Negroes be integrated into our educational system. Since that time the Supreme Court has placed upon the district courts the responsibility for implementing that historic decision. Its directive reads in part:

> In fashioning and effectuating the decrees, the courts will be guided by equitable principles. Traditionally, equity has been characterized by a practical flexibility in shaping its remedies and by a facility for adjusting and reconciling public and private needs. These cases call for the exercise of these traditional attributes of equity power.

Judge Baker will search his soul. What is equity? Whence derive equitable principles? What is the relation between law and human dignity and Christian ethics? Between Sunday Mass and Monday morning court hearings? Between Christ my Saviour and my colored brothers in Christ?

The judge graduated from our State university and put in a semester or two at Georgetown during the war. How much basic philosophy and theology did he get? What impact did it make on his undergraduate mentality? What continuing, maturing intellectual life has parish or Church offered him since he left the college campus? And how much idealism remains after fifteen years of real life"? Now in his early forties, he has twenty years on the bench before him, twenty years of devious argumentations and weighty judgments.

Mary Mackay called last Saturday right at lunchtime. She wanted to discuss T. S. Eliot's *Murder in the Cathedral* as a possible presentation by the dramatic quartet. There are some technical difficulties, but all are surmountable because the language and message and dramatic impact are such as to impel one to vault any barrier.

Saturday morning, Dr. Bozek called. Another parishioner, 40-year-old past president of our area's medical society. He wanted the address of a priest from Wichita, Kansas, a recent visitor to our parish to whom he had loaned two tape recordings. By letter he will ask him to forward the tapes to an inquiring doctor in Muskogee, Oklahoma.

These tapes record some of the dozen or more discussions in which Dr. Bozek has engaged with three other doctors and a few other interested persons this past year, discussions on the rational psychology of St. Thomas applied to modern medicine. They used *The Image of His Maker* by Rev. Robert E. Brennan, O. P. (Bruce, 1948), as their major idea source. It proved an excellent choice.

For hours they rubbed their minds together. What is

the intellect, the will? Does spirit really exist? What are emotions and habits? For the first time these products of materialistic medical schools began to glimpse man as a spirit-and-matter, body-and-soul, time-and-eternity composite. A Methodist surgeon observed: "Gosh, if only I had gotten something of this whole view where I studied medicine."

Out of these exchanges a Catholic Physician's Guild has been activated. *The Image of His Maker* and other volumes have found their way into the uppermost levels of our State medical-school faculty. Tape recordings have been played back a dozen times to as many doctors. The question naturally arises, where do we go from here?

These experiences of one pastor over one week-end belabor a point which needs belaboring: the need for bestirring intellectual life at the parish and community level, with emphasis on the apostolic formation of lay leaders.

Here are Catholics with talent and creative gifts. But what vehicle for these are they offered by parish or Church once they get their diplomas? We rage about the shallowness of our U. S. Christian culture, the spectator passivity and tinsel brittleness of secular recreation and entertainment. Culture is self-reflection socially expressed. Culture grows out of a community conscious of itself. Little sense of community exists in too much of our parish life, and less community self-reflection. Our constantly moving families offer no seed bed for cultural roots. How shall a Christian art be evoked in *suburbia Americana?*

First we need to understand the changes occurring in our suburbs. Then we must uncover what intellectual resources our community actually has and how they may best be mobilized. A third step is to exchange experiences among pastors and parish leaders over the nation. Through these exchanges we can profit from each other's experiments. To my mind the individual parish cannot meet these needs. Had we not best project a community-wide movement? Spearheaded by whom? With what structure and emphasis?

There have been experiments and some successes in this field in Pennsylvania and Delaware, California, Ohio and Canada. The experiments take a variety of forms under a variety of auspices. Patterns set in several European countries are worthy of inspection, perhaps of adaptation. The adult-education section of the National Catholic Educational Association can tell us much. So can the intellectual's movement of *Pax Ramana.*

We must continue our communication through every means. The lower echelon of the Church, pastors especially, need to grasp the deep yearnings of our maturing laity. With this grasp, priests and people will certainly create whatever new or modified entities our growth and age and apostolate demand.

We have closed Friendship House. Local indignation against the House, enflamed by headlines and editorials of the Shreveport *Journal,* led us to the racking decision.

Crusades have suffered defeat before, and have often undertaken strategic withdrawals. Never have I known crusaders more remarkable than the Friendship House staff; really thorough-going followers of Christ. Historically the thorough-going Christian has often been unpopular, starting with John the Baptist. If the staff had their way they wouldn't object to enduring even more abuse and threat, imprisonment and intimidation. But the time came to answer the question we must constantly re-phrase: Is it the best way here and now? the best way to promote justice and love for the Negro? Might someone get hurt—what with the evening daily egging on potential violence?

The recent Till murder case emphasizes a burning reality: since May 17, 1954 we have witnessed in the South a revival of the most virulent Southern NATIONALISM. The Northerner has become *ipso facto* disqualified in racial matters. In the South he has no voice, no leg to stand on with the public opinion he would wish to influence.

Even before the Supreme Court decision this held true. Now this Southern xenophobia has multiplied a hundred fold. In this question the Yankee is regarded a foreigner from north of the border. When Friendship House was established eighteen months ago I requested that the staff should be of Southern extraction at least in part. But such staff were not available. This so-called invasion by "Northern agitators" presented the classic handle for rabble rousers to hang on to.

The taint of Yankeeism is so deadly that it tended to nullify the work of the staff. Worse yet this Southern nationalism degenerating into xenophobia cancels out the effectiveness of Southerners, white and Negro, who join hands with the Northerners for the great goal of interracial justice and Christian brotherhood. The Louisianian who supports the U. S. Supreme Court becomes a local traitor.

Friendship House had become something of a symbol. In losing that symbol we lose much. But how mistaken are the opponents of desegregation who think that this little squall can turn aside the Bark of Peter from its appointed course toward the fullness of Christian justice and love. We should thank the paper for headlining the Church's condemnation of racism as heresy, for showing that the Church established by Christ condemns Southern racism as well as Hitler's. I wonder how many Shreveporters knew this till now.

Friendship House was a means to an end. In our judgment public events and peculiar local circumstances rendered it no longer beneficial in our city at this time. So we employ other means. The determination to strive for interracial justice and a more perfect Christian society will not wane or flag in consequence of the closure. News reports of the day from New Orleans bear this out.

2. Catholic Teachers and Racism

IN NOVEMBER 1955 Bishop J. B. Jeanmard of the Diocese of Lafayette excommunicated two persons for having violently attacked a catechist in the Parish of Our Lady of Lourdes, Erath, Louisiana. The complaint arousing the violence was that the religion class was composed of white and Negro children. These events received wide notice in the nation's press, rating a front page story in the *New York Times*. Happily the two excommunicated persons made public amends within the week and were welcomed back into the Church.

I cite these happenings in order to recall the public temper in our state during the Fall of 1955, and in order to place in proper perspective this opening address given to the Annual Teachers' Institute of the Diocese of Lafayette. Monsignor Ignatius Martin, the Diocesan Superintendent of Schools, had directly requested that I speak to his teachers specifically on the racial issue. He and Bishop Maurice Schexnayder, then Auxiliary of Lafayette, were with me on the platform. In May 1956 Bishop Schexnayder succeeded Bishop Jeanmard as Ordinary of the Diocese.

The talk is slightly shortened to reduce repetitions of thoughts previously expressed in this JOURNAL.

Why are five hundred teachers, clergy, religious and lay, gathered for this teacher's institute of the Diocese of Lafayette?

Why do we have a Catholic school system?

What is a Catholic teacher? Who are you?

Why have you the religious left parent and family and home? Why do you the laity sacrifice gold and seniority, pension and tenure to teach in the Catholic school?

How and why are you different from every other educator?

St. John answers our questions in his Gospel prologue. St. John, the patron of your diocese, points out your distinctive character. St. John sings out the nature of your exalted calling.

You are bearers of the Light of the world. You are bearers of that True Light which enlightens every man who comes into the world. You continue the message and mission of Jesus Christ in space and time. You beget, upbuild and nurture Our Lord's Mystical Body. You are the Voice of the God-man speaking forth His way and His Truth *hic et nunc,* in the *here* of the Diocese, in the *now* of September 1955.

You are vessels of election, bearers of a great power— the power of becoming sons of God.

A Catholic teacher is all this and more. What do we mean by the word "Catholic"?

Catholic from the Greek word *katholike* means universal, katholike means all-embracing.

Katholike means geographic wholeness: Go and teach all nations.

Katholike embraces all the human family: Preach the Gospel to every creature.

Katholike designates the whole of Christ's teaching: to observe all things whatsoever I have commanded you.

Katholike looks to the whole of man, all his faculties and potencies, intellect and will, appetites and emotions: whether you eat or drink, or whatsoever you do, do all for the honor and glory of God.

Katholike envisions the totality of society and the institutions composing society: the family, the economy, the body politic, education, the arts; in the words of Pius Eleventh, all things must be restored to the dominion of Christ Our King.

Katholike stretches through the whole of time: the year 33 to the year 1955, 1955 to the consummation of the world.

We then are the Church Katholike. We are Christ living on in time and space. We: Bishops and Priests, Religious and Laity, Pastors and People, Teachers and Taught.

Through us Christ lives on, through us the Light shines in the darkness, through us Christ speaks to the world, to this embattled, bleeding world which knows Him not.

Look at this world, this human family scattered over five continents and seven seas, these two and one-half billion brother humans for whom Christ died. Look beyond your classroom and school, look beyond your diocese and state, look beyond our southland and our nation. Look and behold—what do we see?

In the fall of 1954, exactly one year ago, I spent three weeks in Copenhagen, Denmark, attending a UNESCO

Seminar on Adult Education. We stayed in a small college near the Danish capital. For three weeks sixty-five delegates from thirty-two countries lived and worked together. Besides the seven or eight hours of daily workshops and lectures, committee meetings and reports, we profited, as you might imagine, from informal discussions beyond number, bull sessions far into the night. We exchanged ideas and principles; with the passing of the days, we became friends, chatting by the hour over tea and crumpets. For the first time I came into personal contact with the rest of the world, with the thought and aspirations of men like Dr. Datta of Hindu India; Mr. Shafig, an Arab Mohammedan from the Middle East; Mr. Mao, a French-speaking Buddhist from Indo-China; Mr. Quansah from a colony of the African tropics; M. Nazet, a public school administrator from Paris; I was the only Catholic priest.

Through their eyes, their lips and from the outpourings of their hearts I saw this world which we would win for Christ. I saw a world in revolution.

Look at a map of this world.

Here is the Communist bloc, that one-fifth of the world's surface covered by Russia and China, with the satellites clustered-round, within the Iron Curtain. Eight hundred million people inhabit this huge land mass: one-third of the world's population. They know not Christ; they deny the very God Who would make them His Sons.

Here is the free West, Western Europe and the Americas flanking the Atlantic Ocean. Six hundred million people, heirs of the culture of Greece and the law of Rome, half-heartedly Christian, frequently repudiating in the name of agnostic scientism the God of Abraham and Isaac and Jacob. Our Western World, our Atlantic Community, that minor fraction of our globe in which Christ the Light of the World has shone for nineteen hundred years to an uncomprehending twilight.

And look at the remnant third, Africa and South Asia. Over one thousand million people, one billion brother humans, disciples of Buddha and Mohammed, followers of Hinduism and witch-doctor fetishes. One billion people torn between the ideologies of East and West. Listening to the clarion call of Karl Marx; barely hearing the murmured voice of Christ, His "Come, follow me!" muffled by our own curses and incriminations, by those acts of hate and discrimination sounding louder than the Voice of the Savior.

For three hundred years we of the so-called Christian West have lorded it over the rest of the world. Africa, Asia and Oceania have been our colonies and territories carved into the British and Dutch, French and Belgian empires. Less than two hundred million people of these four European countries have held sway over the work and destiny of one and a half billion people in Asia and Africa. We of the U. S. have been partners with our European allies. We shall not attempt just now to evaluate colonialism. It had its good points. The fact of the matter is that people of Africa and Asia are now in revolt. India and Pakistan, Egypt and Burma, Morocco and Java have reached *their* 1776.

Economic and political freedom compose only part of the picture. More important still is the question of race. Look at this human family for whom Christ died. Seventy-five percent of Adam's children are colored, three-fourths of our human brothers are non-Caucasian, black and brown, yellow and red. For three hundred years the white minority has dominated the colored majority through our colonies and empires; our armies and navies have enforced our will. The non-white majority is in revolt against the heel of the so-called Christian West, against the pernicious heresy of a superior race. 'Non-white,' we say even in our official U. S. census. "Why do you call us 'non-white'?" an Asian educator asked me. "Why do you designate us with a negative epithet? We don't call you 'non-black' or 'non-yellow.' "

In short, my dear friends with Christ, the racial question rears uppermost in the mind of most of the world, an embattled, bleeding world.

Keeping this global background in mind, let us now turn our eyes to our own nation and region, our own state and area. Here too the racial question is of prime concern. It headlines our newspapers and dominates the covers of our weekly magazines. It forms a major plank in all gubernatorial platforms and will be a major issue in the presidential election. A topic of heated conversation over the canasta table and party line, over farm turnrow and back yard fence.

Small wonder that your diocesan superintendent of schools wanted this racial question discussed at this opening session of your institute. Despite the gnarled knots of intertwining difficulty, despite our preference for a complacent status quo the Light we bear must shine forth, willy-nilly we must face this changing world bought with the Precious Blood of Jesus Christ. We cannot indefinitely hide from the truth, we who are bearers of the Truth.

In this question of world shattering import you hold the key. The Catholic educators of Louisiana will set the pattern for the future; as seldom happens in the course of the centuries your acts can determine the course of world events. Again so many depend for so much upon so few.

This is not a shabby indulgence in histrionics. This is not hysteria. Look at the facts. The question of racial equality stands uppermost in the mind of the whole wide world. Among nations the test case, the *cause celebre* is the United States. Within our country the South is the dominant factor. And where in the Southland will the decision be made? In south Louisiana, if we are true to our claim as teachers of the Church Katholike, bearers of the Light, bearers of the power to become sons of God.

South of the Mason and Dixon line in this area stretching between Louisiana and Virginia there reside one and one-half million Catholics. But more than half of these Catholics, eight hundred thousand, reside in south Louisiana. The pattern of justice or injustice, of Christian love or racial heresy, the pattern established here will affect irrevocably the whole Southland, the whole nation, the whole world.

A heavy responsibility then burdens your shoulders. The eyes of the world are upon you. We Catholics of Louisiana shall be judged by history—and by the Divine Judge of the living and the dead.

The time has come to set our compass. We must determine once and for all the direction in which we must move. This journey will not be without its delays and detours; this journey will take time and patience, effort and sacrifice.

We Catholics must deliberately move toward the complete integration of the Negro, welcoming him as our brother in Christ and fellow son of God in all the areas of our society.

Whenever it befalls that a human being must undertake a difficult task it is only natural that he should inquire as to the necessity of the task. Despite the discipline in religious obedience shared by most of us we react the same way. The integration of the Negro into our Catholic school system is surrounded with such difficulty that we rightly ask, "Why should it be? Why change a system which existed for fifty years and more? Why stir up all this trouble and agitation?"

There are many reasons why the Negro must be integrated. This morning I shall indicate only four.

If a lawyer were addressing you he would logically advance reasons of a legal and juridical nature. He would point out the guarantees of our federal constitution, so clearly set forth by the Supreme Court. Were a statesman like John Foster Dulles addressing you he would plead the cause of our nation as leader of this embattled world, 75% of which is colored. I am neither lawyer nor statesman. I am a Catholic priest, an Alter Christus, speaking to Catholic teachers, bearers of the Light of the world, bearers of the power to become Sons of God. The reasons I advance are accordingly the reasons of Christ; I plead the cause of the Church of Christ, the cause of all who are and can be Sons of God.

First, we must receive the Negro, on a status fully equal and without reserve, into our Church and school and society for the advance of the world-wide mission of Christ. Surely we still hear the command of Christ: Go and teach all nations. You, Sister Mary Joseph, might not go to steaming jungles of Malaya. You, Brother Ber-

nard, might not join your confreres on the high plateaus
of Tanganikya. You, Father Smith, might never work in
the Jesuit missions of Ceylon. You might remain the rest
of your earthly days in the schools of this diocese. Strange
as it seems the fabric of history and the network of world
communications are so interlaced that you will teach the
whole of mankind from this secluded sector of God's
green earth. Why? How? Because what happens here affects the South, the way the South goes, so goes the nation. And the nation stands in the spotlight of the globe.
South Louisiana will teach the world. South Louisiana is
a chalkboard upon which we will write the lesson of
Christian charity and fraternal love, or (God forbid!) we
will stone-heartedly chisel out the heresy of hatred and
racism. We can move only in one direction. Christ gives
us no choice.

Secondly, we must strive toward receiving the Negro
on a status fully equal and without reserve into our
Church and school and society because to deny the Negro
such status is to be guilty of the heresy of racism. Yes,
heresy *is* a hard word. Heresy is a frightening word when
used before Catholic teachers who are bearers of the
Light of the world. Could it be that some among us are
guilty of heresy? Perish the thought! We must not judge
persons. But we can judge doctrine.

Our Holy Father, Pope Pius the Great, devoted the
first encyclical of his reign to this problem of human
solidarity. He offers:

"A marvelous vision, which makes us see the human race
in the unity of one common origin in God, 'one God and
Father of all, Who is above all, and in us all' (Ephesians
IV, 6); in the unity of nature which in every man is equally

composed of material body and spiritual, immortal soul; in
the unity of the immediate end and mission in the world;
in the unity of dwelling place, the earth of whose resources
all men can by natural right avail themselves, to sustain
life and develop life; in the unity of the supernatural end,
God Himself, to Whom all should tend; in the unity of
means to secure that end."

What is the heresy of racism? It has various manifestations.

To believe that the Negro people are cursed by God
is heresy.

To believe that the Negro people are predestined by
God to an inferior status as hewers of wood and drawers
of water, janitors, field hands and cooks is heresy, a blasphemy against the one God and Father of all, making
mockery of the Lord's Prayer.

To believe that we Caucasian people are possessed of
some innate superiority, endowed with qualities of intellect or will, faculties of spirit and genius unique in
nature, differentiating us from other consequently inferior peoples, forming a height of excellence unattain-
able by such inferior peoples—all this is heresy.

To judge a person's rights and to choose one's neighbors primarily and habitually on the basis of thickness
of lip and straightness of hair and degree of pigmenta-
tion, to relegate Sons of God to a position of inferiority
precisely because God made his children in a particular
form and appearance—all this is living heresy.

To acquiesce supinely in a social system derived from
slavery, a human bondage with bought and sold human
flesh as chattel—this is to acquiesce in heresy.

Negro people have made greater cultural, educational
and social progress in a shorter time than has any other

ethnic group in recorded history. How can we ever understand the debilitating effects of the slavery from which they had to recover? Read a copy of the Black Code, the slave law promulgated by Bienville, first governor of Louisiana, and published in this volume by Harper's in 1851. A few excerpts:

"Slaves shall be held in law as movables . . . ; they shall be equally divided among the co-heirs." Art. 40.

"Movables" by law. I presume the original French was *"meubles,"* the French word for "furniture," mere furniture bought and sold, bequeathed and inherited like a four-poster bed or marble top dresser.

Another article in this our Louisiana law:

"We declare that slaves can have no right to any kind of property, and that all that they acquire either by their own industry, or by the liberality of others, or by any other means or title whatsoever, shall be the full property of their masters." Art. 22.

"We forbid slaves belonging to different masters to gather in crowds either by day or by night, under the pretext of a wedding, or any other cause . . . under the penalty of corporal punishment, which shall not be less than the whip . . . and should there be aggravating circumstances, capital punishment may be applied. . . ." Art. 13.

"Thefts of importance, and even the stealing of horses . . . or cows, when executed by slaves . . . , shall make the offender liable to corporal even to capital punishment, according to the circumstances of the case." Art. 29.

Such was the depth of inhumanity from which our Negro brothers have so gloriously risen in these ninety years. This is an admirable accomplishment.

We know by Faith that there is no master race destined forever to rule and no inferior race destined by God to subjection. By Faith this heresy of racism is condemned *a priori*. Our Negro brothers in Christ have proved racism erroneous in practice *a posteriori* from the very progress they have made toward equality.

It is now for us to receive them into the fullness of Our Father's House which they so richly merit.

Thirdly, we must receive our Negro Catholics into the full life of the Church and society because they are members of the Mystical Body of Christ. The Mystical Body of Christ! Time permits but a mention of this fundamental dogma of the Church of Christ.

"Know you not that you are temples of the Holy Spirit?"

St. Paul tells us that the baptized human in the state of grace is the temple of the Holy Spirit. God dwells within him. Who are we to refuse association with him in whom God dwells, because his body is brown, his hair kinky and because *his* grandfather was bought and sold like furniture by *my* grandfather?

In his 1942 encyclical Pius Twelfth teaches us that the Third Person of the Blessed Trinity is the Soul of Christ's Mystical Body, the Church. This means that we are unified and joined together by the Personified Love of God Himself. This means that as the parts and organs of my human body are inspirited, given life and oneness by my individual soul, we members of Christ's Body are souled, given life and oneness by the Holy Spirit. My left hand is joined to my right hand by my immortal soul as the principle and source of natural life. In like manner, you and you and you and I are joined together by the Holy Spirit, God Himself, into the unity of Christ's Mystical Body.

Discrimination against the Negro is discrimination against the very Body of Christ Himself. Racial discrimination forms a blood clot, an occlusion in the flow of grace and love within Christ's Mystical Body. We must remove this obex, this obstacle to Grace for the full flowering of Christ.

Fourthly and lastly, we must receive the Negro into the full life of the Church and society because this is the way of Christian perfection.

You will note that I have said little about social justice and legal rights. Real as these might be they are secondary reasons, secondary with Catholic teachers, most of whom have by solemn vows set out on the way toward Christian perfection.

"Be you perfect as your heavenly Father is perfect," is the height toward which we strive. "Thou shalt love thy neighbor as thyself," must be our goal, a goal set for us not by a Supreme Court or the NAACP, but by Christ Himself.

You might murmur in your hearts: "This is a hard saying. Who can listen to it?" Grant if we must, this is a hard saying. The way of Christ can be hard. "Thou shalt not kill. Thou shalt not steal. Thou shalt not commit adultery. What God has joined together let no man put asunder. Take up your cross daily." These are all hard sayings. Contrary to our disordered passions and appetites, contrary to our dim intellects and weak wills. Contrary to following the crowd. The way of Christ is difficult. The way of integration is difficult. But it must be

our way because it is the way of Christ, the way of
Christian love and perfection.

In conclusion, my dear teachers, it is not for me to tell
you what means you are to employ to move along this
difficult road. I know little about the local set-up on your
golden prairies of rice-ripened Acadia and Jeff Davis
parishes; I know little about the personalities you must
encounter along the marshlands of the Gulf, along the
banks of storied Bayou Teche.

The Holy Spirit broods over your diocese, the Love of
God personified dwells here within you. He speaks to
you through your Bishops and priests. He speaks to you
teachers, bearers of a great power, the power of becoming sons of God, Bearers of the Light.

3. Natural Law

Dr. Paul M. Hebert, dean of the Law School, set forth the week-end theme, and re-stated the perennial theme, in his greeting to the conference:

> "By heartening contrast with the realism of our day which would exclude morals and objective truths from the solution of human problems, you will in the three days allotted to this conference consider some of the current problems in our society from the viewpoint of a bedrock philosophy of religious dogma which accepts man as a creature of God with a dignity and with a destiny in the hereafter. . . ."

A critical discussion of segregation, re-assessment of "right-to-work" laws, the doctrine of national sovereignty and the world community were among the problems to which the dean referred. He was welcoming a hundred Louisiana lay leaders to our November conference on "Catholic Social Principles and the Body Politic."

The State Council of the Knights of Columbus sponsored the conference with the local university K. of C. council and L. S. U. Newman Club as hosts under Monsignor Robert Tracy, chaplain. The University graciously allowed us use of its excellent facilities. That the Louisiana Knights of Columbus should sponsor such a gathering of fourteen lawyers, twelve workingmen, ten educators, four full-time union officials, and sixty students, professional and business men right along the banks of Ole Man River presents *prima facie* evidence that "the old order changeth."

However, changing social patterns, daily headlined and daily deprecated by "Southern gentlemen," were not the main concern of the gathering. Of deeper import than the *fact* of social change is the *why*. The profound significance of this conference is that practical men came together to seek out the roots of present change and to dig channels for the future.

In 1948 the American bishops in their annual statement deplored the prevailing secularism which exiles God from the world He has created and keeps Christ in the sacristy, sealed off from the social life where men work out their salvation.

French-settled Catholic Louisiana tends to play down the Church's *social* teaching to a degree even greater than American Catholics generally. To account for this emphasized secularism we might adduce two ideological reasons: a Voltairean this-worldly rationalism among the non-religious; a Jansenist, disincarnate spirituality among the religious-minded. We Catholics of French descent inherit Voltaire's world, a world without the spiritual, and Jansen's spiritual life, a life isolated from the taint of the world. This supplies historical background for our public criticism of papal social doctrine based on natural law morality, and for public resistance to its *ad hoc* interpretation by the teaching Church and apostolic laymen. In consequence, politics is politics, business is business, social customs are social customs, and Sunday Mass and sermon have but slight connection with Monday morning deals.

Thus, our week-end conference needed first to establish the truth that political or social acts, of citizen or body politic, are human acts subject to the moral law, and that this moral law derives from the Creator and from the very nature with which He endowed man.

The Baton Rouge conferees, whether professors or ward politicians, constantly witnessed to this current agonizing reappraisal of political morality and jurisprudence. Dean Hebert recounted that last month he attended a legal-research institute at the University of Michigan in the company of many scholars and law school administrators. There the dean of a Midwestern State law school, criticizing the propriety of planting a listening device in the jury room in connection with certain University of Chicago studies of the jury system, stated: "I think that there is a moral issue involved. I repeat—in our zeal for research, we must recognize that not everything scientifically possible is morally justified."

"To my knowledge," continued Dean Hebert, "this was the interjection of a new word. It was the first time it had been used by any speaker at the conference. It was the word 'moral'."

A learned federal judge, he went on, had objected strenuously. Quite a verbal tiff ensued: "We had an almost visible rebellion at the idea of the interjection of any concept of morals as a standard in a discussion of law improvement through legal research." Who won the debate is beside the point; that two deans of State university law schools should have publicly departed from the prevailing realism and insisted on moral norms in law was news sufficient for the day.

This trend of the times was further documented for our week end by a faculty member of Tulane University, Maurice D'Arlan Needham. This professor of political science and editorial writer for the *Times-Picayune* of New Orleans presented findings on "Religious Truth and the Root Concepts of the Body Politic," drawing heavily on two recent books: Walter Lippmann's *The Public Philosophy* (Little, Brown, 1955) and Eric Voegelin's *The New Science of Politics* (University of Chicago Press, 1952). Professor Voegelin teaches jurisprudence at Louisiana State Law School.

Professor Needham traced to its sources and tributaries that classic natural law flowing from the intellectual stream of Sophocles, Socrates, Cicero, the Christian Fathers, Aquinas, Suarez and Thomas Jefferson, now rediscovered and proclaimed by Lippmann as the "public philosophy" to which we must return.

Government as a positive good, and not a mere necessary evil, received able treatment from Rev. James J. Maguire, C.S.P., director of the Wayne University Newman Foundation in Detroit. This led rugged individualists to reassess Rousseau's dicta on the freedom of unfettered primitive man in the light of the Catholic concept of man's essentially social nature.

Mixed in with this theorizing were down-to-earth panels on day-to-day subjects: racial integration, labor law and the United Nations.

This our fifth week end on social principles in as many years turned out to be our most successful to date. Our purpose is not just vaguely educative in a general way. The institute's aim is to form a cohesive "school of thought" on pressing social problems among leaders throughout the State in order that they may acquire that sense of mission and solidarity needed to carry Christ into the market place. It seeks to extend its influence upward into the higher realms of social and political theory, and downward into the hourly human decisions of big business, big government, big labor, Jim Crow.

The conferees publicly expressed their mind in this unanimous statement:

1. We are grateful to the teaching Church for the social doctrines given to us as applying to economic and social problems which involve moral issues. It is the sense of the conference that we all recognize our responsibility as citizens to inform ourselves and to apply the teachings of Christ and His Church on these issues according to our position and status in life.

2. The changing of the traditional pattern of segregation in race relations is a critical problem of our day. This conference recognizes that the ending of past injustices is right and proper under God's law and the supreme law of our country. As laymen and as citizens we dedicate ourselves to work for just solutions to the problems presented, realizing that the full acceptance of Christ's teachings would immediately ease the unusual tensions created by the grave issues involved.

3. Moral issues are involved in the economic problems of our society. The teachings of the Church on such questions are authoritatively expressed in the encyclicals of the Popes and the official statements of our bishops. It is the duty of each of us to inform ourselves on such teachings and to work for right and just solutions in accordance with this spiritual guidance.

4. All of the problems of our interdependent society find their solution in the application and acceptance of the moral law. We live in a world community because of

modern day technology and communications. As members of the human family redeemed by Christ, we must proclaim the universal truths and moral bases for an international order rooted in justice and brotherhood under God.

Perhaps these are old thoughts clothed again in the same old well-used words. But in the given ensemble of Louisiana, 1955, they are not without significance. At the moment most ears in the deep Deep South are deaf to the faintest echoes of the Word made Flesh. For the long pull ahead Christ and His Church need a body of formed Catholic laymen, full of justice and love, who will speak and act. Such men are at hand.

4. The Collegium

DURING EASTER WEEK each year the National Catholic Education Association draws five to eight thousand participants to its national convention. Monsignor Fred Hochwalt, N.C.E.A.'s secretary general, asked me to come up to the annual gathering in St. Louis this April to tell the diocesan superintendents something about our collegium experiment:

With the increasing maturity of the Church in our country we must focus increasing emphasis upon the deepening of the intellectual life of the whole Church, both clergy and laity. We now hear repeated variations of this refrain from voices like Bishop John Wright, Fathers Murray and Ellis, M. Jacques Maritain, Christopher Dawson, Dean Hugh Taylor and others. The published talks, articles and books of these men and their associates are the soil and soul from which my thoughts this evening rise forth. I invoke what they stand for as an introduction to my thesis, confident that this audience needs no introduction to these distinguished men whom I dare call upon to introduce my subject.

I address myself to only one area of their thesis: the

bestirring of the intellectual life of the *laity* at the level of parish and community. I am not *now* concerned with the clergy and religious. I am a pastor, not an educator in the strict, formal sense. I shall not discuss scholarship or curriculum, degrees or credits from a faculty or campus point of view. I concern myself with the graduate of your high schools and colleges after he moves into our parish, after he is married and has begun his family, after he has established his work and business or professional status, after he has become a citizen of the bodies politic, after he assumes his full role as an adult member in the Church Katholike, Our Lord's Mystical Body.

I shall speak about your alumni, my parishioners, presuming to class some fraction among my parishioners within the intellectual ladder at the bottom rung position.

Six months ago in this very city Bishop Wright said in his Founder's Day address at St. Louis University:

"At a moment when the word 'intellectual' has become a reproach and when the vocation of the intellectual has become obscured or even discredited, is it not time to reflect prayerfully on Christ the Divine Intellectual, the Eternal LOGOS of the Father . . . the Word of God.

"Meditation on Christ so understood . . . will throw new light on the Christ-like function of the genuine intellectual, called to imitate Christ by making incarnate in each generation and each culture something . . . of the treasures of eternal wisdom and knowledge, the divine ideas summed up totally and perfectly in the Person of the Son, the LOGOS, *the Verbum (quod) caro factum est et habitavit in nobis. . . .*"

(End quote from Bishop Wright, CATHOLIC MIND, March 1956, p. 126.)

Bishop Wright then rallies the thin ranks of Christian scholars to (I quote him again): "The battle for the minds of men, for the furtherance of ideas rather than political boundaries or military spheres . . . a battle in which the Holy Catholic Church not only belongs but must be victorious if God's will is to prevail." (*Ibidem*, p. 128.)

I perceive and heartily agree with these pleas for the intellectual apostolate at Harvard and Princeton, Chicago, Oxford, and other top level campuses—an intensification of the immeasurable work Maritain, Dawson, Murray, Gilson and others have begun so auspiciously. This intellectual apostolate touches my parishioners because the deans of Louisiana State, Texas A. and M. and Tulane universities, as well as the brighter lights among these faculties, received their doctorates from these top-level institutions; whence, too, come numerous text books, reference works, theories and "schools of thought."

My further plea is that we invigorate our apostolate to intellectuals not only from the top trickling downward, but also from the bottom percolating upward, presuming that even some parishioners may be classed within the intellectual ladder *at the bottom rung position*. I hold that we can have a grassroots ferment of cultural and intellectual life. That we can and we must.

Suburbia Americana is the new sociological darling. The beguiling character and traits of *suburbia* and *exurbia* are now the object of affectionate attention from swarms of statisticians and social researchers. Very properly our Catholic sociologists, all too few in number, Fathers Thomas, Fichter and Fitzpatrick, Professors

Kane, Clark and others begin to analyze this suburban setting in which hundreds of new Catholic parishes and schools have been established in the decade since the War.

Seven years ago my Bishop assigned me to the establishment of such an upper middle class parish in a city of 160,000, a city typically Southern in religious and racial complexion, only 7% Catholic. Our suburban people are lawyers, doctors, engineers and geologists, corporation officers and department heads, educators, bankers, contractors, brokers, realtors, sales managers and regional big-brand franchise holders.

As I came to know my people this striking fact stood out: the high percentage among them who had college and university backgrounds. In order to guide me in my pastoral role in breaking the bread of life, in order to determine vaguely what bill of fare my people could best digest and assimilate, the milk of babes or the meat of adult men, we began asking in the parish census questions about educational background. Unfortunately, I am not a sociologist. These surveys were non-professional, amateurish, inaccurate beyond a doubt. But they are sufficiently accurate to reveal an overall picture.

The best sampling which I shall report was taken by two major seminarians, theological students, in summer 1955. They called upon 160 families, a 30% cross-section of the parish, for interviews of thirty to sixty minutes.

We found that of the 160 husbands 123 had attended college for an average of three and one-half years each.

Of the 160 couples 84 were mixed marriages. In our survey we interviewed non-Catholic spouses as well as Catholics. We found that among the 123 college men only fourteen, or 12%, had gone to Catholic colleges, while 109, or 88%, were products of non-Catholic campuses. A higher fraction of the college wives, 18%, attended Catholic institutions.

Data about place of birth, occupation, number of moves since marriage, converts, elementary and secondary education, et cetera, was also obtained. Time and place tonight do not permit comment. The focus must remain upon the astonishing concentration of college alumni we find in our suburban American parishes. And making all allowance for deficiency in our methodology and interpretation I do submit that having 76% of the fathers of the parish with three and one-half years of college work presents a fact and a challenge of prime import for the Church in America and presents a fact and a challenge of prime import to you, the good stewards of our burgeoning educational system.

We who are the Church continue Christ in time and space. Christ the Vine lives on in our own age and culture. We must cultivate a vineyard which proliferates verdant foliage into the airy reaches of scholarship and erudition. But likewise a healthy plant must sink its roots into the more earthy soil of the workaday world.

The perceptive student of history pierces beyond the surface debris of mere war and dynasty to discern in human events close interrelation between the dominant ideas of a given period, the ideals and values derived by society's thinkers from their concept of truth, and the cultural temper to which these ideas and ideals give birth. The study of history is primarily the study of the incarnation of ideas, the idea becoming the flesh of the social body. As *Alteri Christi,* Other Christs, priests of the LOGOS, we might summarize our mission with this

Ciceronian phrase: *Verbum incarnandum est.* The lay-man partakes of the same mission. He must incarnate Christ.

I submit that the ideas generated by "American aca-demic circles" take on flesh, become incarnate in the managerial, professional, political and work life of my parishioners; in the Monday morning real life situations of the operating room, editorial staff, court chamber, bar-gaining table, board of directors, labor halls, country club barbecues, and legislative floors. By their agency the idea becomes the act, social theory becomes the contract, po-litical ideal the statute.

We must conceive of education as a life long experi-ence. We must acknowledge that the present tenor of parish and Catholic community life offer little to the college man who would continue the quest. The graduate leaves an intellectual campus climate with its lectures and library, seminars and bull sessions. The world he enters of business and politics, diaper-changing and country-clubbing is an intellectual wasteland. His mind is after all still a tender plant and finding no suitable en-vironment, the life of the mind quickly withers and dies. He needs prepared ground to sink his roots; he needs nourishment; he needs communication with others for cross-fertilization.

To nourish the life of the mind fifteen minutes from the pulpit are wholly inadequate time-wise and perforce our pulpits address themselves to a broad embrace of ages and conditions, on subjects rather strictly religious. Most study groups and discussion clubs are kindergar-tens. Pamphlets only whet, or frustrate, appetites. Our monthly Catholic culture series featuring big-name lec-turers offer hors-d'oeuvres without meat and potatoes.

Hopefully, serious books and periodicals like AMERICA and COMMONWEAL begin to reach a wider audience, but recent surveys show that we read less than any other nation in the West. Cities fortunate enough to boast a Catholic college find until now that radiation from the campus barely reaches the adults of the area. Educational TV is a baby question mark.

Faced now with the striking concentration of college alumni cited earlier, faced now with a Catholic people a generation and more removed from our ancestral migrant slums, and due to other causes I am not now able to recite, this drab scene of parish and community life can and must and will be reconstructed. The curtain has raised on the new setting. Beginnings, pioneer efforts, experiments are under way.

We know something of the adult education section of our own National Catholic Educational Association. Monsignor Cox continues the expanding night school at St. John's in downtown Philadelphia. Some five hundred adults meet weekly for non-credit courses in the five centers of the institute begun by Cardinal Stritch last September with Russell Barta as director. Father Henri Foltz of Wilmington has been assigned by his Bishop to offer adults evening courses in philosophy and liberal subjects. The Thomas More Institute of Montreal continues full blast. The labor schools now broaden their offerings. Extension courses currently receive closer attention from college faculties and administrators. PAX ROMANA comes of age under Dean Taylor of Princeton and Father Rooney of Catholic University.

I undertake no exhaustive survey of these manifestations. They are many and varied. They are woefully needed.

To meet our own pastoral need we are experimenting in our own city with what we term the collegium.

The collegium is a loose affiliation of men and women of the community associating together to bestir their intellectual, cultural and vocational life as adults. The roots of the collegium go back some five years when I began fortnightly confabs with ten selected men, men with innate and developed traits of leadership, men thirty to forty years of age who shared a common concern for the social problems of our city and region: the integration of the Negro, labor-management relations, problems in the body politic, educational theory, the family breakdown, et cetera.

These ten lawyers, doctors and business men had little knowledge of the encyclicals and the Church's social teachings, and even less grasp of the philosophical and theological sources of social justice and charity. They perceived the inadequacy and rootlessness of the basic ideas motivating the social institutions in which they fulfill their role. They began asking: What are human rights? Whence derive duties? Why do men work? Why did God create natural resources? What is life all about? What is matter and spirit? the intellect and will? How do they operate? What of immortality? Good and evil? Who *is* God? Who *am* I? What is society? It's purpose and institutions? What is the meaning of history? of today's crisis? Where do I fit in? What is my role and vocation in the plan of Christ and His Church?

I am now convinced that a high percentage of men will cry out for these ultimates given the challenge and the atmosphere. Essentially our people are not as shallow and superficial intellectually as might be concluded from the husks we and the pundits offer them. A goodly number *will* drink from that grandly flowing stream of Plato and Aristotle, Justin Martyr and Augustine, Albertus Magnus and Aquinas, Bellarmine, More and Maritain, Suhard, Leo and the Piuses.

Evolving from this first group the collegium, I must insist, is still in the experimental stage. With pardonable presumption we incorporate elements of Newman's IDEA OF A UNIVERSITY and Hutchin's Great Books conversation, with the pragmatic realities of *our* people and city, *our* nation and world.

The collegium structure is simple: an executive committee of four laymen and myself, appointed by the Bishop upon our nomination. Later we hope to acquire a full-time director, probably a layman, and to incorporate under a state educational charter.

The embryonic collegium now sponsors four principal offerings: the soirée, the group, the newsletter and the library. Ten soirées this winter at eight o'clock on alternate Sunday evenings each brought together 60 to 140 persons. Basic ideas are presented by a three to five man panel, then explored and kicked around seminar-fashion by the twenty to thirty more vocal audience participants. The executive committee selects the subjects and panellants some months in advance. Our first concern is for *ideas,* then we strive to perceive how these ideas influence issues and social institutions like the economy, education, race relations, the U. N., the family. We often use books as idea sources.

About every two weeks we mail out a mimeographed newsletter to 600 persons. This heralds the coming soirée, gives panel background and the ideas likely to be aired; it reports on the last discussion with emphasis again on the ideas exchanged and principles drawn; it calls attention to new books and magazine articles on hand in the parish center where the soirée meets.

Leafing through the newsletters:

Soirée subject: *The Twentieth Century Capitalist Revolution,* discussing ideas drawn from A. A. Berle's book of the same title. Are corporations developing "consciences?" A sense of morality and public duty? Accepting the moral concept of right and wrong? The corporation's world impact? The corporation and "the City of God."

Twenty-one articles are cited in resumé from the collegium magazine rack, e. g. "For Man to Know," by Vannevar Bush from the *Atlantic Monthly;* "Science and Philosophy" by Pius XII from *The Pope Speaks;* Barbara Ward from the *New York Times;* "Psychoanalysis and the Christian" by Karl Stern from *Commonweal;* articles on education from *Saturday Review, America* and *Harper's.*

Another soirée: *What is Man?* Man as a matter-spirit, body-soul composite. Nature of the intellect and will. Mostly ideas drawn from the *Image of His Maker* by Brennan. And on this panel were four couples, including four medical doctors, who had met together semi-monthly in their homes during the past year to pore over the relation of Thomistic rational psychology to modern medicine.

Another soirée: *The Origin and Nature of Law* with a panel of five lawyers drawing principally from Lippmann's recent *The Public Philosophy* which pleads for a return to natural law. Three of these lawyers are non-Catholics. None of the panel ever attended Catholic high school or college. None had encountered affirmative treatment of the natural law philosophy at Tulane,

Washington and Lee, Harvard and Louisiana State Universities.

Other soirées—a hurried glimpse—

The U. S. and the U. N.

Is Modern Day Education Effective? chaired by the Presbyterian dean of our city's Methodist college, with a panel including one of his faculty, the supervisor of our county's public school teachers, a Jesuit high school priest, and a parent.

The Philosophical and Historical Roots of Communism.

The Family: Origin, Nature and Purpose. Parents as co-creators with God; child to youth to adult development, chaired by a Baptist psychiatrist.

What Makes Music? Introducing the symphony, led by our local city symphony conductor, with members demonstrating instrumental families, technique, and historical development.

Geology—A Blueprint of God's Creation, with five petroleum geologists, two non-Catholic, one of whom was still worried about the six days of Genesis.

The soirée lasts two and a half hours with a midway break for coffee and tea and chatter. Let's readily admit the impossibility of digesting such pretentious palaver in a couple of hours. Let's admit that some do not follow all that goes on. Still they come to know that the world of the mind still exists; they desert TV for an entire evening: *they revive that nigh-lost art of conversation.* And the pervading tone and temper is: God and man and the world we live in, today through the lens of eternity, the impact of Christ the God-Man upon our society, all the while seeking that True and Good which give meaning to life.

"The Spirit breathes where It wills." All do not grasp to the same depth, all do not grow to the same height. Think of the collegium in concentric circles. A small intense nucleus of five persons, the executive committee; a larger nucleus of thirty to forty who conduct the panels, exchange books and articles, meet at noontime luncheon to talk about Citizens Councils and the NAACP, or to plan a soirée—the five geologists met four times in two weeks, the doctors still meet, other groups as well.

Then a third concentric circle of a hundred and more who participate in the soirées, many of whom have something to say there and elsewhere in programs and conversation. The six hundred who now receive the newsletter form a final circle of affiliation.

The collegium is of the laity, by the laity and for the laity. Only three of the forty-one panellants have been priests. The collegium is for the whole community; about one hundred fifty non-Catholics receive the newsletter; a quarter of the participants are not of our Faith, and sixteen of the thirty-eight lay panellants were non-Catholic. But we must not make the mistake of thinking only in terms of the individual. Ours is a social movement; we aim at influencing the whole of society and its institutions through ideas. We believe that all things will be restored to Christ when the Truth of the Eternal IDEA becomes incarnate in society.

The collegium is not a panacea, it is an experiment, a freshly conceived embryo. Your counsel and prayers through gestation and delivery, until viability and maturity, would be deeply appreciated.

5. A Profile in Courage

THE CITIZENS COUNCILS' party line goes like this: "The Southern Negro wants to continue segregation. He's satisfied with 'separate but equal'. He knows how to keep his place. All this integration talk comes from Northern agitators."

Our most local of elections just interjected a startling rejoinder to this comfortable theory. By secret ballot Southern Negroes in two precincts voted 478 to 43 against segregation. The secret ballot offers a much safer opportunity for truck drivers and teachers, domestics and shopkeepers to express their inner convictions than does open talk, which might reach the ears of the white bossman, school board and landlord.

This chance to voice their opinion by vote came to the Negroes of our city in last week's general election for police jury. In Louisiana the parish police jury corresponds by and large to the county commission of other States, with legislative and executive authority in parish (county) affairs.

Twenty-two men sit as jurymen for four-year terms. Fourteen of these were to be selected for Ward Four, comprising the city of Shreveport, from a slate of 18 candidates. General elections normally mean little here; the Democratic nominees have been shooed in without opposition for half a century. However, for the first time since Reconstruction days, Republican hopefuls came to the post to oppose the 14 Democrats.

Three weeks ago, resolutions were offered before the parish jury favoring interposition by the Southern States against the U. S. Supreme Court's anti-segregation rulings and endorsing the principles of the Citizens' Councils. The one dissenting voice was that of Thomas Patrick Fitzgerald, Democratic nominee for re-election. Vivacious discussion ensued for over an hour. Tom responded point by point to the dominant defenders of segregation.

He thought that those favoring interposition were spinning their wheels. We should be thankful, he said, "that the Supreme Court decided the way it did. The way the court is handling it, local conditions are being taken into consideration."

Juror number one said: "I am not thankful that the Supreme Court acted like it did. Some of those members don't measure up to the stature of a justice of the peace. Their decision was based upon opinions of the left wing, psychiatrists, psychologists, sociologists and bubbleheads."

Tom replied: "As a lawyer, I am in favor of justice; as a conscientious citizen, I am in favor of upholding the law. We should not condemn the Supreme Court of these United States for an action in which they have considered the Southern States to the point of turning over to local Southern courts the method by which integration . . . can be accomplished."

Juror number two: "I believe that God, not the Southern States, made segregation."

Tom again: "I don't believe God made any separate

creations. I believe He made one big human race, and the differences are due to climate and geography." The story was carried in the Shreveport *Journal* for March 22 and the Shreveport *Times* for March 23.

The debate continued in the public press, over TV and radio, and in conversation everywhere. For once a local Southern voice had opposed the segregationists. Other voices joined in through letters to the editor. Louis Rains, juvenile probation officer, wrote to the morning *Times* that he believed many Southerners yet to be heard from did not favor interposition, nullification, economic pressure or the legal-murder approach. He commended Archbishop Rummel and Fitzgerald, "the good Christian citizen of our own city," for "putting Christian principle and justice before prejudice."

The next evening's *Journal* had a banner headline in monstrous two-inch letters: JUVENILE PROBATION OFFICER QUITS. Maybe Louis Rains did remember all the while that the juvenile court is financed by the parish police jury; that he had criticized the public body which employed him.

The *Journal* of March 27 replied in a lengthy editorial note to a letter from Mr. Rains similar to the one he wrote to the *Times*. This excerpt reflects the paper's temper:

> In connection with his (Rains') obvious reference to the Emmett Till case, his law-enforcement experience also should have taught him that one of the surest ways for ANY male of ANY age or ANY color—white, black, red, brown, pink or green—to get a bullet through his head is to become intimate with another man's wife, with or without her consent, and let her husband hear about it! The "unwritten law," right or wrong, has been upheld by juries

in Mississippi, Louisiana, New York, California and throughout the nation.

Public opinion was whipped up against Tom Fitzgerald. The way to oust him became a slogan: 13 and 1. The *Journal* editorialized on April 13.

> Citizens of Ward Four (Shreveport) will have an opportunity to make membership of the Police Jury 100 per cent in favor of segregation. . . . Registered Democrats who are satisfied with all of Ward Four's Democratic nominees for the jury except Mr. Fitzgerald will vote for 13 of the 14 nominees listed in the Democratic party column on the voting machine and ONE nominee—Charles T. Beaird— listed in the Republican party's column.

This well-qualified young industrialist from an old family of community leaders protested that he had been singled out without his consent. Nevertheless, "13 and 1" became the crusade cry to oust Tom. On election eve another *Journal* editorial reproduced a sample ballot effectively marked 13 and 1, and identified Mr. Beaird as an avowed opponent of integration.

And so it was done. Fitzgerald was 15th in the race, with 3,294 votes, against 5,552 for Mr. Beaird, number 14.

Still in his early forties, Tom already had a fine record for Catholic leadership. He was president of the Serra Club and of his parish Holy Name Society, a fourth-degree Knight of Columbus, an executive committeeman and co-founder of our collegium. He is an alumnus of St. John's, our local Jesuit high school, of Spring Hill College, Georgetown University and Centenary College. He has now won another distinction. He lost the fight, but his cause has won.

The *Times* wrote of the election: "Fitzgerald's defeat was generally attributed to his anti-segregation views. . . . Significantly, the two predominantly Negro precincts in Ward Four gave Fitzgerald an overwhelming vote. . . . He received 324 votes in (precinct) 39, compared to 23 for Beaird, and 154 in (precinct) 40, compared to 20 for Beaird." That makes 91.7 per cent. And—what was just as startling—37 per cent of the citizens voting favored this Southern espouser of desegregation.

How many really share Thomas Fitzgerald's convictions? How many merely admire his courage? One way or the other, where there exists such courage and such admiration, there is hope.